CARVING
TOTEM POLES &
MASKS

CARVING TOTEM POLES & & MASKS

Alan & Gill Bridgewater

Sterling Publishing Co., Inc.   New York

We would like to thank all those people and companies who helped us with this book:

Peter Bridgewater, The Studio, Alfriston, East Sussex, England—for his map.

Henry Taylor Tools, England—for tool sponsorship.

Gregg Blomberg, Kestrel Tools, Lopez, Washington, United States—for general help and for supplying the crooked knife.

Mr. Lee, Lee Valley Tools, Ottawa, Canada—for his information and inspiration.

Glyn Bridgewater (Glyn De Bonk)—for searching out exhibition material.

Fowey Library, Cornwall, England—for hunting up research material.

Edited by Laurel Ornitz

Library of Congress Cataloging-in-Publication Data

Bridgewater, Alan.
    Carving totem poles & masks / Alan & Gill Bridgewater.
        p.   cm.
    Includes bibliographical references and index.
    ISBN 0-8069-8214-4
        1. Wood-carving.   2. Totem poles—Northwest, Pacific.   3. Indians
    of North America—Northwest, Pacific—Wood-carving.   4. Indians of
    North America—Northwest, Pacific—Masks.   I. Bridgewater, Gill.
    II. Title.   III. Title: Carving totem poles and masks.
    TT199.7.B73   1991
    730'.028—dc20   91-726
                                                                                       CIP

10 9 8 7 6 5 4 3 2 1

© 1991 by Alan & Gill Bridgewater
Published by Sterling Publishing Company, Inc.
387 Park Avenue South, New York, N.Y. 10016
Distributed in Canada by Sterling Publishing
% Canadian Manda Group, P.O. Box 920, Station U
Toronto, Ontario, Canada M8Z 5P9
Distributed in Great Britain and Europe by Cassell PLC
Villiers House, 41/47 Strand, London WC2N 5JE, England
Distributed in Australia by Capricorn Ltd.
P.O. Box 665, Lane Cove, NSW 2066
Manufactured in the United States of America
All rights reserved

Sterling ISBN 0-8069-8214-4

Contents

Color section follows page 64.

Preface

The Indians of the Pacific Northwest coast of North America established one of the most remarkable artistic cultures known to man.

When we first saw examples of Northwest coast Native American carving—a collection of eighteenth-century masks—we could do no more than stand back in awe and admiration. Such perfect symmetry and such power! With the forms, motifs, and colors being wonderfully counterbalanced, and with the designs and colors running in harmonious swaths across the various pieces, we marvelled at the confidence, power, and skill of the carvings. And, of course, trained as we are in the English tradition to think of wood carvings as either polished or gilded, we were completely taken aback by the use of brilliant primary colors. The crispness of the forms, the graphic balance of shape and color, and the sweeping beauty and control of the craftsmanship—it was breathtaking!

From then on, we began, by way of searching through old bookshops and visiting museums, to become more and more absorbed and interested in Native American wood carving. However, the more we saw, the more apparent it became to us that of all the Native American tribes and cultures, the Indians of the Northwest coast were unique in that they were the only group to have concentrated their arts and crafts skills almost entirely on wood carving.

They lived in wooden houses (Illus. 4), boiled water in wooden boxes (Illus. 5), and ate from wooden plates and bowls. Many of their weapons were made of wood; they travelled in wooden canoes; even their hats were carved from wood. From this, we concluded that the Indians of the Pacific Northwest lived in a society that was singularly, almost completely wood-oriented.

Very soon our interest, first in the patterns and motifs (Illus. 6) and then in the actual wood carving, led us into trying our own hand at some *Kwakiutl* mask carvings. Of course, there's no denying that our initial efforts were considerably less than beautiful.

At first we copied and reproduced, and then we

Illus. 1. A Tlingit chief wearing his robe of office—the rings on his hat bear witness to the number of potlatches (gift-giving ceremonial feasts) he has attended.

Illus. 2. The four views of a steam-bent food tray. The design consists of a series of stylized views and profiles of a bird. The tray is joined at the A's.

modified and improvised, until there came a point when we felt that we were learning afresh. It was as if all our preconceived notions about wood carving were being stripped away and replaced with a new awareness. Free from the Western wood-carver's self-conscious obsession with tools, tools, and yet more tools, we were able to get back into close, harmonious contact with the basic materials. With not much more than a crooked knife and a small selection of gouges, it was as if we were at last being given the chance to work with our gloves off.

Our encounter with Northwest coast Indian wood carving has been an inspiring revelation, as well as a unique pleasure that we would like to share with you.

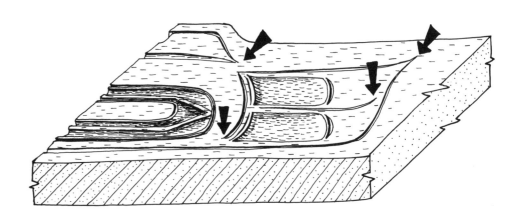

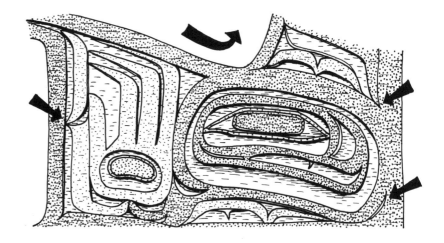

Illus. 3. Characteristics of Native American wood carving. Top: The depth of the V-section trenches subtly varies in some areas, feathering out into delicate quiffs. Bottom: The overall design elements are bent and stretched so as to create easy-to-work shapes that fit the tools, the materials, and the natural rhythm of the work.

8

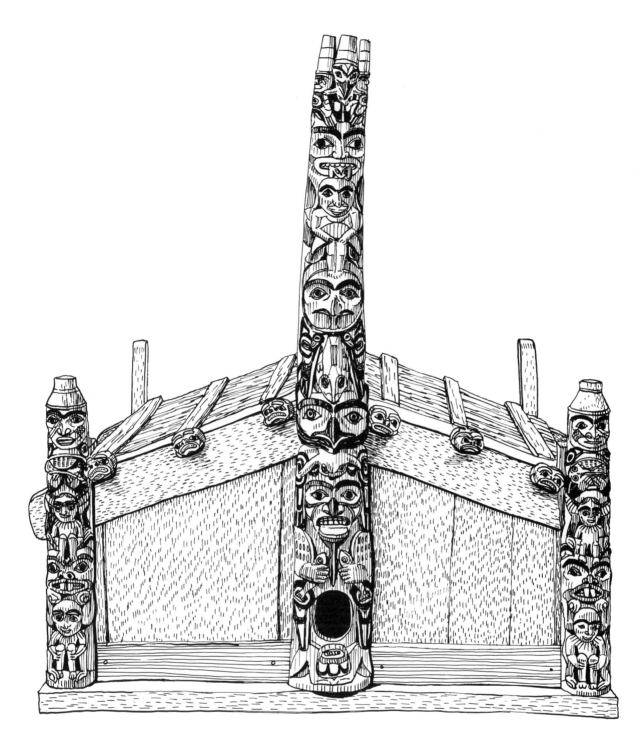

Illus 4. Model of Haida *house—carved and painted in red, green, and black. (Carved by Charles Edenshaw in 1920.)*

In the Introduction, we set the scene by telling you a little bit about the Northwest coast Indian culture. Then we have a section describing all the basic tools, materials, and techniques. After this, we go straight into the 20 very detailed, step-by-step projects. Among the projects are charms, amulets, bowls, and steam-bent boxes, as well as clan crests, dance masks, totem poles, and shaman's rattles. At the end of the book, there are additional motifs and patterns.

Each project opens with a brief introduction to place the carving in a cultural context. Then with accompanying detailed drawings, all the stages of the project are explained—from studying Indian originals, deciding whether you want to copy the project directly

9

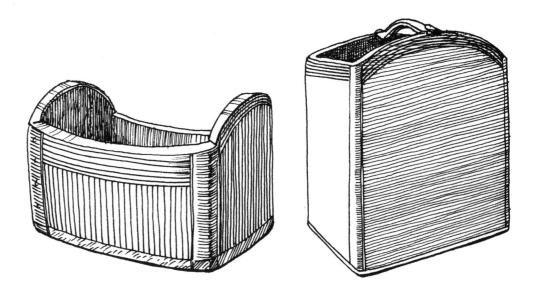

Illus. 5. Kwakiutl *food tray and bucket—kerf-cut and steam-bent.*

or make modifications, selecting the wood, setting out the designs, cutting in the primary forms, and using the knives and gouges, to sawing, carving, whittling, painting, and burnishing.

Each project will give you new insight not only into a culture that was dedicated to wood carving, but also into your own skills and wood-carving potential. Each and every project will, in some way or other, present you with a challenge.

By working through the projects—some indeed authentic replicas and others modified to suit our own needs—you will gradually increase your wood-carving skills and along the way create uniquely beautiful carvings and sculptures.

Illus. 6. *Painted design on the four views of a steam-bent box—also shows a section through the plank thickness.*

The Indians of the Pacific Northwest

The largest wooden sculptures ever carved were made by the Indians who lived along the Northwest coast of North America (Illus. 2). Using archetypal tools—the adze and the crooked knife—they created wood carvings that are not only incomparable in their size, but also in their colors, power, and beauty. They made totem poles well over 70 feet high, steam-bent boxes that are so perfectly formed that they hold water, and magnificent canoes carved from a single tree, as well as all manner of chests, dishes, masks, caskets, hats, rattles, and ceremonial staffs. All were carved, decorated, and painted with almost unbelievable virtuosity.

When European travellers out West first saw the wood carvings during the eighteenth century, they were amazed and not a little puzzled. Line upon line of totem poles stood along the beach (Illus. 1). Thunderbirds, ravens, frogs, bears, beavers, and wolves—with staring eyes and proud arched brows—looked out to sea. The totem poles, houses, and canoes, and just about everything else the Indians possessed, were made from red cedar wood.

These Native Americans lived in a wood-carver's paradise. The forests of easy-to-carve, fine-textured, straight-grained wood provided for all their material needs. In addition, the sea gave them unlimited amounts of salmon, cod, halibut, shellfish, otters, and

Illus. 1. Drawing from a photo taken at the end of the nineteenth century— Haida village, Queen Charlotte Island.

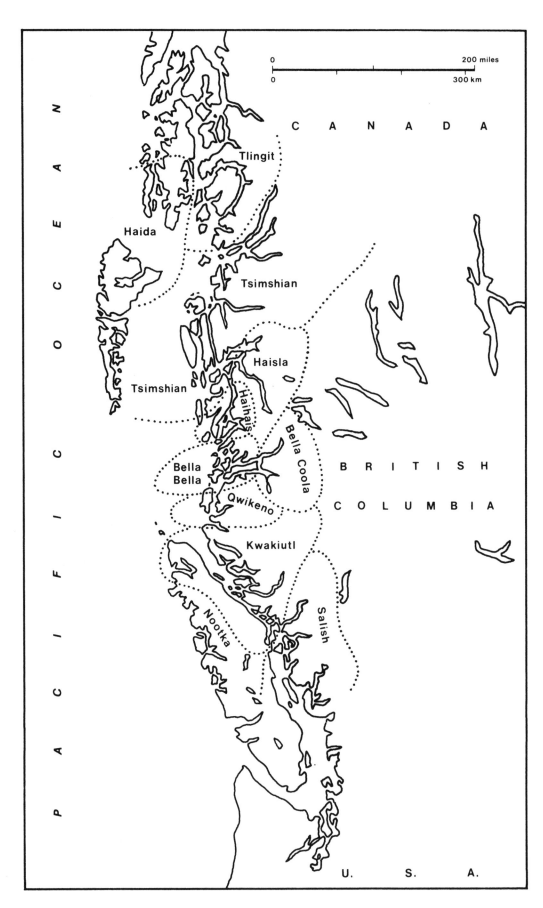

Illus. 2. Map of the American Northwest coast—territories and tribes.

seals. So abundant were the sea and the forests that in a few months they were able to gather, preserve, and store more than enough food for the rest of the year.

Once the food was stored away, the Indians withdrew into their houses, into themselves, and into the supernatural period or season known as the *Tseyeka*. At this time, names and personalities were changed, masks were worn, and long dance dramas as well as spiritual rituals and ceremonies were performed. The people took on new identities that had to do with the supernatural legends and myths that governed their lives. By means of wearing masks (Illus. 3) and reenacting dramas, they spent the long winter months in the firelit confines of their communal houses, working through the various stories that told of their legendary and mythical status (Illus. 4).

Puppetry, shamanistic trances, elaborate tricks and articulated masks and strings, transform themselves into beings that were half-human and half-animal. All this was made possible by the work of the wood-carver.

The Indians developed a particular motif system in which the name of the clans, their relationship with the spirits, and all the related hereditary myths and privileges were expressed in flat-relief-carved and painted symbols (Illus. 5). It was necessary for a man to proclaim his lineage and accompanying entitlements not only by erecting totem poles but also by having his clan crests carved and painted on all his possessions. Just about everything he owned, from the walls of his house down to the smallest bowls and boxes, were decorated and embellished with totem figures and crests (Illus. 6, 7, and 8). In much the same way as European armorial banners and shields show with stylized imagery the glories and status of the family, all the carvings, crests, and images of the

Illus. 3. The Crooked-Beak-of-Heaven mask, worn by women during the cannibal dances.

illusions, and all manner of dressing up were employed in these dramas, intended to link them with the beings and spirits of the supernatural world. Masked cannibal spirits would rush out of the shadows biting and clacking, blood would appear to flow, the dead would seem to rise, and various characters would, by means of

Native Americans document the myths, legends, and related privileges of the Indian clan and family.

Contact with the Europeans was a disaster; by the end of the nineteenth century, the Native American population was decimated from an estimated 100,000 down to not much more than 25,000. Words cannot

Illus. 4. Interior of the whale-eagle house (Chilkat-Tlingit tribe), showing the carved-and-painted screens and house-post clan panels.

14

Illus. 5. Tlingit food storage box—22″ high, 13½″ wide, and 13½″ deep. The sides are made from a single plank of red cedar—*kerf-cut, steam-bent, and sewn—and are carved and painted with Kow-E-Ko-Tate sea-spirit motifs.*

15

Illus. 6. Tlingit *shaman's comb with spirit face (front and back).*

Illus. 7. Tlingit *raven rattle, dating from about 1850. It shows the face of a hawk and the figure of a bear, raven, and another bird; the joined tongues symbolize the transfer of the spirit power. Perhaps the most accomplished of all* the wood carvings, rattles of this character were an important part of the chief's ceremonial costume, as they represented the source of his hereditary power.

easily describe the ugly disintegrations that followed into the twentieth century.

The good news is that there is now a glorious worldwide interest in the Native Americans of the Pacific Northwest. With Indian carvers rising like thunderbirds out of the ashes and once again producing inspired works of art, we are now witnessing a grand resurgence of what has come to be known as the strangest, most intriguing, and most dedicated woodworking culture known to man.

Illus. 8. Tlingit food box or tray, dating from about 1882. This carved steambent box has fibre lashings and is painted red, green, and brown.

Tools, Techniques, and Materials

A Wood-Carving Glossary

Abalone Marine shells used as inlay decoration. In North American Indian wood carving, the shells are used to decorate and embellish mask and crest details, such as eyes, teeth, and eyebrows. The shells shine and glitter like mother-of-pearl.

Acrylics Plastic polyvinyl-acetate-type paints that can be mixed with water or used straight from the can or tube. We favor such paints because they are simple to mix with water to make washes, they dry very quickly, and once dry they are completely waterproof. Such paints make good color-wash stains.

Adze A cutting tool that has an arched blade at right angles to the handle. In use, it is swung like a pendulum, with the heavy chisel or gougelike cutting edge removing scoops of wood. The North American Indian carvers use a short elbow adze.

Alder A sapwood tree common in low-lying, damp areas. A wood traditionally used by North American Indian carvers, it is especially good for carving bowls and the like.

Apple A hard, dense, close-grained wood that comes in small sizes, carves well, and takes a good polish.

Awl A small tool with a pointed or fluted blade that is used for pushing and piercing swift holes.

Band saw A power-operated tool, consisting of a metal band running over and driven by wheels—a good tool for cutting out large, thick blanks. If you want to stay away from power tools, then use a bow saw instead.

Beech A heavy, pleasant-to-carve, inexpensive wood that has a yellow sapwood and reddish heart—a good wood for carving.

Beeswax A yellowish or dark-brown wax secreted by honeybees. The perfect wax for polishing and burnishing, it can be purchased in solid or paste form.

Bench clamp, or cramp A screw device for securing wood to the bench or for holding two or more pieces of wood together—variously called a clamp, cramp, C-clamp, hold-down, etc. The North American Indian carvers traditionally use a rope clamp. In use, the rope is passed over the workpiece and looped around the carver's foot; pressure on the rope is sufficient to hold the wood secure.

Bent or curved tools See **Gouges**.

Bird's mouth fretsaw board See **V-board**.

Blank A block, slab, or disc of prepared wood—a piece of wood that has been prepared for carving.

Blocking in To draw the lines of the design on the wood, establishing the primary details of the pattern or form. Sometimes it refers to painting, in the sense that a design can be painted and blocked in.

Bow saw A thin, bladed saw set in a wooden H-frame that is used for cutting curves. In use, the blade/handles can be rotated as much as 360° to enable the carver to clear the workpiece when cutting curves.

Box wood A beautiful, pleasant-smelling, butter-smooth wood that has a hard, dense grain. It can be used for small, special carvings such as amulets and dishes.

Brushes Brushes come in all shapes and sizes. For the projects in this book, it's best to use good-quality artist's brushes—meaning, brushes that are small, soft, and long-haired. Wash them immediately after use and store them bristle-up.

Burnishing Taking part of a wood carving to a hard, high-shine finish. Burnishing is best achieved using oil and/or beeswax, a brush, a fluff-free cloth, and lots of elbow grease.

Calipers A two-legged compasslike instrument used for stepping off or transferring measurements. It usually consists of two legs that are pivoted at the crutch, or two S-shapes that are crossed and pivoted.

Carved in the round A three-dimensional carving or piece that needs to be worked and viewed from all sides—such as a totem pole, rattle, bowl, or mask.

Cherry A close-grained, pleasant-to-work, reddish brown wood that is especially good for small projects. Cherry carves well and can be brought to a high-shine polished finish.

Chip carving A technique for decorating the surface of a carving by chipping out little triangular pockets. In terms of North American Indian carving, many of the long, triangular filler motifs that tie the larger motifs together to make an overall design are chip-carved.

Chisel A flat-bladed, hand-held cutting tool. In use, it can be held in one hand and pushed with the other, or held in one hand and struck with a mallet. Although there are many types—skew, spoon, bit, fishtail, and straight, to name but a few—chisels are characterized by their cutting edge always being flat or straight. With that said, the names of the various types refer to the shape of the shaft; a shaft might be straight, bent, or spoonlike (Illus. 1).

C-clamp See **Bench clamp**.

Clasp knife Just about any fold-up pocketknife might be called a clasp knife. We favor the use of small penknives.

Close-grained This refers to wood that has narrow annual-growth rings. Such woods usually carve well.

Compass A two-legged instrument used for drawing circles and arcs. It's best to get the long-legged, screw-operated type.

Constructed, or built up A carving that is constructed, or built up, from a number of blocks, layers, elements, or parts. So, for example, if a mask consists of a main face, a pivot-fixed jaw, pinned and glued horns, and eyes made from inlaid abalone, it could be described as being built up.

Coping saw A frame saw used for cutting small sections of wood. The G-shaped frame allows you

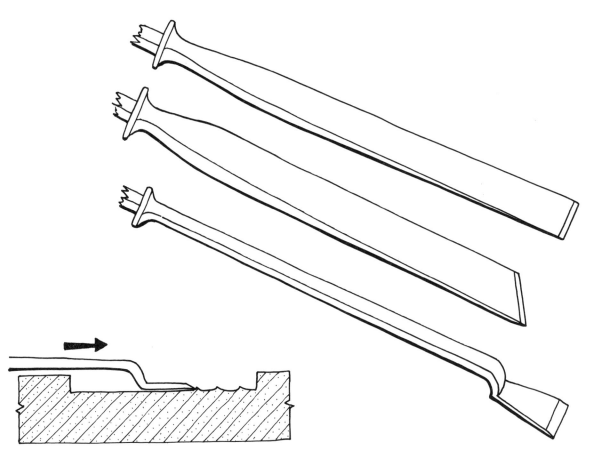

Illus. 1. Chisels. From the top: Straight chisel, skew chisel, and dog-leg chisel. Bottom: The dog-leg chisel is the perfect tool for bringing lowered ground areas to a smooth finish; work with a flat, skimming action.

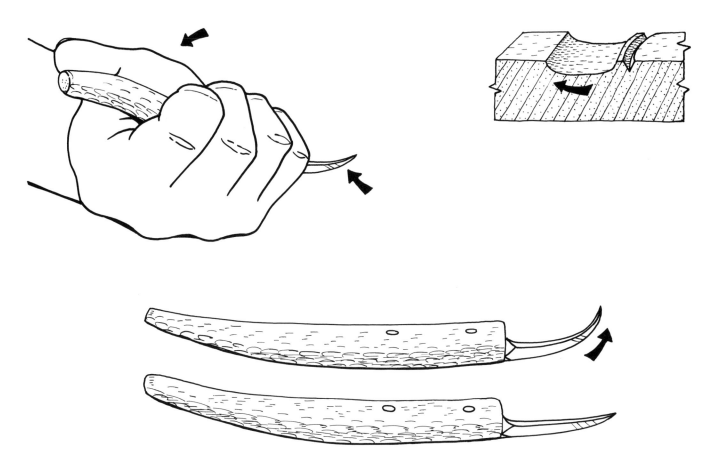

Illus. 2. Crooked knife. Top left: Hold the knife daggerlike and lever against the end of the handle with your thumb, working with a swift scooping-and-hooking action. Top right: The crooked knife is the perfect tool for working *shallow, dished areas such as moats and eye sockets. Bottom: Crooked knives are made left- and right-handed, and with varying blade shapes, ranging from a gradual curve through to a tight half-circle hook.*

to swiftly fit and remove the thin, flexible blades. It's a good saw for clearing out and piercing "windows" of waste, and for making small projects. In use, the work is secured in a vise and the saw is held so that the blade passes through the wood at 90° to the working face.

Crooked or hooked knife A long, hook-bladed, double-edged knife with a curved handle—a tool traditionally used by North American Indians. In use, the knife is clasped daggerlike so that the thumb is pushing and levering against the end of the handle. By rocking the wrist and levering against the handle, it is possible to remove waste wood with a rapid scooping-and-hooking action (Illus. 2).

Cushion A leather or canvas bag loosely filled with sawdust, sand, or old rags. In use, the workpiece is nestled, cradled, or supported by the cushion. It is especially useful for carving small, round-based, lap-supported pieces such as bowls, dishes, and spoons.

Deep-carved Meaning, in the context of North American Indian carving, that the depth of the cuts are deep rather than shallow. A totem pole might be deep-carved, whereas the motifs on the surface of a box would probably be shallow-relief-carved.

Deep V-section gouge See **Gouge**.

Designing In the context of this book, this means working out a structure, pattern, or form by making sketches, outlines, models, or prototypes that are based on museum originals.

Dog-leg chisel See **Chisel**.

Dowel pegs Wooden pegs used in much the same way as nails. A pilot hole is drilled through mating pieces of wood, and then the dowel is driven into the hole. It's best if the dowel is cut with a knife, many-sided, and a tight friction fit.

Drilling holes Boring holes. It's best to use a small, inexpensive hand drill, with a main grip handle, large drive wheel, and self-centering chuck.

21

Elevations   In a drawing, the views of an object. Thus, a particular view might be described as "top," "end," or "side" elevation.

End grain   Cross-section grain at the end of a piece of timber, which is often difficult to carve and needs to be approached with care.

Enlarging grids   See **Gridded working drawing**.

Finishing   Scraping, rubbing down with sandpaper, detailing with the point of a knife, painting, waxing, burnishing, and otherwise enhancing the appearance of a project.

First cuts   The very first stages in the carving after the initial designing, drawing, and transferring. This usually refers to the first incised setting in, or stop-cuts, and the V-section trench.

Flat-curve gouge   See **Gouges**.

Forstner bit, or saw-tooth cutter   A large-diameter drill bit used for drilling out flat-bottomed holes. Sizes range from ⅜ to 3½″ diameter. This is a useful tool for clearing out large and deep areas of waste.

Found wood   Wood that can be found, such as beach-combed or salvaged wood. For the projects in this book, you might use wood from logs or fallen trees, old building joists, and the like.

Fretsaw   Fretsaws are akin to coping saws; the only real difference is that they have larger frames, finer, more fragile blades, and an absence of end-blade pins.

Front-bent gouge   See **Gouges**.

Gouges   The most important of all wood-carving tools, the gouge is a curved-sectioned, hand-held cutting tool. It can either be held in one hand and then pushed with the other hand, or held in one hand and banged with a mallet. All cutting tools of this sort—regardless of whether the blade is so shallow-curved as to be almost flat, or whether it is deep U-sectioned—fall in the gouge category. In the context of this book, gouges are named or classified by the shape of the cutting edge, and the shape or curve of the shaft. So, for example, a gouge might be described as a "large, deep U-section

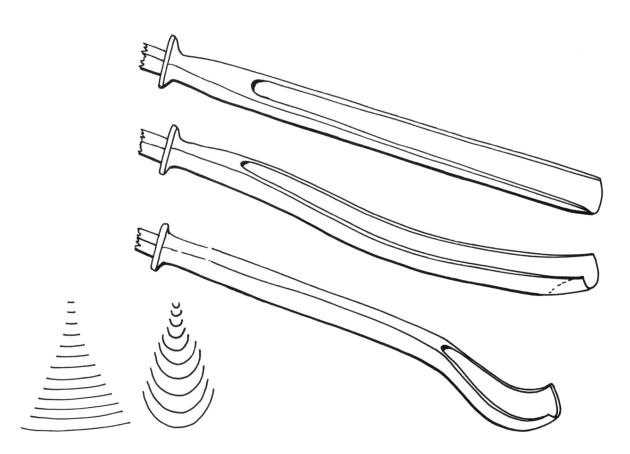

Illus. 3. Gouges. From the top: A straight gouge, a curved gouge, and a spoon-bit gouge. All three gouges are the same width and have the same U-section blade—only the shafts *are different. Bottom: Gouges range from having a shallow, almost flat curve section to having a deep U-section.*

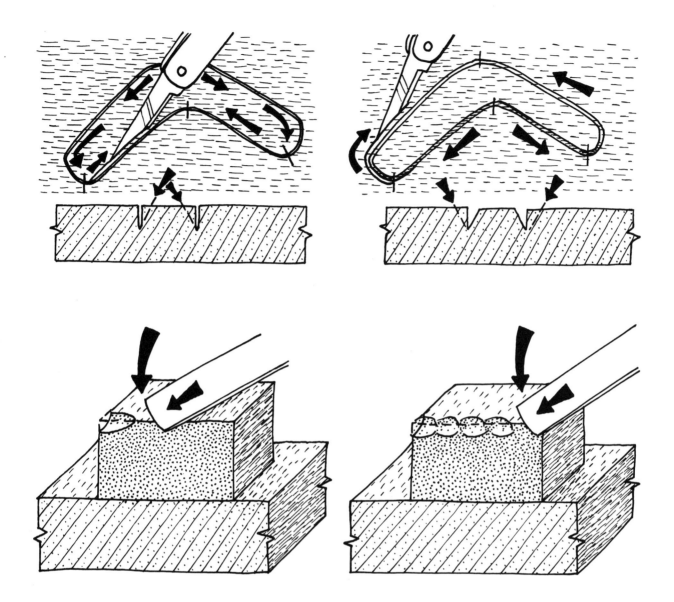

Illus. 4. Cutting across the grain. Top left: First sink a stop-cut that follows the design, and then cut at 'an angle into each side of the stop-cut so as to remove a V-section sliver of waste. Being watchful of the run of the grain, first run the blade around the inside of the stop-cut. Top right:

Make a second angled cut to complete the V-section trench. Note the change in the direction of the cut. Bottom left and right: Modelling the end grain, use a slicing downward cut, removing only small amounts until the required form is achieved.

spoon bit," a "shallow-curve straight gouge," or a "large U-section scoop gouge," and so on. With a "large, deep U-section spoon bit," "large" refers to the width of the cutting edge, "deep U-section" describes the shape of the cutting edge, and "spoon" describes the curve of the shaft. It's worth noting that North American Indian carvers have been using modified European steel/iron carving tools for the last hundred years or so (Illus. 3).

Glues and adhesives Although there are all manner of glues and adhesives, from animal glues to instant tube glues and resins, we recommend using PVA (polyvinyl acetate) glue, because it is easy to use, can be washed off when wet, and is not smelly or wasteful.

Grain This refers to the annual rings that run through the wood as well as to all the lines, colors, and textures that characterize a piece of wood. Wood-carvers spend much of their time trying to angle the thrust and direction of their tools so as to cut the grain to best advantage. Ideally, you need to cut either across or at a slight angle to the run of the grain (Illus. 4).

Gridded working drawing A scaled square grid

23

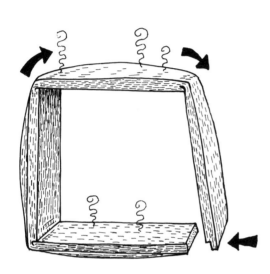
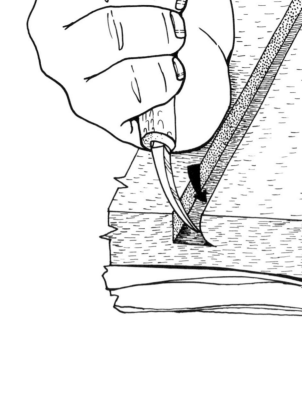

Illus. 5. Kerf-cut and steam-bent. Top right: The kerf joint needs to be worked with a saw and knife. Use the point of the knife to cut away the waste from under the overhang.

Bottom left: Once the wood has been kerf-cut at the corners, it can be steamed and bent into shape.

placed over a working drawing. In use, the object illustrated can be reduced or enlarged simply by changing the scale of the grid. So, for example, if the grid is described as "one square to 1"," and you want to double the scale, then all you do is make each square equal 2". When you come to transferring the drawing to the wood, you just draw out a grid to the suggested size and directly transfer the contents of each square. At one square to 1" you draw a full-size 1" grid, at two squares to 2" you draw a full-size 2" grid, and so on.

Grounding or wasting Cutting away the wood in and around the main design and taking it down to a lower level so that the design is left in relief.

Hold-down Of all the wood-holding tools, such as the vise and the clamp, for example, the bench hold-down is probably the most useful for the projects in this book. In use, the shaft is fitted into a hole in the bench, the swivel arm pad is set on the workpiece, and the screw thread is tightened up.

The mechanism allows for a swift release of the work.

Hollow-carved, or dished This describes areas that have been lowered and modelled so that the resultant cavity is curved, or dishlike, in shape.

Holly A beautiful, close-grained, ivory-white wood that carves well and takes fine details—a good wood for small delicate carvings such as amulets, bowls, and rattles.

Incised A shallow, knife-worked V-section trench or scoop cut. You first make an initial stop-cut, and then cut at an angle into each side of the stop-cut so as to remove a tapered V-section sliver of waste.

Inlay In the context of North American Indian wood carving, an inlay nearly always refers to decorative abalone, semiprecious stones, or strips of copper that have been inset so that they are flush with the surface. The North American Indians use inlay to give dramatic emphasis to primary features such as eyes, teeth, lips, and claws.

Kerf-cut In the context of this book, a partial cut made by a saw and/or a chisel and knife that is meant to encourage a "fold" or a bend in a length of wood, rather than a straight-through severing cut (Illus. 5).

Keyhole saw, or pad saw A small knifelike saw used for removing "windows" or cutting holes. It is especially useful for areas that are too thick or too inaccessible for a coping saw or a fretsaw.

Knife A carver needs a good selection of knives. It's best to collect and adapt knives as dictated by your needs; if a small kitchen knife, a penknife, or a scalpel does the job, then it's the one to use.

Knots These are termed as dead, hollow, loose, spiked, and so on. Knots are unpredictable, so do your best to avoid them.

Lime A close-grained, knot-free wood that is easy to work and can be cut and carved in almost any direction—the perfect wood for beginners.

Mallet A wooden-headed hammer that is used primarily with a chisel or gouge. You could also use a small club, such as a baseball bat, or a European type of sculpting mallet.

Maquette A working model that can be made of clay, Plasticine, or scrap wood.

Marking out Using a pencil with a sharp point to make crisp, clear guidelines.

Masking tape A general-purpose tape that is used to secure various parts while they are being glued, nailed, pegged, sawn, or otherwise worked. It's also, of course, used to secure paper to the drawing board and tracing paper to the wood. Avoid using transparent tape because it's too sticky and sometimes leaves a mess.

Measure This could be a wooden ruler, a tape measure, or a steel ruler. It's best to use a steel ruler because it can also be used as a cutting guide.

Moat A shallow U-section trench often employed in carvings around eyes and joints. Within the context of North American Indian carving, moats are important features that characterize the work.

Modifying Changing or redesigning a project so that it is smaller, larger, worked from thicker or thinner wood, or whatever—altering details to suit your own preferences or needs.

Paints and painting Before painting, always clear away bench clutter, wipe up dust, and carefully set out your tools and materials so that they will be conveniently close at hand. North American In-

dian carvers traditionally use basic, bold colors, such as red, blue, black, and white. The paint tends to be applied in thin matt washes rather than in solid gloss colors. We recommend using acrylics or even watercolors, and then rubbing them down with a fine sandpaper and applying a coat of wax polish.

Pear This wood is pinkish brown, has a close grain and a satiny finish, and cuts in just about any direction. It's a good wood for carving.

Pencil-press-transferring Tracing a master design and then pressing through the tracing so that the lines of the design are transferred through to the wood.

Piercing saw A small large-frame saw that is similar to the coping saw and fretsaw. Such a saw is particularly useful for delicate work, because the blades are fine and free from end pins so that they can be passed through minute pilot holes.

Plateau wood When the ground wood in and around a design feature has been cut away and lowered, then the remaining high-relief, flat-topped feature could be called a plateau. Such details as eyes, eyebrows, and lips, carved in high relief, characterize North American Indian wood carving.

Plum A beautiful pink-brown wood. Pleasant to carve, it has a tight grain and a hard, smooth finish.

Profile A form, blank, or cutout might be called a profile. The term is also used to describe the flat silhouette, or side view, of a workpiece, just after the waste has been cleared and just prior to modelling.

Prototype The initial model, or mock-up, made prior to buying and cutting your wood. For your prototypes, you could use Plasticine, clay, or inexpensive throwaway wood.

Riffler files Small, shaped files that are used for working small, difficult-to-reach corners, holes, and curves.

Rope quoit A coil of fat rope used to support a round-based item while it is being carved—helpful in making dishes, bowls, rattles, and masks.

Roughing out Swiftly clearing away the bulk of the waste with a saw or large gouge—the carving stage prior to modelling.

Rubbing down Rubbing the wood down with a series of graded sandpapers so as to achieve a smooth, ready-to-paint finish. In terms of North American Indian carving, the wood needs to be smooth to the touch, but not so overworked that you blur the crisp marks left by the cutting tools.

Sandpaper An abrasive used in the rubbing-down process, which is purchased in graded packs and used in a rough-to-smooth order. Sanding is a pleasurable but dusty task that is best carried out well away from the painting and designing area. We usually do our sanding outdoors.

Scale The ratio between the working drawing and the carving to be made. For example, if the scale is one grid square to 1″, then you draw a full-size 1″ grid and transfer the contents of the working-drawing squares through to your full-size squares.

Scalpel A slim-handled, fine-point, razor-sharp knife used for cutting, carving, and whittling fine details.

Setting in Meaning, to cut in along the design line, separating the ground wood from the relief design. A design could be set in either after or before cutting the V-section trench; it depends upon the character of the work. Thus, you could cut a V-section trench to the waste side of the drawn line, set in on the line, and then clear away the small amount of waste between the set-in line and the trench; or you could set in on the drawn line, cut the V-section trench, and then remove the small amount of waste.

Setting out This refers to transferring the traced lines through to the wood, as well as to generally preparing the wood, the tools, and the working area prior to carving.

Shallow-relief-carved Areas that have been wasted and lowered to a shallow depth—a design that travels over the surface of a carving without changing the basic shape of the piece.

Shaving knife A knife that is used like a scraper. The knife is held at both the point and handle, and dragged over the surface of the wood so as to remove fine shavings and wisps of waste.

Sharpening One of the secrets of wood carving is knowing how to keep your tools razor sharp. There's no problem with chisels. You simply set them in a little wheeled cradle (as sold by most tool manufacturers), run the cradle backwards and forward over the lightly oiled stone, and then, apart from a couple of swift strokes with the strop to remove any burrs, the job is done. Gouges are rather more tricky. Hold the gouge up to the light in your left hand, as if to peer closely at the cutting edge; then take the stone in your right hand and stroke the bevel of the gouge, while at the same time rolling the gouge so that the full arc of the bevel comes into contact with the stone. By seeing the shape of the bevel in silhouette, and by seeing the light shine between the blade and the stone, you can adjust the angle of the stone and/or the tool, and thus sharpen the cutting edge to best effect (Illus. 6).

Short grain Meaning, areas of wood where the structure of the grain is such that the wood is fragile and liable to split. In terms of North American Indian carving, the high points of such features as noses, lips, and nostrils, and of bowl rims, are usually short-grained.

Skew chisel A pointed chisel where the cutting edge is set at an angle of less than 90° to the side of the shaft—a good tool for cutting V-section trenches and for clearing difficult-to-reach areas of waste.

Spoon bit, or spoon gouge See **Gouges.**

Square A term used to describe wood that is square angled, clean faced, and altogether well prepared. Such wood might be described as being "fair and square."

Steam-bent In the context of this book, wood that has been kerf-cut, steamed, and bent. The thinner the wood and the longer the steaming process, the easier it is to achieve the bend (Illus. 5).

Stop-cut An initial cut straight down into the wood, a cut into which subsequent cuts are made. A stop-cut defines the length of subsequent cuts and acts as a brake, literally stopping the cut.

Straight saw Just about any straight-bladed, fine-toothed woodworking saw—a tenon or a gents, for example. It means a flat-bladed saw rather than, say, a thin-bladed coping or bow saw.

Sycamore A hard, light-colored wood that has a firm, compact grain and carves and finishes well. A traditional, nontoxic, low-taint wood, it is often used for storing dairy products and kitchenware.

Template A pattern or cutout made of wood, plastic, or cardboard—a shape that is used to reproduce a number of identical shapes. North American Indian carvers traditionally use thick hide templates for stylized motifs that they want to reverse and symmetrically repeat—such as for eyes, eyebrows, wings, hips, and elbow and knee joints.

Timber faults There is no such thing as a perfect piece of wood or any guarantee that a particular block of wood is workable throughout. If wood is discolored or spongy, it could be decayed. If there are end cracks or "checks," the wood is best avoided. If the wood is stained by, say, oil, rust, or grease, then look for another piece. The list goes on and on. The best we can do is to look out for problem indicators and try to spot the flaws and faults at an early stage.

Try to be on the lookout for such faults as foreign bodies within the wood, hidden cavities, cup shakes, unwanted waney bark, unexpected grain twists, and so on. Always double-check your wood before you start carving, and if you have any doubts as to its quality, put it aside and look for another piece (Illus. 7).

Tool-textured Meaning, the marks left by the tools. For the projects in this book, tool marks are de-sirable. It's best to give the finished carving a swift rubdown with fine-grade sandpaper, so as to leave the surface feeling smooth and yet at the same time dappled and rippled with tool marks.

Tracing paper A strong, translucent paper used for tracing. We usually work up a good design, take a tracing with a soft 2B pencil, line in the reverse side of the tracing, and then use a hard pencil to press-transfer the lines of the design through to the working face of the wood.

Trenching The procedure of sinking a stop-cut and then using a knife to cut into each side of the stop-cut so as to remove a sliver of waste. If you prefer, you can use a V-section tool rather than a knife.

Undercutting Sinking the waste so as to make a plateau, and then gouging out a cavity from the

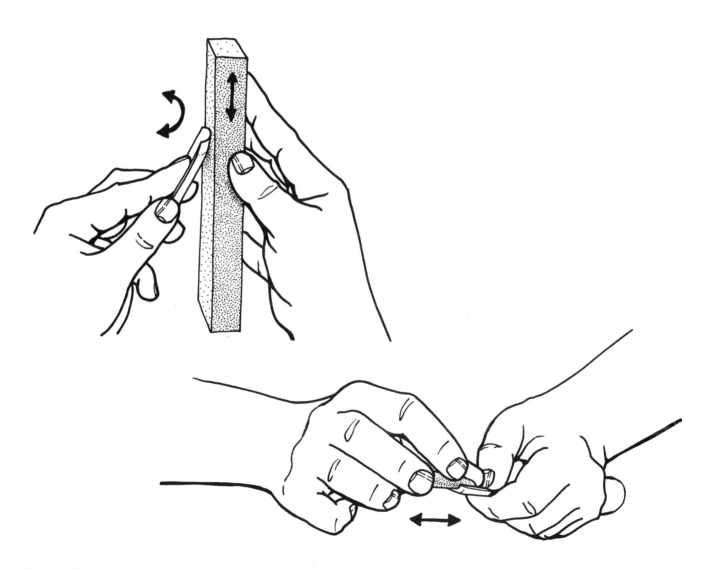

Illus. 6. Sharpening a gouge. Top: Hold the gouge up to the light and stroke the bevel with the stone, gently swivelling the gouge so that the whole arc of the bevel comes into contact with the moving stone. Bottom: Stroke the inside curve of the gouge with the small, tapered slip stone so as to remove the edge-of-blade burr.

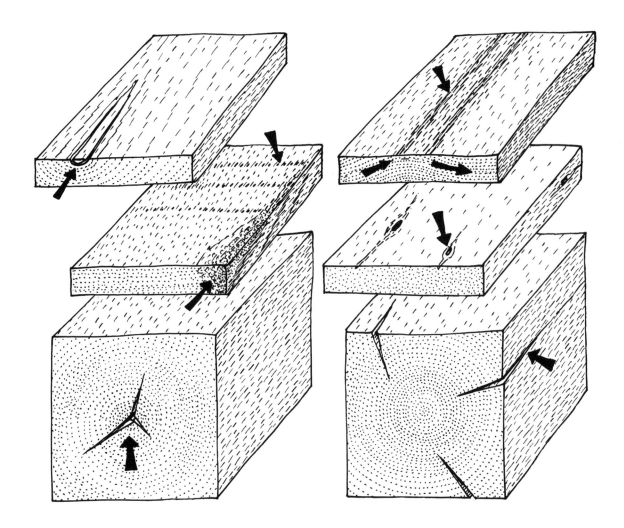

Illus. 7. Timber faults. Faulty timber is best avoided. Top left: Cup shake—here, the heart of the wood is split and unstable. Top right: Distorted out-of-character grain—such wood is likely to be difficult to work. Middle left: Soft edges and fungal stains suggest that the wood has started to decay. Middle right: Dead knots can be a problem in that they are likely to drop out. Bottom left: Heart shakes are the result of old age and shrinkage of the heartwood—such timber might well contain large cavities and splits. Bottom right: Star shakes are usually the result of severe artificial seasoning.

side of the plateau so as to achieve an overhang or undercut.

Vegetable oil   Just about any plant oil that you might use to protect and burnish the wood—corn oil, nut oil, soya oil, etc. It's best to apply a couple of coats, let them soak in, give the wood a swift rubbing down, and then burnish with a brush and cloth.

V-board   Also called a V-table or a bird's mouth fretsaw table. In use, it is clamped to the work surface so that the V-notch extends beyond the surface; the sawing needs to be done near the vertex of the V-notch.

V-section tool   Also called a veiner, a V-section tool can be used to carve fine V-section cuts or trenches.

Vise   A bench-mounted clamp that comes in all shapes and sizes. There are engineer's vises, carver's chops, and so on. The vise needs to be strong enough for the job at hand.

Waste ground   The areas in and around the design that need to be lowered, wasted, or otherwise cut away.

Whittling   Generally taken to mean cutting and carving with a small hand-held knife. You carve with the workpiece being held and supported in one hand and the knife being held in the other. It's best to work with a comfortable-to-hold, sharp-edged knife, and to employ a careful thumb-paring action.

Workbench Regardless of whether you use a specially designed carpenter's bench or a strong kitchen table for a workbench, it needs to be strong enough to take a variety of clamps.

Working drawing A scaled and detailed drawing that shows sizes, sections, details, and so on. Never cut the original drawing—always take a tracing.

Working face The best side of the wood—the side on which you draw the face that is in full view, for example, the front of a panel, the front of a totem pole, and the outside panels of a box.

Work-out paper Inexpensive paper that can be used for initial roughs and work-out drawings. It's best to use a slightly matt white paper.

Workshop In the context of this book, your workshop can be just about any place, from a spare room or a garden shed to the garage. Ideally, the room needs to have a workbench, a water supply, good ventilation, power, good natural light, plenty of shelf space, a heater, a bin for rubbish, a corner set aside for rubbing down, a painting area, and so on. If you are a beginner, it's best to start with the basic space and then organize the surfaces and areas as the work progresses and you come to understand your own needs. You might decide, for instance, to do the working drawings in the kitchen or bedroom, the sawing in the garage, the rubbing down in the garden or yard, and the painting and waxing in the garden shed. Your workshop needs to be well considered.

Remember that wood-carving tools are sharp and best kept away from small children. Please be warned and organize your workshop accordingly.

PROJECTS

1
Whale–Eagle Dish (Haida)

A "grease" dish with whale-eagle imagery
used at potlatch ceremonies

Saw, gouge, and knife
Hollow-carved, shallow-relief-carved, and incised
Oiled and burnished

During the Indian potlatch, or ceremonial "giving away" feast, it was customary for chiefs and clan dignitaries to demonstrate their importance by lavishly distributing gifts and food. With a great deal of singing and dancing, guests would be led into the great feast house and invited to sit around an enormous fire. Once everyone was carefully seated in order of importance, hosts and guests alike would give speeches and take part in dance dramas.

It was during these self-glorifying dramas, when hosts and guests would vigorously uphold their claims to hereditary status by reenacting traditional events from family and clan histories, that the food was served.

Superior status was also claimed and demonstrated by individuals as well as entire clans by offering and accepting eating challenges. Thus, the host might single out a rival individual and then try to humiliate

Illus. 1. Project picture—a Haida "grease" dish with whale-eagle imagery, worked in cedar.

him by suggesting that he was so inferior that he had never experienced a good meal. Once the challenge had been made and accepted, mounds of food would be brought in and set before the individual who had accepted the challenge. Large, carved heirloom dishes, huge bowls, and sometimes whole canoes full of food would be brought in. And, of course, as the name of the game was making sure that there was an overwhelming superabundance, the challenging group always had a great deal more food than was needed.

Finally, to further justify his status claim, the host would be extravagantly wasteful with the excess. It was at this stage—during the great grease feast—that expensive oil in huge "grease" dishes would be brought in and carelessly splashed about. Then, as a parting who-cares-anyway gesture, the host would start pouring the oil onto the fire. And so the potlatch continued, with the oil-fed fire blazing higher and higher, with more speeches being made, and with more gifts being presented.

Eventually, after days of excessive eating, drinking, making speeches, and acting out dramas, everyone would go home, either happy and content with the proceedings or at least determined to hold a bigger and better potlatch next time around.

DESIGN, STRUCTURE, AND TECHNIQUE CONSIDERATIONS

Take a good long look at the project picture (Illus. 1) and the working drawings (Illus. 2), and see how at a grid scale of about two squares to 1", the bowl is about 12" long, 5 to 6" high, and 6" wide.

Note how, at one end, the round-nosed design represents a whale, while at the other end, the sharp down-turned beak represents an eagle. The dual nature of the crests suggests that the clan to whom the bowl belonged laid claim to both an eagle and a whale as being part of their supernatural heritage.

Working from a single, carefully selected block of cedar, the carver has skillfully reduced the bowl walls to an overall thickness of about 1/2" at the rim and to 1 to 1 1/2" at the end and sides.

Apart from the whale and eagle heads that are obviously carved in the round, the rest of the design is shallow-relief-carved and incised. Looking carefully at the incised imagery, you will see that the central side motif shows both the whale's flipper and the eagle's wing.

If you get the chance, visit a museum to see *Haida* bowls of a similar type and period. If you have any doubts as to how the form will look in the round or how the details need to be worked, get yourself a small block of Plasticine or clay and make a model.

Now, draw the project out to size and establish clear profile views of the top, ends, and sides.

TOOLS AND MATERIALS

For this project you need:

- a block of straight-grained, knot-free cedar that's about 6 1/2 × 6 1/2" square and 12 to 14" long—which allows for carve-back wastage

- a pencil and ruler

- a sheet each of tracing and work-out paper

- a hand drill with a 1/2"-diameter drill bit to fit

- a straight saw

- a large coping saw

- the use of a bench with a vise and hold-down

- a good selection of gouges and knives, including a deep U-section scoop gouge, a large, wide U-section gouge, a small V-chisel, a crooked knife, and a scalpel

- a pack of graded sandpapers

- a small amount of edible vegetable oil

SETTING OUT THE DESIGN

When you have a good, clear picture in your mind's eye of how the carving needs to be worked—the overall form, the depth of the bowl, the beautiful full shape of the two heads, and the subtle cuts and curves that go into making the patterns and imagery—then set the block of wood down fair and square on the workbench and check it over for any possible problems. Avoid wood that looks in any way to be stained, knotty, waney, or, worst of all, split.

Once you have checked out the wood, trace the outer-limits views and elevations from the master design, and pencil-press-transfer the traced lines through to the faces of the wood (Illus. 3, top). At this stage, don't bother with all the small designs and details; just concentrate on the main profiles. When this is done, go over the transferred lines to make sure that they are clear and well established, and then cross-hatch all the waste areas that need to be cut away. Label the various views "whale," "eagle," "top," and so on.

Now, pin up the drawings so that they are in full

Illus. 2. Working drawings. The grid scale is two squares to 1".

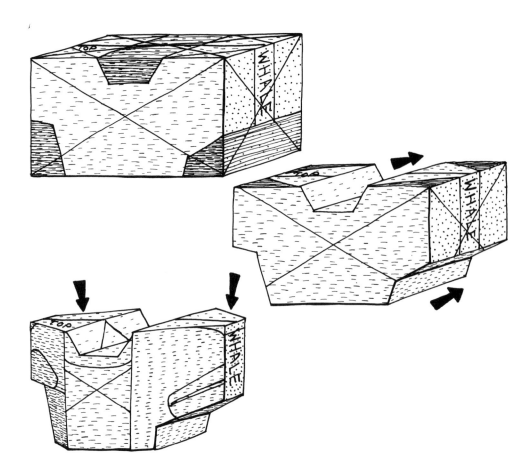

Illus. 3. Top: Transfer the outline profile through to the wood and label the faces "top," "eagle," and "whale." Middle: Cut away the wood from under the two heads and across the top of the dish. Bottom: Establish the "boat" shape.

view, clear all the clutter off the workbench, and set out all your tools so that they are comfortably close at hand.

ROUGHING OUT

With the block of wood held secure in the vise, take the straight saw and the coping saw and start to clear away the areas of unwanted wood. Thus, you can cut away the wood from under the two end heads and across the top of the dish (Illus. 3, middle). Then establish the boat shape of the bowl (Illus. 3, bottom). Don't try to get too close to the envisaged form; just settle for clearing away the large areas of waste. When this is done, use the tracings and the master design to reestablish the lines of the design.

Once you have removed the bulk of the waste and have established the rim level, the bowl width, and one or two main reference points, take a pencil and ruler and mark in what you consider to be the top-of-the-bowl middle point. Now take the drill bit, use a piece of masking tape to mark it off at a point about 2½″ from its tip, and then sink a pilot, or depth, hole down into the bowl where you made your mark (Illus. 4, top right). Reckoning on a base-to-rim height at the middle of about 3½″, the 2½″-deep pilot hole should stop short about an inch away from the bottom of the bowl.

Having cleared away the rough and sunk the pilot hole, secure the wood to the bench and prepare to clear away the waste area in the middle of the bowl. Mark in clearly the rim thickness of the bowl and establish a stop-cut; then take the deep U-section scoop gouge and, working from the sides to the middle, begin cutting out the central waste (Illus. 4, bottom). Working with short, controlled, wood-scooping chops, cut right around the inside rim. Continue in this manner, all the while measuring and assessing as the bowl gets deeper and the walls get thinner.

When you get to the bottom of the pilot hole, you can assume that the base is only 1″ thick. Finally, using a crooked knife, round and work the inside of the bowl. Continue paring away fine slivers of wood until the inside bowl is smooth but slightly dappled.

CARVING THE WHALE AND EAGLE FORMS

After you have chopped out the inside-bowl waste comes the challenging and skill-stretching task of trying to carve the outside form of the whale and eagle.

Draw in the middle lines, and then, with the coping saw, gouges, and crooked knife, cut, carve, and shape the beautiful, broad sweep around the whale "nose" (Illus. 5, top left). In like manner, carve the proud and thrusting hook of the eagle's beak, the slightly concave dishing of the four main eye areas, and so on (Illus. 5, right).

There is of course no single, easy, sure-fire way of carving a project of this sort. With that said, you won't go far wrong if you keep your tools sharp, settle for removing the wood a little at a time, and cut and work either across or with the grain. It's also important to never dig too deeply into the wood, push the point of the gouge or knife into end grain, carve with an uncontrolled slashing stroke, or try to extricate the point of a tool by levering down.

Now, hold the dish on its side and carve the side edges on the bottom to a smooth curve.

As you get nearer and nearer to the envisaged form, you will have to keep the bowl turning, all the while keeping one eye on the working drawings and pencilling in and reestablishing the main shapes and interior lines. You will also have to spend more time standing back and assessing your progress, bearing in mind that with every stroke you are getting closer to the limits of the wood and of course to the finished form that is hidden just below the surface. Therefore, you will have to proceed cautiously and settle for only removing small amounts of wood.

As the animal forms emerge from the wood, the carving will become more fragile, and so you will have to think of ways of holding it secure other than by putting it in the vise or clamping it with the hold-down. At this stage it's best to cradle the workpiece in your lap or support it on, say, an old rag-filled cushion or on a bag half-filled with sand.

Finally, when you are happy with the overall form and shape of the carving, go over it with a knife held on its edge and scrape the surface to give it a slightly rippled, tooled finish.

DETAILING AND FINISHING

Having worked the form, meaning the overall shape of the bowl, you can start to cut in all the little details that make up the wraparound design. Take another look at the project picture (Illus. 1) and the working drawings (Illus. 2), and then transfer the lines of the

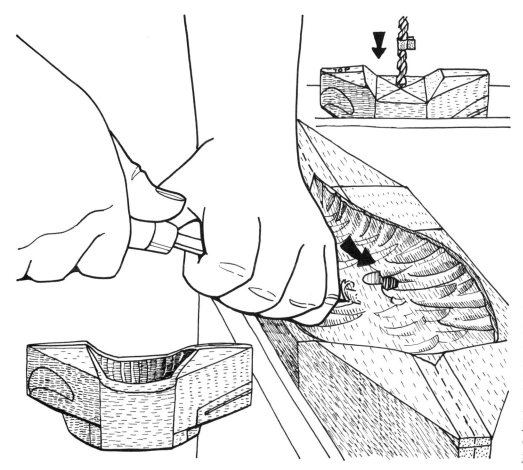

Illus. 4. Top right: Use masking tape on the drill bit to mark the 2½″ depth of the hole. Sink the hole in the middle of the bowl. Bottom: Take the deep U-section scoop gouge and, working from the sides to the middle, cut away the unwanted wood from inside the bowl.

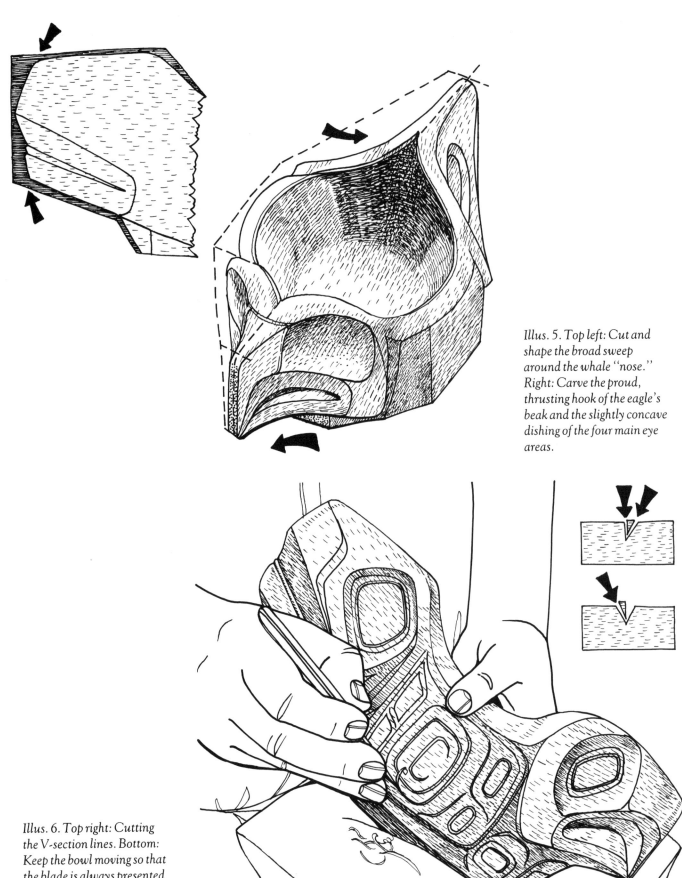

Illus. 5. Top left: Cut and shape the broad sweep around the whale "nose." Right: Carve the proud, thrusting hook of the eagle's beak and the slightly concave dishing of the four main eye areas.

Illus. 6. Top right: Cutting the V-section lines. Bottom: Keep the bowl moving so that the blade is always presented with the line of the next cut; brace your arm by tucking it into your waist.

design through to the sides of the dish. See how the pattern motifs are made up of incised lines and very shallow relief-carved depressions.

The incised V-section lines are pretty straightforward—all you do is make three cuts for each line. First you make a single cut to establish the position of the line, and then you work secondary angled cuts at each side of the initial cut so that a V-section sliver of waste falls away (Illus. 6, top right). Of course, you could always use a V-section gouge, but since the lines taper and vary, it's probably best to use either a small penknife or a scalpel. Work with a tight, controlled action, all the while keeping the bowl moving so that the blade is always presented with the line of the next cut, and keeping your arm well braced by tucking your elbow into your waist (Illus. 6, bottom).

When you come to cutting the shallow depressions or dishings, start by shading in the area that needs to be sunk or lowered. When this is done, use a knife to run a V-section line around the area (Illus. 7, top right), and then use the tool of your choice to cut away the waste. Of course, the tool you choose will depend on the size and shape of the area being lowered, but, generally speaking, you will need to use the

crooked knife and/or one of the small shallow-curve spoon gouges. Cut away the waste with shallow scooping or shaving strokes (Illus. 7, bottom), watching out for the run of the grain and adjusting the angle and direction of your cut accordingly. And so you continue, variously cutting in V-section lines, outlining areas that need to be lowered, and sinking areas of waste.

Finally, when you feel that the bowl is finished, rub it over with the finest sandpaper, wipe it down with the vegetable oil, and burnish it to a dull-sheen finish.

TROUBLESHOOTING AND POSSIBLE MODIFICATIONS

- If your knife or gouge starts cutting up roughly, then it needs to be sharpened. It's best to develop a rhythm of working: a few minutes spent carving, a few seconds honing the knife or gouge on the stone, a moment or two to stand back and consider your progress, and so on.

- Don't be too slavish about following the design—if you need to adjust a feature or detail because of a fault in the wood, or maybe because of an over-enthusiastic cut, or simply because you want the design to go in a slightly different direction, then don't hesitate to do so. Always be prepared to veer away from the design and to modify your work to suit your own needs.

- When you are cutting the V-section grooves around the edge of the eye plateau, be careful so that the thin band of wood between the incised cut and the edge of the relief area doesn't crumble away. It's important to have the edge of the plateau strengthened and buttressed by having the high wood running down into the dishing cut in a smooth curve.

- The bowl should be sharp-edged, chamfered, and slightly undercut along the inside rim—spend time getting this right. Looking at the various details should be helpful.

- If you become anxious about the carving and don't know whether you should continue working on it, consider it finished, or throw it out, then it's best to call a halt for a day or two and then go back to work with a fresh eye.

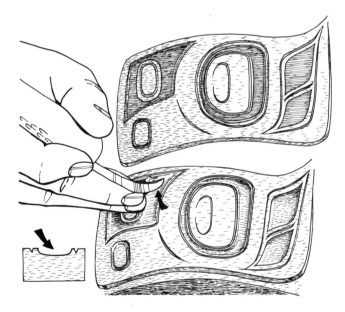

Illus. 7. Top right: Run the knife around the areas to be dished—the shaded areas. Bottom: Remove the waste with shallow scooping cuts.

2
Shaman's Staff (Tsimshian)

A staff with crest figures and motifs used during curing rites

Knife-shaped, set in with stop-cuts, incised, shallow-relief-carved, and whittled Oiled and burnished

A shaman's power had a great deal to do with his showmanship and his dramatic use of sleight-of-hand tricks. This is not to say that he was thought to be a trickster or in any way fraudulent, but rather that there was a general, unspoken understanding that the shaman's palming skills were themselves supernaturally controlled.

Like a conjurer, he would appear, surprise and mystify his audience with his awe-inspiring performance, and then attempt to use his powers to cure his patient. Certainly, the audience might have doubted the shaman's powers, but, just as we know that a magician can't really pluck live rabbits out of thin air, yet we are still struck with awe when we see these tricks done, so the Indians were equally stunned with the shaman's performance.

A shaman's staff, sometimes called a "talking stick," was more than just a badge of office; it was part of his curing regalia. With a carefully staged buildup, including much drumming, rattle shaking, and singing, the shaman would announce his approach by tapping his staff on the ground.

Imagine a firelit room and relatives gathered around a sick man's bed. Without warning, the chanting and drumbeating stops. A faint tap, tap, tapping is heard—which grows louder and louder. Suddenly, the shaman enters the room, with his staff of office in one hand and a rattle in the other. His painted-and-oiled mask glistens and glints in the firelight. Long coils of hair, bone amulets, and feathers fall in plaited swaths over his shoulders. His headdress of bear claws and bones make him look at least a head taller than the tallest

man in the room. Suddenly, he plucks a "disease" object out of the air—the cause of the illness—and begins to sing and plead with the spirits. Who could doubt the supernatural powers of such a man!

DESIGN, STRUCTURE, AND TECHNIQUE CONSIDERATIONS

Take a look at the project picture (Illus. 1) and the working drawings (Illus. 2), and see how, at a scale of four grid squares to 1″, the carved-staff detail measures about 7″ long and about 1¾″ in diameter at its widest point. Note how the motifs are carved in such a way that they give the illusion of being deeply worked. However, if you study the forms closely, you will see that they are no more than surface-incised and shallow-relief-carved, with the deepest detail being cut to a depth of no more than about ¼ to ⅜″.

Consider also how although the forms look to be in the round and three-dimensional, they are actually more of a surface design that wraps around the staff. Note the shape and form of the characteristically stylized *Tsimshian* motifs—the ears, the eyebrows, the almond-shaped eyes with the big, round pupils, the side eyes that mark the shoulder joints, the long, extended beak and mouth, and the infill of feathers. Of course, we have only shown the 7″ carved section, but take into account the staff being about 7′ long, with the 7″-long carved section set about 6 to 7″ down from the top of the staff.

When you have studied all the details and consid-

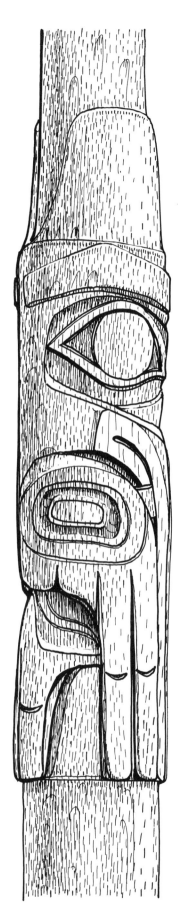

ered all the possibilities, sit down with a pencil and a pad of work-out paper and draw the design up to full size.

TOOLS AND MATERIALS

For this project you need:

- a 7'-long piece of square 2 × 2″ wood—for example, a strong, easy-to-carve wood such as pencil cedar

- a sheet each of work-out and tracing paper

- a pencil and ruler

- a good selection of knives, including a crooked knife, a heavy craft knife, a stout shaving knife, and a scalpel or fine-bladed penknife

- a small amount of vegetable oil and a cloth

CHOOSING THE WOOD AND ROUGHING OUT

Once you have studied the various drawings and details, and have a clear understanding of how the project needs to be worked, pin the drawings up and out of harm's way and prepare your working area. Of course, as this project is worked with no more than a clutch of knives, your working area might be anyplace, from a nice shady spot out in the garden to a chair on the porch or a stool by the fire. One of the pleasures of working a project like this is that you can easily take it up and put it down, as the mood strikes you.

Now, take the 2 × 2″ square section of wood and check it over for faults. The 7' length needs to be smooth and straight-grained, strong, and completely free from splits, knots, and twists. If the wood looks in any way to be less than perfect, then put it to one side and choose another piece.

When you have selected your wood, take your largest and sharpest knife and set about shaving the 2 × 2″ square section down to about a 2″-diameter round section. As with any carving process, don't be tempted to rush through the task, trying to rip away the waste. Approach it nice and easy, all the while making sure that the blade of the knife doesn't run too deeply into the wood (Illus. 3, top). If by chance the knife does appear to be running into the grain, turn the staff around and approach the cut from the other direction. Continue shaving and turning, shaving and turning,

Illus. 1. Project picture—a Tsimshian shaman's staff with crest figures and motifs.

41

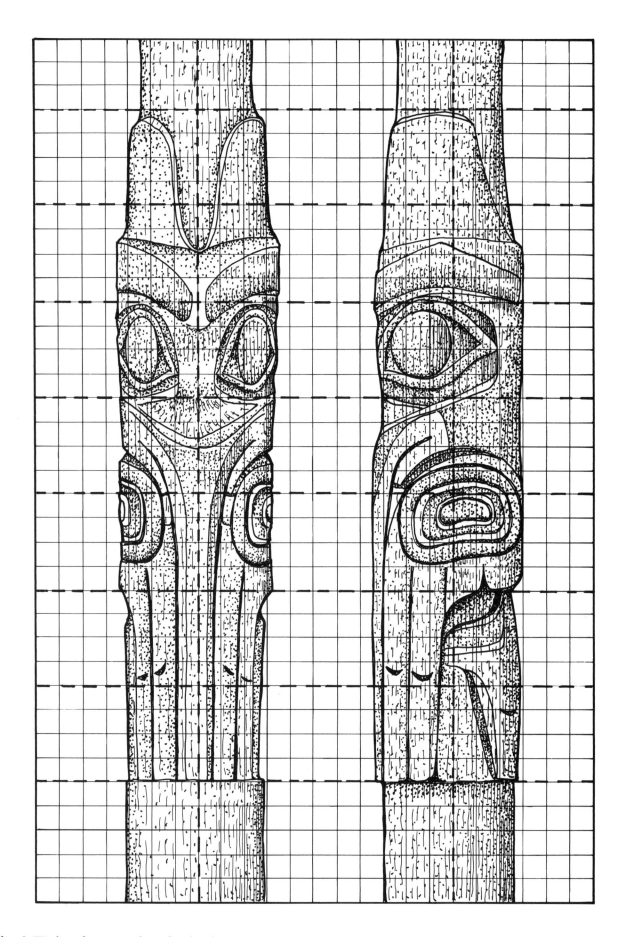

Illus. 2. Working drawings. The grid scale is four squares to 1″.

42

until the wood takes on a pleasant, slightly rippled, round appearance.

SETTING OUT AND CUTTING IN THE DESIGN

When you have achieved a good, clean section of wood, measure down about 6 or 7″ from the top end of the staff and then pencil in the 7″ section that needs to be carved. Wrap a thin strip of paper around the staff, cut it to fit the circumference, and then fold it in half and in half again so as to divide its length into equal quarters. Having decided on the position of the main central line, use the strip of paper to run four quarter-circle lines down the shaft (Illus. 3, bottom right). Label the lines "front center," "left," "right," and "back." Now, starting just above the "ear" motif and working down the shaft at 1″ intervals, run lines around the area that is to be carved (Illus. 4, top).

Having drawn in the guide grid and having made sure that the grid checks off against the grid of the working drawings, take a fine-pointed hard pencil and very carefully draw in all the primary lines that make up the design.

Now, take a sharp, comfortable-to-hold medium-sized knife and cut in the lines of the design to a depth of about ⅛″ (Illus. 4, bottom). In the main,

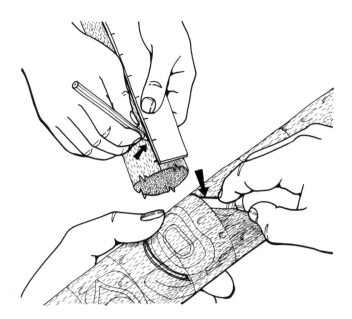

Illus. 4. Top: Starting just above the "ear" motif and working down the staff at 1″ intervals, run lines around the area to be carved. Bottom: Use a medium-sized knife to cut in the lines of the design.

it's best to work in a sitting position, with the bottom of the staff resting on the floor, and with the shaft being held and gripped between your knees. Grasp the shaft firmly in one hand and use the knife with a thumb-braced dragging, or paring, action. Of course, while you are cutting in the design, you will have to roll and move the shaft so that the point of the knife is always presented with the line of the best cut.

MAKING STOP-CUTS AND WHITTLING

When you have cut in the design, have another look at the working drawings (Illus. 2), and see how the carving can be broken down into main areas, or features—the eyes, the ears, and so on. Now, starting with, say, the outline around the top of the stylized ears, take a small knife and cut in at an angle towards the initial stop-cut, so as to remove a V-section sliver of waste (Illus. 5, top right). Aim to leave the edge of the ears looking sharp, crisp, and at stepped right angles to the working face. Once you have established the sharp, stepped profile of the ear, then go back to the larger knife and lower what is now the waste ground, so that the shaft runs from the top of the ear in a smooth sweep and tapers towards the top of the staff. Refer back to Illus. 2—the working drawing on the left.

Still looking at Illus. 2, see how there is another

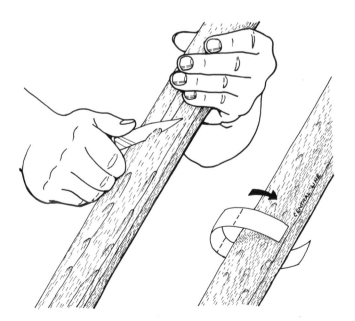

Illus. 3. Top: Shave the 2 × 2″ square section of wood down to a 2″-diameter round section. Bottom right: Decide on the position of the main central line and then use a strip of paper to divide the circumference into equal quarters.

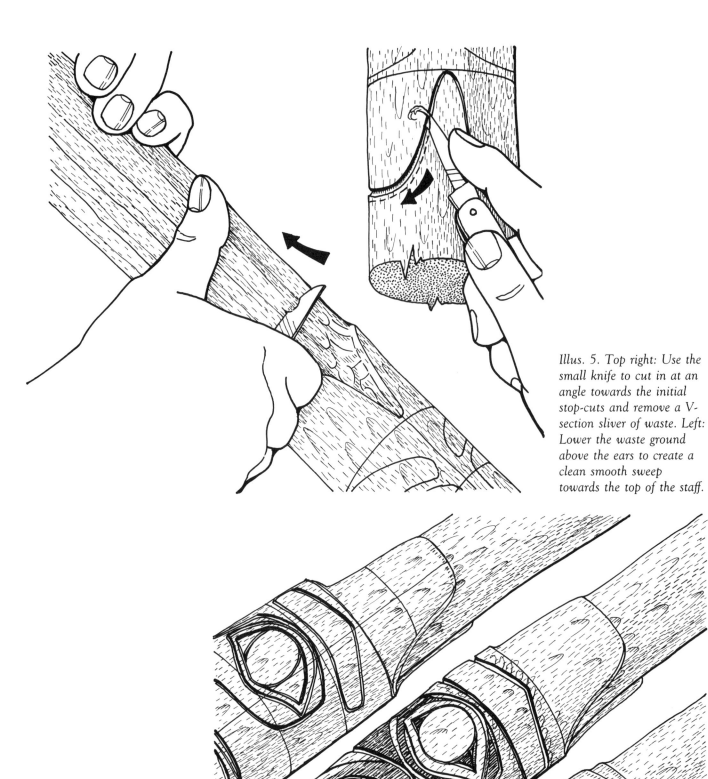

Illus. 5. Top right: Use the small knife to cut in at an angle towards the initial stop-cuts and remove a V-section sliver of waste. Left: Lower the waste ground above the ears to create a clean smooth sweep towards the top of the staff.

Illus. 6. Top: Cut the eyebrows and the other main design lines. Middle: Widen the stop-cuts on the waste side of the design line and shade in the areas that need to be lowered. Bottom: Lower the shaded areas so as to form the characteristic steps and angles.

44

slight step from the top of the eyebrows to the ears. Now proceed as before—first making sure that the line is well established with a stop-cut, then cutting in towards the stop-cut so as to make a V-section trench, and finally lowering the wood on the waste side of the trench so that the design steps down from the forehead towards the ears. The same goes for the eyebrows themselves. If you look at them closely, you will see that they are raised ever so slightly from the surrounding ground, so that there is a step down from the surface of the eyebrow towards the forehead. Again, make sure that the shape of the eyebrow is set in well with a stop-cut (Illus. 6, top), widen the stop-cut on the waste side of the line so as to make a V-section trench (Illus. 6, middle), and then lower the ground on the waste side of the trench so that the eyebrow is left in relief (Illus. 6, bottom).

Continue working slowly down the shaft in this manner. Of course, some of the steps aren't sharp at all but are actually more angled slopes, yet the approach remains the same.

Finally, shave the staff so that it runs in a smooth, easy taper from the carved area on down towards its foot (Illus. 7, top).

FINISHING

When you have what you consider to be a fairly good carving, take a small scrap of fine sandpaper and a scalpel, and work backwards and forward over the various steps, scoops, dips, angles, cracks, and crannies, making sure that they are all free from burrs and ragged edges (Illus. 7, bottom). The success of a small carving like this hinges on its being crisply and precisely worked. Spend time making sure that the raised surfaces are smooth and the bottom of the various V-section areas are free from debris. Finally, when you are happy with the project, wipe it over several times with a generous amount of vegetable oil and burnish the wood to a good smooth finish.

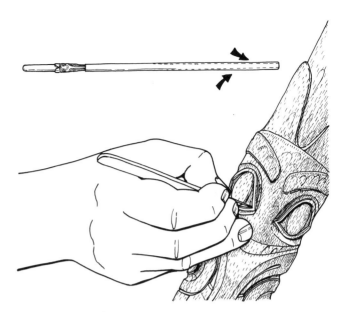

Illus. 7. Top: Shave the staff from beneath the carved area and on down towards the foot, trying to form a gentle taper. Bottom: Use the scalpel to remove the burrs and ragged edges, cleaning out all the angles, cracks, and steps.

TROUBLESHOOTING AND POSSIBLE MODIFICATIONS

- Your choice of wood is of primary importance—it has to be strong, smooth-grained, free from knots, and easy to carve. Certainly, a wood like ash is strong and free from knots, but it is almost impossible to carve. And, then again, although a wood like mahogany is strong and easy to carve, it is completely out of character for this project. If you have a choice, it's best to go for one of the cedars.

- Apart from roughing out and shaving, when the wood is sliced away from you with big, broad, follow-through strokes, the actual motif carving is best achieved with small, tight, thumb-controlled levering-and-paring cuts.

- If you like the overall design but would prefer to make, say, a walking stick, then all you do is change the length of the stick.

3
Rites Charm (Tsimshian)

A shaman's good-luck charm or amulet worn
around the neck

Knife and saw
Fretted, pierced, incised, and shallow-relief-carved
Waxed and burnished

The *Tsimshian* Indians believed that the spirits were present in all things—in the rocks, in the trees, in the elements, in the animals, in every aspect of life. They believed that some of these supernatural beings were friendly and concerned with ordinary everyday activities, such as fishing and eating, while others were malevolent and needed careful watching. Everything possessed a spiritual force or power.

The Indians were always on the lookout for signs of a supernatural presence. A clap of thunder, a flash of lightning, a whistling noise in the trees, an unusual cloud formation, an animal behaving in a certain way—such natural phenomena were all considered to be indications that the spirits were active and close by.

It was necessary to acknowledge, thank, and plead with the spirits by holding rites and acting out special ceremonial dramas. Since so much in their lives depended on hunting, a good many of the rites were related to placating specific animal beings. There were salmon rites, bear rites, bird rites, curing rites, and so on. To assist them in these special acts, the Indians would wear little amulets—such as small carvings, special stones, feathers, and the like—for good luck. If a hunting party or a group making a canoe, for example, felt they needed special magic assistance, they sought the services of a shaman. The charm featured in this project was used by a *Tsimshian* shaman during salmon-curing rites.

DESIGN, STRUCTURE, AND TECHNIQUE CONSIDERATIONS

Take a good long look at the project picture (Illus. 1) and the working drawings (Illus. 2), and see how, at a scale of four grid squares to 1″, the charm measures just under 3″ wide, about 5″ long, and ¾″ thick. Note the way the form is pierced, rounded, incised, and shallow-relief-carved.

The design includes a cranelike bird with a characteristically *Tsimshian*, stylized eye motif, moonlike face symbols on both the wing and tail joints, and various infill forms on the wings and beak. It's worth noting that charms of this size and character were also worn as a set, meaning that a collection of different charms would be suspended from a single, much larger charm. Therefore, you might want to try your hand at carving a number of different forms, and thus modify the project accordingly.

Both sides of the charm need to be carved with the various motifs being worked as near-identical mirror images.

Although, ideally, this small, rounded, rather delicate form should be worked from a tight-grained, pale wood such as box, holly, or even yew, there's no reason why you can't change the size and character of the project and use, say, lime or maybe even a fruit wood such as pear. It's best to consider carefully your carving skills, your tools, and how you envision the proj-

Illus. 1. Project picture—*a* Tsimshian *rites charm.*

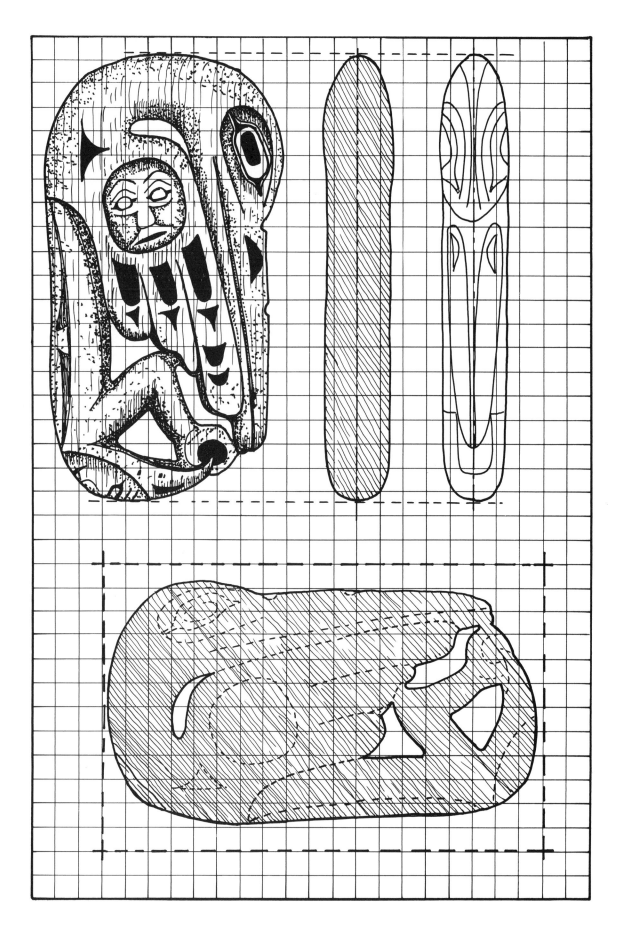

Illus. 2. Working drawings. The grid scale is four squares to 1″.

ect—its size and usage—and then to adjust the design and select the wood according to your needs.

Since this project is small and pierced, you will have to choose your wood with extra care. Avoid wood that appears to be coarse-grained, sappy, knotty, or stained.

If you get the chance, take a trip to a museum to see the range of small *Tsimshian* carvings, from charms and amulets to nose pins, "soul-catcher" tubes, and lip plugs.

When you have carefully looked over the project picture and the working drawings, and have a clear understanding of how the project needs to be worked, sit down with a pad of work-out paper and draw the design out to size. Establish a crisp, workable profile, drawing out the front, back, top, and side views.

TOOLS AND MATERIALS

For this project you need:

- a piece of ¾"-thick, close-grained, knot-free wood at a little over 5 × 3"—box is probably best

- a pencil, a ruler, and work-out paper

- a small hand drill and a ³⁄₁₆" drill bit to fit

- a coping, fretwork, or bow saw

- a pack of spare blades to suit the saw

- a workbench or table, with a vise or a clamp and a bird's mouth fretwork board

- a selection of small knives—perhaps a couple of small penknives and a scalpel

- a riffler file

- a pack of graded sandpapers

SETTING OUT THE DESIGN

Having looked at the project picture and the working drawings, draw the main profile out to size and shade in all the areas that need to be cut away and wasted. When all the lines are well established, use a soft pencil to take a good, clear pencil tracing. Reverse the tracing and tape it in place on the wood with tabs of masking tape.

When you are happy with the overall arrangement, and when you have taken note of the run of the grain and of any awkward knots and the like, take a hard pencil and press-transfer the traced lines through to the wood. Don't worry at this early stage about all the

fine details; just try to transfer the main outline profile and the pierced areas (Illus. 3).

Finally, when you have drawn in good, crisp, clear lines, shade in the areas that need to be cut away, and pin up the working drawings and tracings so that they are out of harm's way yet in view.

CUTTING OUT THE PROFILE AND ROUGHING OUT

Secure the wood in the vise and use the drill to run pilot holes through the middle of each of the four pierced areas, or "windows." When this is done, dismantle your chosen saw, pass the blade through one of the holes, locate and retension the blade, and then cut out the enclosed shape. Aim to cut slightly to the waste side of the drawn lines. Work at a steady, even pace, all the while doing your best to hold the saw so that the blade passes through the wood at right angles to the working face.

Having cut out the holes, secure the wood in the vise and cut away the outside waste in like manner. Again, try to work the cut edge so that it is at right angles, or 90°, to the working face (Illus. 4).

Take another look at the project picture and the working drawings and note how some edges are smooth and round whereas others are relatively crisp and flat. Now take your chosen tool—anything from a large craft knife or a penknife to a clasp knife or even a specially shaped and modified kitchen knife—and remove the bulk of the edge waste.

As you are working, try to cut from high to low wood or across the grain, being careful not to run the blade into the end grain. Continue running the knife across the grain, cutting away the sharp corners, and generally whittling and wasting, until you have achieved a round-edged, pebblelike form (Illus. 5).

Finally, pencil in and reestablish the main lines of the form, and use the riffler file and the sandpaper to rub the wood down to a smooth, rounded finish.

CARVING THE DETAILS

When you have achieved a nicely rounded form the size of a hand, take the tracing and reestablish the lines of the design—the moonlike faces, the eye motifs, the feather details, and so on. Do this on both sides of the wood. Now take the fine-point penknife and cut in the main stop-cuts. Working in the first instance to a depth of about ⅛", cut in the main

Illus. 3. Transfer the main outline profile through to the wood; then shade in the "windows" to be removed.

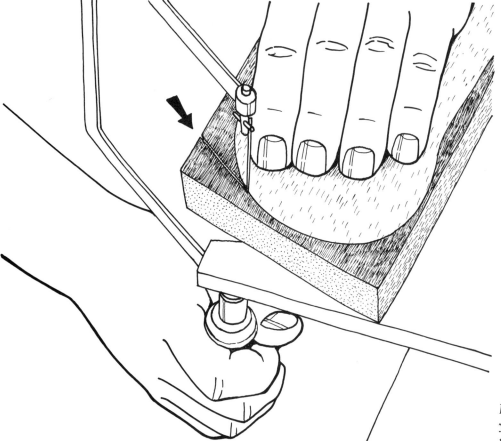

Illus. 4. Make sure that you cut to the waste side of the drawn line.

50

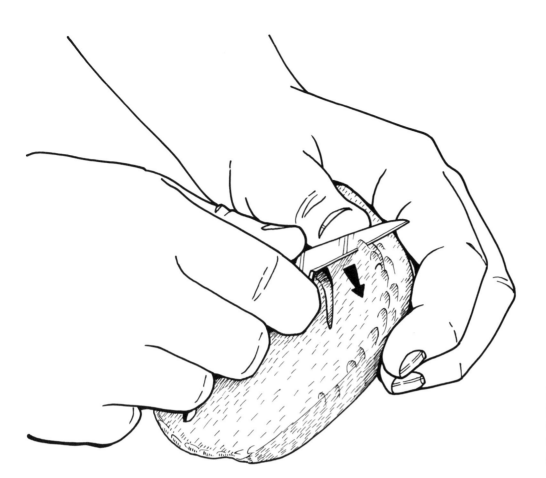

Illus. 5. Use the knife to pare away all the sharp angles and corners, aiming to achieve a smooth pebblelike form.

features—the eye motif, around the moonlike face, around the feather shapes, around the various little half-circles, and the infill triangles (Illus. 6).

Now, using the scalpel, select one of the details, say, the moon face, and set to work, cutting away the waste. Working from the middle to the side, slide the blade down at an angle into the stop-cuts and remove a V-section of waste. Don't try to remove the wood in one great thrust; it's much better to work a small sliver at a time.

The working action goes something like this: You slide the blade down into the stop-cut and remove a sliver of waste, you reestablish the stop-cut and remove a little more waste, and so on. Of course, as the details vary, you will have to adjust your approach to suit the task at hand. For example, the moon face needs to be left slightly domed, the triangular infill pocket just to the top left of the moon face needs to be deep, more like a chip-carved triangle, and the large eye motif has to be worked so that the sharp line at the top of the eye runs in a smooth line through to the beak.

It's all pretty straightforward, with the exception of the main bird-eye motif. This is not to say that it is difficult, but because the carving is so small, you will have to be extra careful not to damage the small peaks of short grain. Take a look at the eye detail (Illus. 7) and see how it is made up of three stop-cut forms set one within another. It's best to cut the outside outline first, next the boat shape with the pointed end that characterizes the eye, and then the pupil. Use the finest scalpel blade and take it easy and slowly.

Finally, use the point of the scalpel to cut in all the little incised lines that go into making up the moon faces.

FINISHING

When you have achieved what you consider to be a nicely detailed form, take the sandpaper and rub the wood down to a good finish. This is not to say that you rub down the whole piece, but rather that you selectively rub down the areas in and around the carved details. So, for example, you should rub down the beautiful, smooth curves at the top of the head, the long, smooth, concave sweep of the beak, and so forth. Work with care and caution, making sure that you don't damage or blur the crisp lines and forms left by the knife.

Finally, give the whole workpiece a generous waxing

51

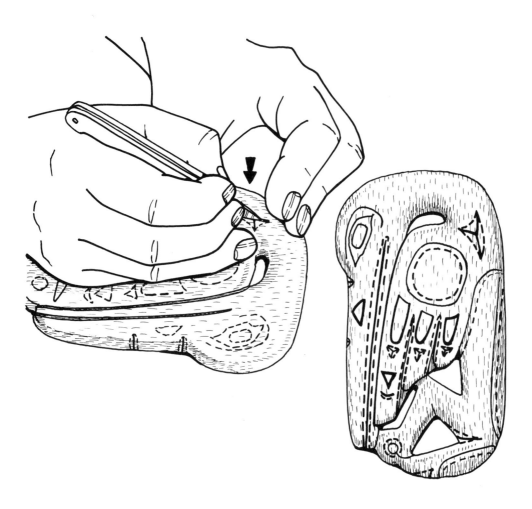

Illus. 6. Cut in all the main stop-cuts to a depth of approximately 1/8".

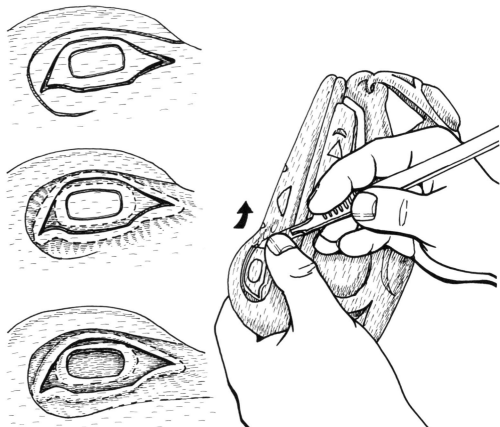

Illus. 7. Left, top to bottom: Make stop-cuts, run the contours down into the stop-cuts, and model to a good finish. Bottom, right: For maximum control, support both the handle and the blade of the scalpel.

and then burnish it to a smooth finish and the job is done.

TROUBLESHOOTING AND POSSIBLE MODIFICATIONS

- It is easy to make most cuts by simple thumb-bracing paring with the scalpel. If the wood cuts up roughly, then either the wood is unsuitable or the knife needs sharpening.
- When you are selecting your wood, it's best to go for a tight, close-grained wood such as box. If in doubt, have a talk with a specialist supplier.

- When you are carving small delicate areas, keep the knife cuts tight and controlled. Be extra careful that the blade doesn't run into the end grain and thus split off areas of short grain.
- Traditionally, carvings of this character were sometimes painted and/or inlaid with small pieces of shell. You could inlay selected areas with a hard wax.
- If in the final stages you split the wood, make a mend with a wood glue, bind the mend with fine cotton thread, let it stand for 24 hours, and then go back to work.

4
Sea-Otter Bowl (*Kwakiutl*)

A bowl for food carved in the shape of a sea otter, or sea beaver

Gouge, drill, and knife
Deep-hollow-carved, carved in the round, and relief-carved
Stained, painted, oiled, and burnished

Known as sea otters, sea beavers, and sometimes even seal otters, this little mammal played a pivotal role in what was to become a three-way trade between Europe, the Northwest coast of North America, and China. Up until the last quarter of the eighteenth century, the Native Americans on the Northwest coast had very little contact with the outside world. Certainly, they had been visited over the years by a number of Russian and Spanish trading and exploratory expeditions, but the contact was so minimal and fleeting that it made very little impression.

All this changed in 1778 when Captain Cook arrived with his two ships, *Discovery* and *Resolution*. After a month spent repairing his ships, mapping, and collecting artifacts, Cook was so pleased with his dealings with the Indians that he decided to give one man in particular a small gift as a token of gratitude. As the story goes, the Indian in return gave him a sea-otter, or sea-beaver, skin. Although Cook didn't have much use for the skin, he was so moved by the gesture that he presented the Indian with yet another gift. The Indian then swiftly took off his own best sea-beaver-skin cloak and presented it to Captain Cook.

Anyway, the end result of all this spontaneous present giving was that Cook gave the Indian his own rather special sword and the Indian invited him to return for as many sea-beaver skins as he cared to carry away. And that might have been that had Cook not, on his way home via China, discovered that the Chinese were prepared to pay vast sums of money for the soft and delicate sea-beaver skins.

When the news eventually reached Europe, it triggered a mad rush in terms of ships and trade—a rush that completely changed the Northwest Indian way of life. It's enough to say that the sea otter, or beaver, was an important animal among the Indians, and as such, it was a much favored subject for the Indian carver.

DESIGN, STRUCTURE, AND TECHNIQUE CONSIDERATIONS

Take a look at the project picture (Illus. 1) and the working drawings (Illus. 2), and see how this bowl is characteristic of many other *Kwakiutl* bowls in that it looks like more of a naturalistic sculpture than a piece of functional domestic ware. In other words, it appears to be more of a three-dimensional sculptural carving of an otter that contains a bowl than a bowl that is decorated with applied sea-otter, or sea-beaver, imagery. The carver has obviously designed the carving so that the animal form takes precedence.

See how, at a scale of one grid square to 1″, the beaver measures about 12 to 13″ long from the back of the head to the tail, 10″ wide across the belly, and about 10″ high from the base up to the top of the head.

Consider how, although the primary feature is the carved-in-the-round animal shape, nevertheless the surface of the animal has been decorated with a small amount of stylized pattern and motif imagery. Note, for example, that not only has the front leg-to-body joint been realistically carved in the round, but it has also been surface-decorated with the typical moated-circle motif that the *Kwakiutl* use in painting and other flat work to represent limb joints.

54

When you have studied the form and considered the various tool and material implications of carving a hollow-form project of this size and character, draw the design out to size, find a suitable piece of wood, and prepare all your tools for the job.

TOOLS AND MATERIALS

For this project you need:

● a block of well-seasoned, straight-grained, knot-free wood that's about 12 to 13″ long and 10 × 10″ square—for example, an easy-to-carve wood such as lime or cedar

● a pencil and ruler

● a couple of sheets each of work-out and tracing paper

● a large straight saw

● a large bow saw

● a workbench with a vise

● a bench hold-down

● a mallet

● a power drill

● a 1½″-diameter Forstner or machine-saw type of bit—one that bores a flat-bottomed hole

● a good selection of carver's gouges, including a large shallow-curve straight gouge, a front-bent spoon bit, a front-bent long-curved gouge, a small spoon bit, and a small spade gouge

● a large pair of calipers

● a leather or canvas cushion filled loosely with sand or a fat rope quoit

● a full-curve crooked knife

● a good selection of small knives

● a selection of riffler files

Illus. 1. Project picture—a Kwakiutl food bowl with sea-otter imagery.

- a pack of graded sandpapers

- a small amount of water-based black-brown wood stain

- a small amount of acrylic red-ocher paint

- a couple of artist's soft-haired brushes—a broad- and a fine-point

- a small amount of vegetable oil

- a stiff brush and a cloth for polishing

SETTING IN THE DESIGN AND ROUGHING OUT

Once you have studied all the drawings, stages, and details, clear your working area, set out your tools, pin up your designs, and set your block of wood down fair and square on the work surface.

Bearing in mind that the project is hollow-carved and noting just how thin the bowl walls are in relationship to the total size of the form, spend some time making sure that the wood is in perfect condition. Look at the end grain and make sure that the 10 × 10″ section is free from splits, look at all the top and side faces and make sure that they are free from knots, and generally give the wood a supercritical going-over. If it is anything less than perfect, select another piece.

With a pencil, mark the wood "tail," "head," "top," and "side." Draw in crossed diagonals and establish a central line, which you can use when you are trying to keep the carving symmetrical (Illus. 3, top left). Trace off the main side view, and pencil-press-transfer the traced profile through to the side face of the wood. When this is done, shade in the areas that need to be cut away and set the wood in the jaws of the vise. Now, bearing in mind that cutting through the massive 10 × 10″ section is going to be a difficult task, take the straight saw and begin to cut away the areas of waste (Illus. 3, top right). It's best to restrict the straight-through cuts to clearing away the bulky corners of waste, and then to work the trickier areas—on top of the belly, around the sides, and in front of the beaver's nose—with a gouge (Illus. 3, bottom).

Don't try to work hard up against the drawn line. With the workpiece now secured with the hold-down, take the mallet and gouge and being very careful to only carve from high to lower wood that is across or at an angle to the run of the grain, clear the waste from around the outside curve of the beaver's back, from across the belly, from around the head, and so

on. Continue until you have cleared away the bulk of the waste (Illus. 4).

CARVING THE FORM

When you have cleared away the rough, set the profile on its side on the workbench and keep it secure with the hold-down. Now take the mallet and one of your large deep-section scoop gouges, and work around the flat-faced profile, clearing away the secondary waste—meaning, the area around the bowl "body." Make sure that you leave the area around the arms lower so that they are left in high relief. As you are working, be watchful for the run of the grain and be ready to adjust your angle of approach and/or the position of the work (Illus. 4, top left). When you have cleared the bulk of waste away from one side, turn the workpiece over so that the uncut side profile is uppermost, support the partially rounded face on either the sandbag or the quoit, and set to work clearing away the waste from the other side.

Once you have achieved the basic roughed-out and partially rounded sea-otter form (Illus. 4, bottom right), clear away the mess, set the workpiece up on the sandbag, and look to your working drawings. See how the front legs are rounded and undercut, and how the area between the legs and the neck is pierced through so that the legs are only attached at the elbows and paws.

When you have a good understanding of how the various details and surfaces relate to one another, then take your range of small scoops and gouges and work towards the finished form. Cut and shape the tail, cut the beautiful, full bulging curve of the back and side belly, model the back of the head and the face, detail the paws, and so on. Carving the arms and paws is somewhat tricky, but only because you have to keep chopping while changing tools and the direction of the cut to suit the changing run of the grain. It's best to lower the waste around the arm by deepening the stop-cut (Illus. 5, top left), and then sliding a bent gouge into the stop-cut so as to scoop out the waste (Illus. 5, bottom left). Be careful when you are cutting out the underarm waste that you don't lever on the increasingly fragile bridges of wood that are the arms (Illus. 5, right).

CUTTING THE BOWL

With the sea-otter form more or less fully rounded and finished, support it on the cushion/quoit and use the ruler and the calipers to measure from the top of

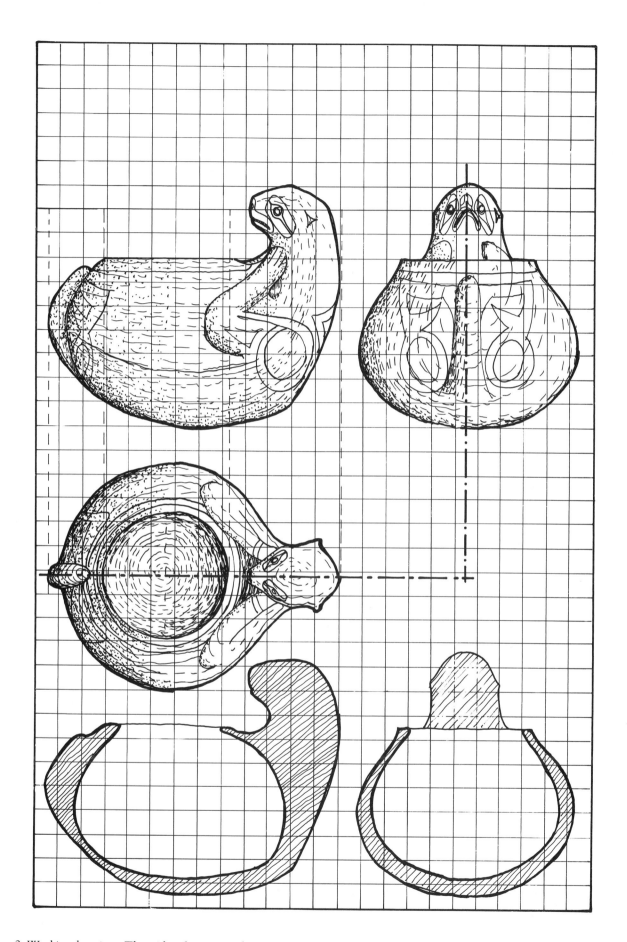

Illus. 2. Working drawings. The grid scale is one grid square to 1″.

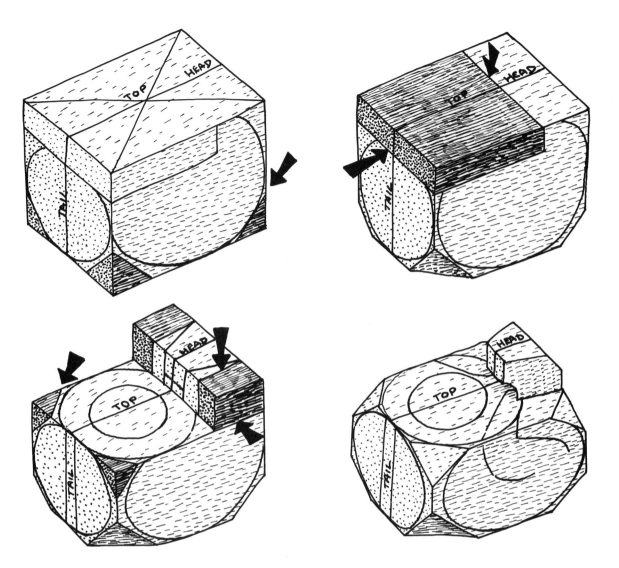

Illus. 3. Top left: Draw in the diagonal lines and the central line as well as the side view and profiles, and label the faces "top," "head," and "tail." Top right: Cut away the waste corners and shade in the area of top waste.

Bottom left: Remove the top waste to reveal the top of the bowl. Then draw in the bowl shape and mark off the head and corner waste. Bottom right: The roughed-out block with the bulk of the waste removed.

the rim down to the bottom of the base. If all is well, the rim-to-base measurement should be about 7″. Based on a measurement of 7″, take the 1½″-diameter Forstner type of drill bit (it must cut a flat-bottomed hole) and use a strip of masking tape to mark it off at 6″.

Making sure that the round-based workpiece is carefully and safely supported (it's best to ask a friend to hold it secure), run a 1½″-diameter pilot hole from the middle of the rim down 6″ into the wood (Illus. 6, top left). Now, reckoning on the bottom of the pilot hole being about an inch short of the bottom of the workpiece, take a front-bent spoon gouge and work around the rim of the hole, clearing away the waste (Illus. 6, right). The working procedure should

go something like this: Work around the rim of the hole scooping out a ring of waste, work around this initial ring scooping out another ring, and so on, until, at about 2½″ out from the middle of the pilot hole, you come to the inside-rim edge of the bowl. When you have lowered the inside surface of the bowl to the depth of one spoon-gouge cut, you go back to the pilot hole and repeat the procedure. And so you continue, removing the waste layer by layer until you come to the bottom of the pilot hole (Illus. 6, bottom left). Be ready to change tools, depending upon the depth of the cut. Also, be ready, every few minutes or so, to spend time honing your tools to a razor-sharp edge.

When you reach the bottom of the pilot hole—that is, when you have cut a straight-sided, 5″-diameter,

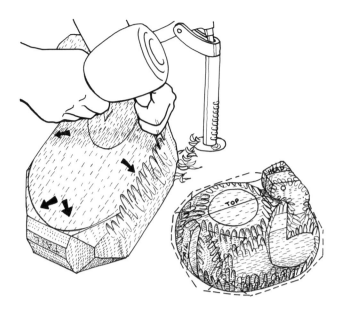

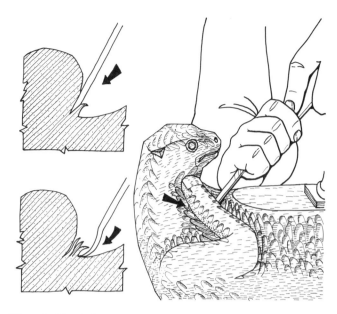

Illus. 4. Top left: Use the mallet and the large scoop gouge to reduce the secondary waste. Bottom right: The roughed-out sea-otter form.

Illus. 5. Top left: First sink a deep stop-cut. Bottom left: Then slide the tool into the initial stop-cut so as to cut away the waste. Right: Reduce the area between the legs and the neck.

6″-deep sinking down through the wood—take a full-curved gouge and start to carve the inside shape of the bowl. By "full-curved," we mean any one of a number of deep U-section gouges that have long,

curved shafts. The carving action is much akin to scooping out the inside of a hard-boiled egg. Slide the gouge from the middle of the rim down and around the inside of the bowl, until the gouge handle

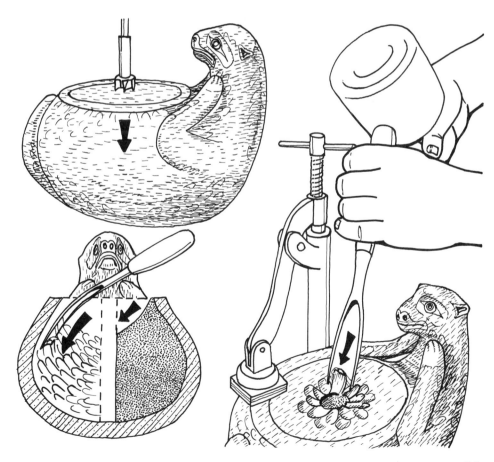

Illus. 6. Top left: Sink a 1½″-diameter pilot hole. Bottom left: Reduce the waste inside the bowl. Right: Use a bent scoop or spoon gouge to work around the rim and clear the waste.

stops short against the rim. Be careful, when you are finishing a cut, that you don't lever the shaft of the tool on the fragile rim of the bowl.

Continue scooping out the waste, assessing the thickness of the bowl side, scooping out a little more wood, and so on, until you have what you consider to be a well-formed bowl interior.

FINISHING

Now clear away the clutter and then stand back and have a good long look at the carving. Ask yourself, Does the otter form look convincing? Could the walls of the bowl be just a shade thinner? Is the outside curve of the back of the neck right? Do the sides of

the outside of the bowl run in beautiful smooth-sweeping curves? Spend time making sure that the details are just right.

Use the riffler file to give emphasis to the form. Don't overwork the surface; just run a furrowed "fur" texture over and around the various dips, curves, and sweeps that go into making up the design (Illus. 7).

When you have what you consider to be a well-worked carving, take the black stain and give all surfaces, inside and out, a generous coating. When the stain is dry, take a scrap of fine-grade sandpaper and rub selected areas, such as the rim of the bowl, down to a smooth finish. When this is done, mix a little red-ocher paint and highlight the details with a fine brush. Finally, rub the whole workpiece down with a generous amount of vegetable oil and use the brush and the cloth to burnish the surface to a dull-sheen finish.

TROUBLESHOOTING AND POSSIBLE MODIFICATIONS

- It is possible to change the order of the carving and cut the inside of the bowl before carving the outside otter form. Although this would make cutting the bowl easier, it would restrict the amount of force you could put into carving the outside form.
- If you like the idea of the project but would prefer to use knives rather than gouges, then it would be better to settle for a half-size otter—make it about 7″ long and worked from a 5 × 5″ section of wood.
- You can make your own carving-support quoit using a coil of fat rope—all you do is coil up the rope and bind it with twine. This makes a good support for carving round-bottomed forms.
- When you are carving the interior of the bowl, be extra careful that you don't lever on and thus break the relatively fragile rim. Especially watch out when working the short-grain areas at the tail and head.

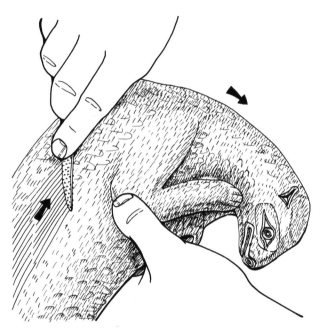

Illus. 7. Use a riffler file to work the outside of the bowl, moving in one direction so as to achieve a texture that looks like fur.

5
"Soul-Catcher" Toggle (Tsimshian)

A small togglelike tube used by shamans for catching wandering souls

Knife and saw
Shaped, pierced, shallow-relief-carved, incised, and painted
Waxed and burnished

One of the shaman's principal pieces of equipment was the small togglelike tube known as a "soul-catcher."

When, like a modern psychotherapist, he was called in to cure a disorder that was more mental than physical, the shaman would first "look through" the patient and give a diagnosis. If it was thought that the illness was caused by a malignant spirit, or perhaps by a harmful object being placed in the patient's body by a sorcerer, he would then need to use the soul-catcher to affect a cure.

Having first ritually set out his equipment, he would gather the relatives around the sickbed, and then use the hypnotic beat of a drum to work himself and the patient into a trancelike state. After various payments had been made, and when the spirits had been successfully contacted, then the shaman would set about doing battle with the supernatural powers.

He might use the soul-catcher tube to suck out the harmful object(s) that had been injected into the patient by an enemy, or use the tube to try to catch the patient's soul. If the soul was thought to be lost, then the shaman would travel spiritually into the Other World—a dangerous supernatural realm where all manner of spirits and souls were on the loose—and there he would search out the confused and wandering soul. In his struggle with the supernatural powers, the shaman might well need to be physically held down and restrained.

Having done battle and having successfully enticed the lost soul into the tube, he would swiftly stop up both ends and then carry it back to the sickbed.

Finally, the shaman would come out of his trance, blow the captured soul back into the patient, and thus, it was hoped, effect a cure.

DESIGN, STRUCTURE, AND TECHNIQUE CONSIDERATIONS

Take a good look at the project picture (Illus. 1), the working drawings (Illus. 2), and the various details. The original toggle that we modelled this after was made of several parts, but you can see that we modified the design by working it as a solid toggle. This is not to say that we have in any way diminished the integrity of the design—the motifs, the size of the toggle, and all the details are authentic and faithful to the original.

Note how, at a grid scale of about four squares to 1″, this particular soul-catcher is about 6″ long and 1½″ in diameter at its widest point.

The design is symmetrically placed on both axes—meaning that the design is not only mirror-imaged from the middle to the ends along the length, but also around the circumference. Note that the thong holes run from either side of the top center through to the slotted mouths. Take a close look at the work-

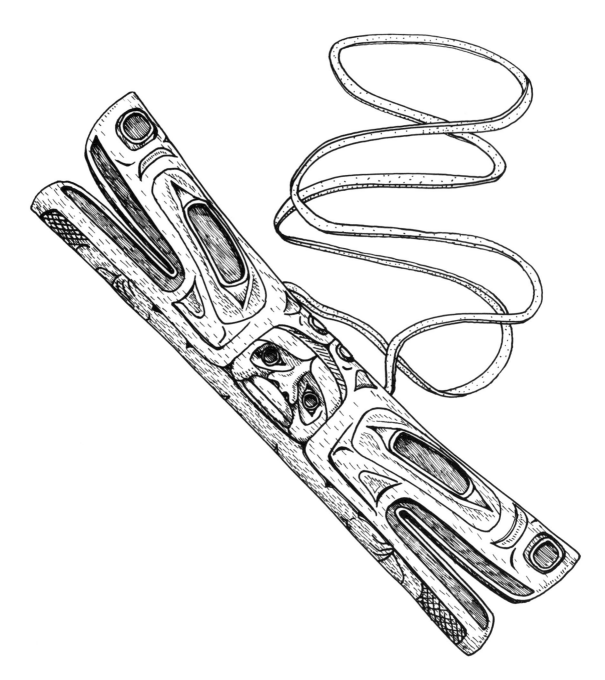

Illus. 1. Project picture—a Tsimshian shaman's "soul-catcher" tube.

ing drawings and see how the "unwrapped" design is based on a quartered repeat, with the actual lines of the design being variously scratched, incised, shallow-relief-carved, and stained.

When you come to making the toggle, make sure that the form tapers from the ends to the middle. It's best to start with a section of 1¾″ square wood and then whittle it down to size and shape. Aim for a round section that gently tapers from, say, a 1½″-diameter at the ends to slightly over 1″ diameter at the middle. Note how the mouth feature at each end slices in about 1½″.

Bearing in mind the small size of the project, choose your wood with extra care. Go for a tight, smooth-grained, white, knot-free wood such as holly or box.

TOOLS AND MATERIALS

For this project you need:

● a piece of 1¾″ square wood that's slightly over 6″ long—a good choice is box or holly

● a pencil and ruler

62

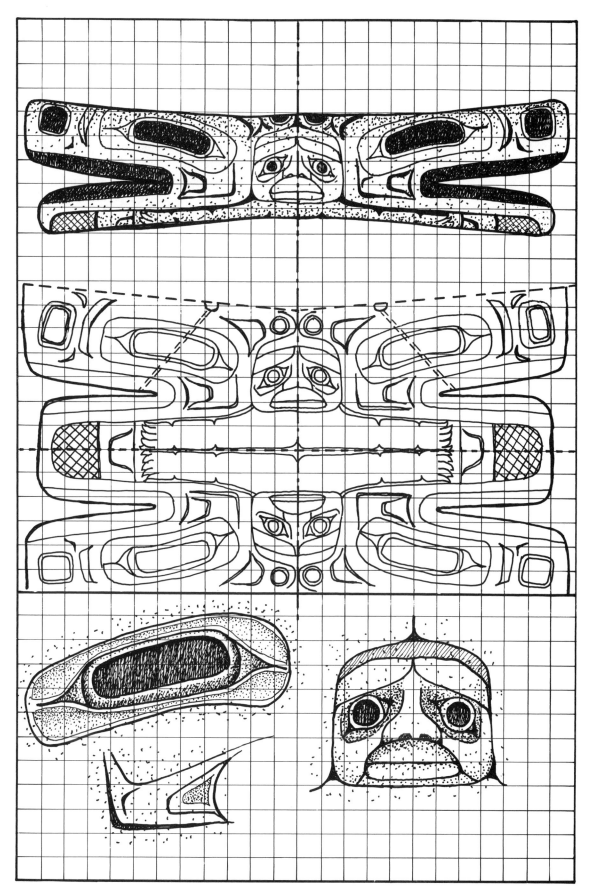

Illus. 2. Working drawings. The grid scale is four squares to 1". Note the sections and details.

- a compass
- a pair of calipers
- a sheet each of work-out paper and tracing paper
- a hand drill with a ⅛″ drill bit—or you could use an awl
- a coping or piercing saw
- a pack of spare blades to fit the saw
- a selection of knives, including a large clasp knife and a scalpel
- a box of watercolor paints
- a couple of artist's soft-haired brushes—a fine-point and a medium broad
- a pack of graded sandpapers
- a small quantity of beeswax polish

WHITTLING THE BASIC FORM

Having noted how the toggle shape needs to be rounded, symmetrical, and tapered towards the middle, take the 6″ length of 1¾ × 1¾″ wood, and mark out the ends with crossed diagonals. When this is done, set the compass to a radius of ¾″, and then scribe each end of the wood out with a 1½″-diameter circle. Use the knife of your choice to whittle the square section of wood down to a round dowel section. It's best to trim off the corners so as to make an octagonal section, and then carefully whittle down until you reach the required 1½″ diameter (Illus. 3, top).

Take the 6″ long, 1½″-diameter dowel and use a pencil and ruler to mark it off halfway along its length. Run the mark right around the wood. Set the calipers to a fixed distance of about 1⅛″. Now take the knife and run it around the wood at the halfway point so as to make a stop-cut. Sink the cut into the wood to a depth of about ⅛″. When this is done, run a slicing angled cut around the wood on either side of the stop-cut so as to make a V-section groove, or trench. Repeat this procedure a couple of times until you have a V-section stop-cut that is about ¼″ wide and 3/16″ deep.

Now, working from the end to the middle, slice in towards the central stop-cut and cut away the waste so as to achieve the characteristic toggle shape that is tapered towards the middle (Illus. 3, bottom). Aim for a total form that looks smoothly curved and or-

ganic, with the underside of the toggle a shallower and more subtle shape.

SETTING OUT THE DESIGN

Take a look at the project picture (Illus. 1) and the working drawings (Illus. 2), and see how the design is mirror imaged and quartered. Now take a 3″-wide strip of tracing paper, wrap it around one half of the toggle, secure it with small tabs of masking tape, mark it, and cut it to fit. With a pencil, label the "around middle" edge. You should finish up with a tracing-paper pattern that is about 3 × 3″ and slightly fan shaped. Fold the paper in half, so as to create the distance that's halfway around the wood, and use tabs of masking tape to secure it flatly over the design.

Now take a soft 2B pencil and carefully trace one half of the wraparound motif, making sure that the "around middle" edge of the tracing paper runs through the middle of the central face motif. Be prepared to modify and "stretch" the design to fit your pattern. If everything works out right, the two half-face motifs should be aligned on the "around middle" edge and arranged so that they are distanced by the long armlike motif and set chin to chin.

Once you have achieved a good clear tracing, set the traced design around the wood, secure it with tabs of masking tape, and pencil-press-transfer the traced lines. Repeat and reverse this procedure on both sides

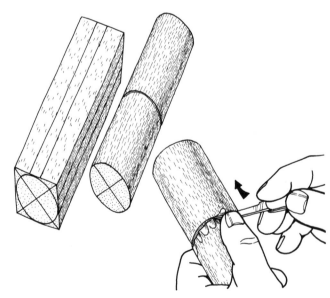

Illus. 3. Top: Scribe each end of the wood out with a 1½″-diameter circle; then whittle down the waste to make a round dowel section. Bottom: Slice in towards the central stop-cut and taper in towards the middle to make the toggle shape.

The small shaman's rites charm or good-luck amulet worn around the neck is project 3.
The shaman's mask representing the moon is project 13.

A

Project 7, this decorative panel was used on burial boxes.

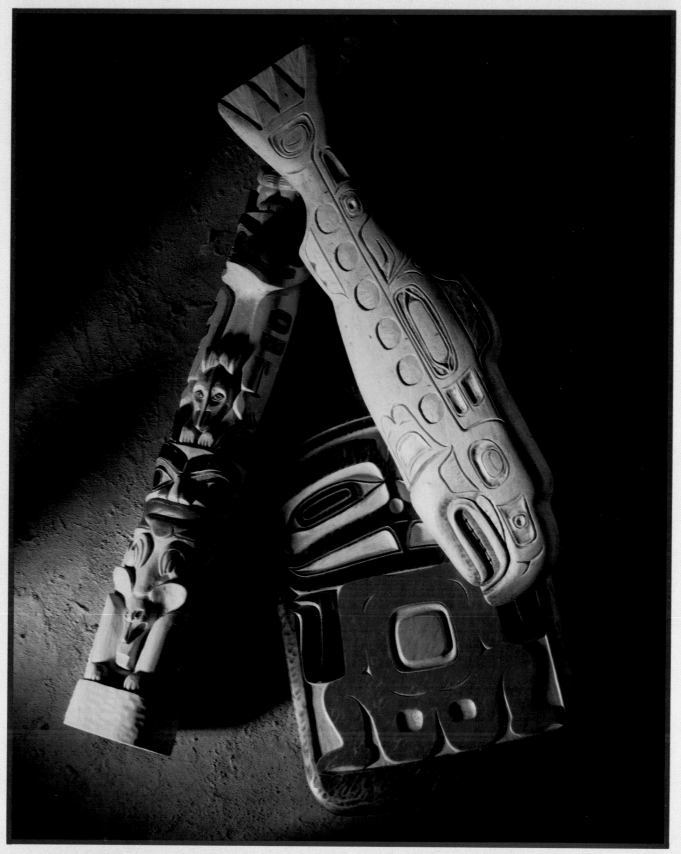

The salmon totemic clan crest on the right (project 17) is a wall-mounted plaque.
The house board in the middle (project 18) shows ancestry and social position. On the left
is a miniature totem pole (project 19), a prototype made prior to carving the full-size pole.

Clockwise from the top are a knife handle (project 10), a spindle whorl used for spinning fibres (project 11), and a shaman's necklace charm (project 15).

D

of the "around middle" line to achieve the total design (Illus. 4). Finally, go over the transferred designs with a pencil, making sure that they are clear and well set out.

CUTTING IN THE PROFILE

Having noted how the mouth motif at each end of the toggle curves and travels down into the wood at a slight angle, set the workpiece securely in the jaws of a muffled vise. Now take your chosen saw and cut away the long, curved wedge of waste. Make an initial pilot cut straight down through the middle of the mouth, and then follow it up with a cut at each side (Illus. 5). Aim for a beautiful, smooth-sweeping curve. Work around the end of the wood, down the underside of the top lip towards the tight wedge at the end of the mouth, back up the bottom lip, and then out and around at the end. Try to make the saw cuts smoothly curved and positive.

Once you have sawn out the mouth wedges, take the knife and trim the sawn surfaces to a smoothly tooled finish. Then cut the length of the bottom jaw back slightly.

CARVING THE DESIGN

Once all the lines of the design are clearly established, take another close-up look at the project picture and

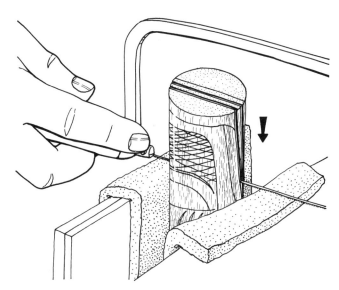

Illus. 5. With the wood supported in the muffled vise, run a pilot cut straight down through the middle of the mouth. Then saw down each side of the pilot cut to form the wedge-shaped mouth.

the working drawings (Illus. 1 and 2). See how, in the main, the design is made up not so much from scratched lines but rather more from shallow-incised cuts. Note how the incised cuts are V-sectioned and how they taper out at the ends. With this in mind, go over the wood with the point of the scalpel and set the design in to a depth of about 1/16″. For example, with one of the main sharp-ended "eye" motifs, run the point of the knife into the wood at one of the sharp ends, gradually increase the depth of the cut as you approach the halfway point, and then gradually draw it out as you reach the other sharp end. The cutting action is—slice in, apply more pressure, and then slice out. Try to work the various lines with swift, smooth, slicing in-and-out strokes. If need be, you might support the workpiece on a sandbag—see the previous project for details.

Having set in the design with the point of the scalpel, now comes the pleasurable task of cutting all the little V-section incised lines that go into making up the design. Each incised line needs to be worked with three swift cuts: the initial set-in stop-cut that establishes the form and then the two angled cuts. If everything works out right, the angled cuts should slice into either side of the stop-cut so as to create the V-section incision, or groove (Illus. 6). And so you continue, working the rather subtle incised lines that make up the design.

When you have cut in the incised lines, take another close-up look at the project picture (Illus. 1),

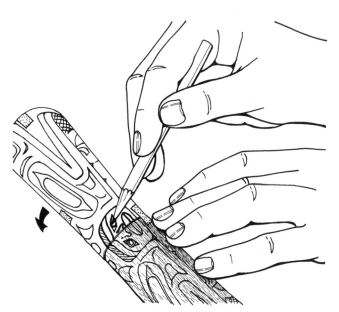

Illus. 4. Wrap the traced design around the wood and secure it with tabs of masking tape. Press-transfer the traced lines through to the wood; then reverse the tracing and repeat the procedure so as to achieve the total design.

and see how some of the details are not only set in with an incised line but also ever-so-slightly lowered, or cut away, in shallow relief. Have a look, for example, at the little triangular detail at each side of the main-eye pupil motifs (Illus. 2, bottom left). Note how the triangular pocket angles down and gets deeper at the corner of the eye. When you come to carve this detail, start by delineating the form with little incised cuts, and then take the scalpel and slide it down from the central eye area into the wood at a flat, slicing angle. Try to work each lowered area by removing a series of flat wisp-thin wedges. Lower the centers of the eyes, the triangular pockets at each side of the eyes, the nostrils, the lips on the large wedge-cut mouths, and just under the nose on the small, central-face motif.

Finally, take the drill or awl, and sink cord holes

PAINTING AND FINISHING

Traditionally, small carvings of this size and character are detailed with inlaid abalone shell, pieces of thin sheet copper, pearl buttons, and paint. When you consider your carving finished, take another look at the project picture (Illus. 1) and the working drawings (Illus. 2), and see how various parts of the design appear to be painted and/or stained.

The lips, pupils, and nostrils are painted a soft blue-green and all the incised lines are highlighted with a small amount of thin burnt umber. When you come to do the painting, aim for an old, worn, and much-handled appearance, with all the colors looking thin and faded.

Start by taking a small fine-point brush and a little burnt-umber paint, and lining in all the incised de-

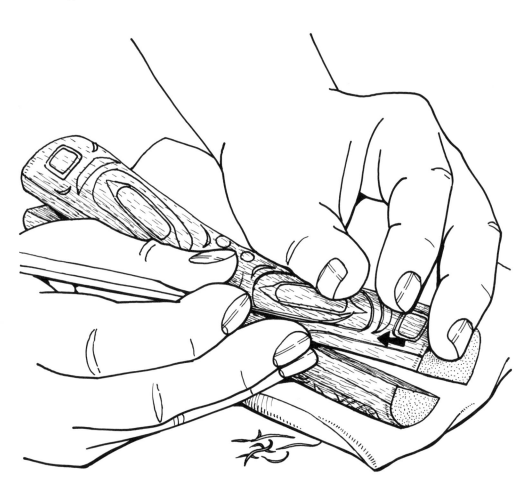

Illus. 6. Make angled cuts on each side of the initial stop-cut so as to make a delicate V-section groove.

down at an angle and through to the mouth slots (Illus. 2, middle). Support the toggle on a scrap of waste and be careful that the drill doesn't burst through and splinter the wood. You might need to ask a friend to support the workpiece.

tails. When this is done, add water to the burnt umber so as to make a thin wash; then take a damp cloth and give the workpiece a couple of all-over coats. Rub the paint well into the pores of the wood, and into all the little cuts and crannies (Illus. 7). Now mix up

66

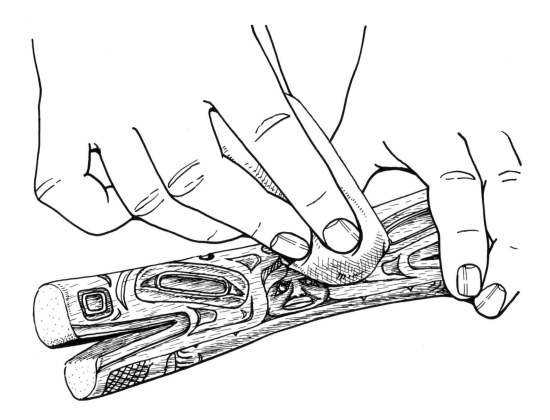

Illus. 7. Rub the paint well into the pores of the wood and then wipe off the excess, leaving the paint in the deep areas.

the blue-green paint and carefully paint in the main feature details such as the pupils, nostrils, and lips.

When the paint is completely dry, take a scrap of the finest-grade sandpaper and rub the whole workpiece down to a smooth-to-the-touch finish. Actually rub through the paint at the sharp edges and the corners and what you consider to be natural "wear" areas.

Finally, apply a generous coat of wax and burnish the wood to a dull-sheen finish.

TROUBLESHOOTING AND POSSIBLE MODIFICATIONS

- When you are choosing your wood, be sure to go for smooth, white, easy-to-carve wood such as holly. Avoid woods that appear to be knotty, sappy, stained, or split. If in doubt, ask the advice of a local supplier.

- If you have any doubts as to the size or design, take a lump of Plasticine, or better still a scrap of wood, and make a quick maquette, or model.

- When you come to sawing out the mouth details, be careful not to twist the blade. Keep your eyes on both sides of the wood, making sure that the line of cut is well to the waste side of the drawn line.

- If, when you are transferring the initial design, the two halves of the motif fail to come together in a good fit, then be prepared to modify the design accordingly. If necessary, reduce the size of some parts of the design or infill with a detail drawn from another project.

- If you want to add an inlaid detail on, say, the pupils and the nostrils, consider using pieces of mother-of-pearl oyster shell or pieces cut from old pearl buttons.

6
"Canoe" Bowl (Bella Bella)

A canoe-shaped "grease" dish used for holding fish oil

Saw and crooked knife
Roughed out, hollow-carved, and detailed
Oiled and burnished

All the Native Americans of the Pacific Northwest ate fish oil, or "grease," with just about every meal. Made from the eulachon, a small sardinelike fish, also known as a candlefish, the grease was obtained by boiling the fish in water, and then repeatedly skimming and reboiling until the resultant oil was of a suitable consistency. The grease was served in special canoe-shaped bowls and eaten as a dip or sauce. However, the grease was more than an addition to a meal—it was also used during various ceremonies as a libation to honor spirits, guests, and dignitaries.

In the context of wood carving, grease dishes are

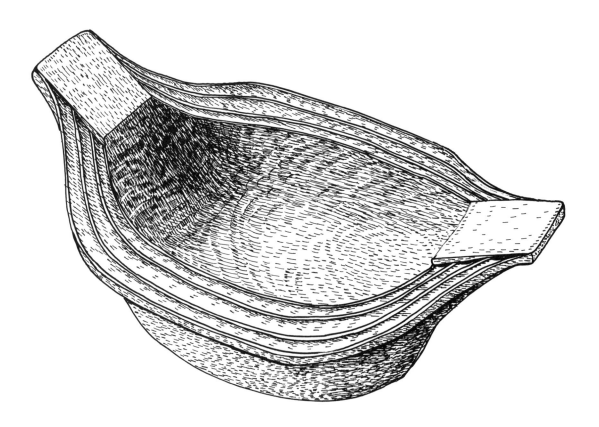

Illus. 1. Project picture—a Bella Bella *canoe-shaped grease bowl.*

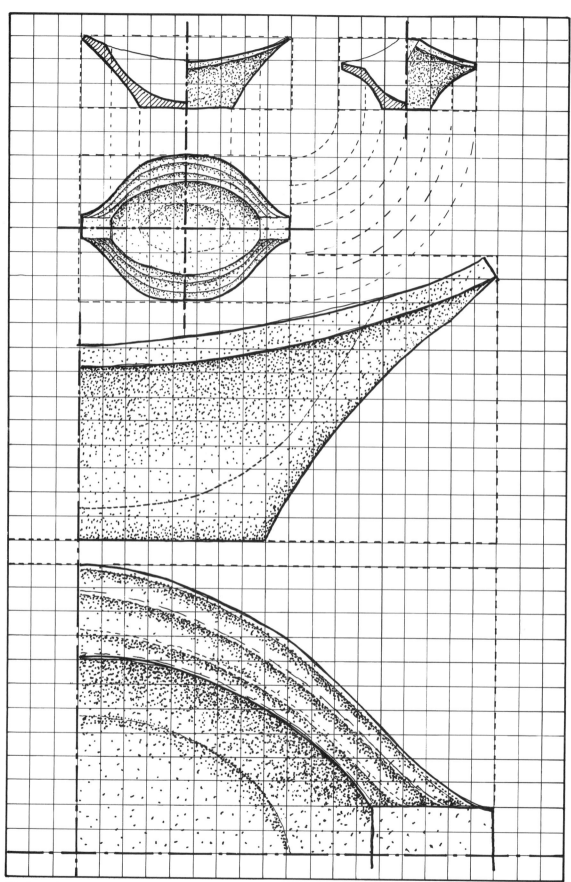

Illus. 2. Working drawings. The grid scale is one square to
1″ for the top and four squares to 1″ for the bottom. Note
the profiles and sections.

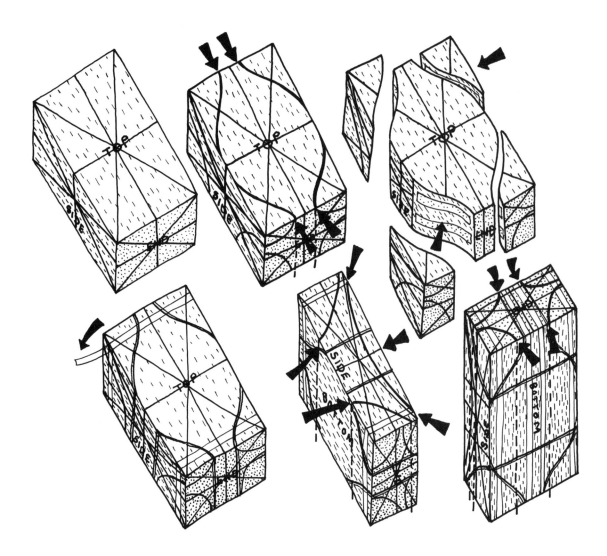

Illus. 3. Top left: Find the middle by drawing crossed diagonals, draw in the central line on all faces, and label all sides. Top middle: Transfer the profiles through to all the faces of the wood. Top right: Cut out the "top" view and use the double-sided transparent tape to stick the waste pieces back onto the block. Bottom left: Having checked that the block is square and well aligned, strap it up with tape. Bottom middle: Cut the "side" view in like manner. Bottom right: Repeat the cutting-and-strapping procedure with all the other views.

particularly interesting in that they are worked almost entirely with the traditional Indian hooked, or crooked, knife. Hooked, curved, doubled-edged, and mounted on a long horn-shaped handle, this knife is a wonderfully efficient wood-carving tool.

In use, the wood to be carved is supported on your lap with one hand, while your elbows are tucked into your waist, your forearms are braced, and the knife is grasped palm-up in your other hand. The carving action is curious in that the knife is held like a dagger with your thumb braced against the hooked end of the handle. The carving technique is one of levering and thumb-pushing the handle while at the same time scooping and pushing with the crooked blade.

The crooked knife is a unique wood-carving tool in that the hooked and double-edged blade allows the carver to cut on both the pull and the push strokes.

DESIGN, STRUCTURE, AND TECHNIQUE CONSIDERATIONS

Study the project picture (Illus. 1) and the working drawings (Illus. 2), and see how, at a scale of (top) one grid square to 1″ and (bottom) four grid squares to 1″, the canoe-shaped bowl is 9″ long, 6″ wide, and 3″ high from the base line to the top of the prowlike rim.

With the inside of the bowl being scooped out and rounded, and the outside shape resembling the traditional Indian canoe, the bowl is both good to look at and pleasant to use. The prow ends make good handle holds, the smooth inside shape is easy to clean, and the furrowed, or fluted, rim is good for depositing shucks and the like when you are eating. All in all, it's a very successful bowl shape.

The low-tech approach makes this a good project for beginners with minimal tools. Certainly, you do need the use of a bench and a saw to clear away the initial lumps of waste around the bowl. But once they are out of the way, then the rest of the carving can be managed on your lap with just a couple of crooked knives. However, you do need to protect your lap with a good thick apron, or better still, a piece of matting or a coverall made of leather.

If you use the crooked knife with a tight, thumb-levering, elbow-braced action as described, then you should have no problem—it's an easy, safe, efficient tool.

TOOLS AND MATERIALS

For this project you need:

• a smooth-faced, square-angled block of prepared, easy-to-carve, straight-grained wood, such as alder or sycamore, that is 9½″ along the run of the grain, 6½″ wide, and 3½″ deep—this allows for a small amount of wastage

• two crooked knives—one with a gentle curve and one with a tight part-circle hook

• a couple of small, straight knives—say, a penknife and a scalpel

• a roll of double-sided transparent tape

• a roll of regular transparent tape

• a band saw—if you don't have one, perhaps you could borrow one from a local workshop or maybe even a school

• a pencil and ruler

• a sheet of tracing paper

• some sort of lap protection, such as a leather apron or a piece of carpet

• a pair of double-ended S-calipers

ROUGHING OUT THE BLANK

Having studied the working drawings (Illus. 2) and the order of work, take your chosen block of carefully angled and squared-up wood, and give it a last checking over, just to make sure that it is free from the more obvious flaws such as splits, sappy areas, and dead knots. Making sure that all the faces and angles are true, find the middle of the faces by drawing crossed diagonals, and then run central lines across all the faces. Now, with the grain running from end to end, mark the faces—"bottom," "top," "side," and "end" (Illus. 3, top left).

Finalize the design, make a good tracing of the top, end, and side views, and then, with the traced views carefully aligned with the central lines, pencil-press-transfer the traced lines through to the wood (Illus. 3, top center). Now, starting with the top and making sure that you cut well to the waste side of the drawn line, run the block of wood through the band saw so as to remove the four pieces of waste on the sides of the bowl. When this is done, wipe the sawdust off all the sawn faces and use the double-sided transparent tape to stick the waste pieces back onto the block (Illus. 3, top right). When the corner pieces are in place, and you are sure that the various pieces are square and well aligned, use the regular transparent tape to strap the block good and tight (Illus. 3, bottom left). Now repeat the sawing and strapping procedure with the other two faces—the side view and the end view. This is the order of work: Saw away the waste, brush down the sawn faces, sandwich double-sided transparent tape between mating faces, and then use the regular transparent tape to strap the block up prior to cutting the next profile.

CARVING THE OUTSIDE SHAPE

When you have sawn out the three views, peel away all the tape strapping and remove all the pieces of waste. If everything works out right, you should be left with a square-cornered bowl blank (Illus. 4, top left).

Pin up all your designs so that they are within view, settle yourself down on a comfortable bench or an upright chair, and cover your lap with a thick apron. Now, take the roughed-out blank, pencil in on the base the desired oval profile, and note all the pieces of waste at the corners of the bowl that need to be cut away (Illus. 4, top right). Hold the crooked knife daggerlike in one hand, use your thumb to lever against the hooked end of the knife handle, support the bowl on your lap, and then start to cut away the waste (Illus. 4, bottom). Work from the edge of the base out towards the bowl sides, all the while removing the waste with small, light scooping cuts. Keep both

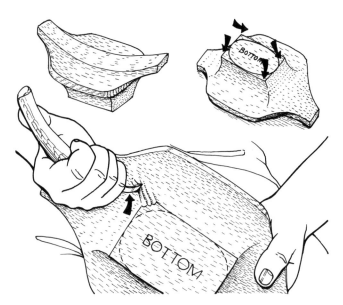

Illus. 4. Top left: The roughed-out sawn blank. Top right: Draw the oval profile on the base. Bottom: Hold the crooked knife like a dagger in one hand and use your thumb to lever the knife handle. Work from the edge of the base down and out towards the bowl sides, employing small, light scoops.

the workpiece and the knife moving so that the blade is always presented with the best angle and direction of cut.

Once you have achieved the base-line profile, change direction so that you are cutting from the rim to the base and start to shape up the sides of the bowl. Not forgetting how the line of the keel needs to divide and fork just before it reaches the top of the prow, draw in a forked guideline, and then work the two sides of the bowl so as to leave the keel and rim lines looking sharp-edged and crisp (Illus. 5, top left). Try to reduce the line around the outside rim to an even thickness of about ¼ to ⅜″, and to have it running like a narrow ribbon around the entire edge of the bowl.

Now, when you have achieved what you consider to be a good outer-bowl shape, run the knife swiftly over the wood so as to leave the carved surface looking crisp and nicely tooled.

CARVING THE HOLLOW INSIDE THE BOWL

Before you start to carve the hollow inside the bowl, take a look at the project picture (Illus. 1) and the working drawings (Illus. 2) and study the way the rim, or lip, runs like a band around the bowl, comes to a

halt against the square-cut prow plate, and drops down sharply along its inside edge. See how, with the rim being about an inch wide, it is necessary to carefully estimate the wood thickness at the edge of the inside rim before you start to scoop out the waste.

Establish the inside-rim edge with a pencil line (Illus. 5, top right) and then, with the bowl nestled right side up on your lap, take the crooked knife and work around the bowl, all the while cutting from the sides to the middle and aiming to set in the line of the inside rim (Illus. 5, bottom left). Don't angle down too sharply or you will cut through what is a relatively slender thickness of wood. It's best to carefully estimate the thickness of the wood at various points with the double-ended S-calipers (Illus. 5, bottom right) and to proceed cautiously, all the while aiming to keep the sides of the bowl hollow-looking, nicely rounded, and smoothly curved.

CARVING THE FLUTED RIM AND FINISHING THE WORKPIECE

Take a look at the working-drawing details (Illus. 2) and see how the rim runs in a beautiful smooth sweep, down from each side of the almost-square prow plate, out and around the full curve of the bowl, and then

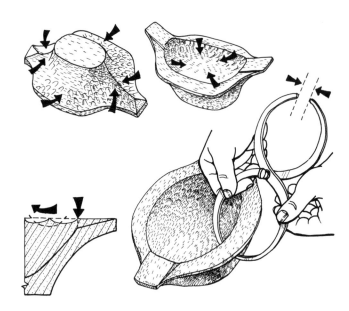

Illus. 5. Top left: Work from rim to base and shape the line of the keel. Top right: Draw in the inside rim of the bowl and use the crooked knife to scoop out the waste—work from the sides to the middle. Bottom left: Gently lower the waste, using shallow, scooping cuts and being careful to set in the inside line of the rim. Bottom right: Use the double-ended calipers to check on the thickness of the sides and rim.

back up to the other prow. Note that, between the three flutes that decorate the surface of the rim, there are very delicate flat-topped ridges. Reckon on having the ridges about $1/16''$ wide and the flutes between, say, $1/4$ to $5/16''$. (These measurements will vary slightly, depending upon the rim position.) Allowing for a ridge on each side edge, use a pencil to mark out the three flutes and the four ridges that make up the total width of the rim (Illus. 6, top left).

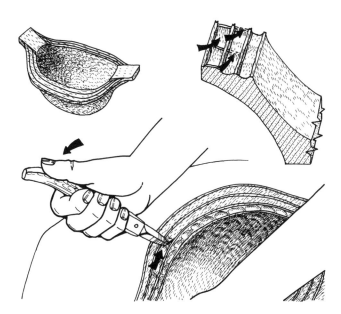

Illus. 6. Top left: Pencil in the four rim ridges. Top right: When you have removed a skim from each of the three flutes, repeat the procedure until all depths and widths are as required. Bottom: Run the crooked knife down between the ridges to achieve the desired flutes and ridges.

With the rim well marked out, take the tight part-circle crooked knife, and with the bowl still nestled and supported in your lap, run the hook of the knife down between a pair of ridges so as to scoop out a thin skim of waste (Illus. 6, bottom). And so you continue, scooping a thin skim of waste from one flute, and then going on to the next, and so on. When you have removed just a skim from the middle of each

flute, return to the first flute and repeat the procedure until the required depth, width, and profile have been achieved (Illus. 6, top right). By working all the flutes at the same time, you can ensure that all the depths and widths will stay more or less constant. Continue until you are left with only about $1/16''$ between neighboring flutes and between the side flutes and the rim.

Trim the prow plates to a good, crisp finish, tidy up the places where the flutes and prow plates meet, and generally work backwards and forward over the entire bowl, bringing it to a good, tooled finish. Make sure that the bowl sits without rocking by cutting a hollow, or "dishing" it slightly, on the underside. Finally, apply a couple of generous coats of vegetable oil, let the oil soak in, and then burnish the wood to a rich sheen.

TROUBLESHOOTING AND POSSIBLE MODIFICATIONS

- It is vital that the block of wood be smooth-faced and square angled. It's best to use a $9 1/2''$-long, machined $3 1/2 \times 6 1/2''$ section for this project.
- It is very important, from face to face in the initial block of wood, to have the bowl profiles symmetrically and precisely aligned with all middle points and central lines.
- When you are running the wood through the band saw, make sure that the block sits squarely on the worktable and that the blade runs through the wood at right angles to the working face.
- For safe, controlled, efficient use, the handle of the crooked knife should be supported by your thumb—with your thumb pointing away from the blade. As you work, you should hold the knife like a dagger. If you slash it like a sword, it could be dangerous.
- If you are a beginner, it might be a good idea not to attempt the rim fluting, as it requires a great deal of accuracy and careful setting out; you could leave the rim smooth, instead.

7
<u>Box Panel (*Tlingit*)</u>

A decorative panel used on a burial box

Saw, knife, gouge, and chisel
Sawn, incised, and shallow-relief-carved
Waxed and burnished

The word "potlatch" comes from the much older *Chinook* work "patshatl"—meaning, to present or give away. Of all the *Tlingit* potlatches— and there were many different types—the mourning, or memorial, potlatch was perhaps the most important.

When a man died, it was necessary to mark the occasion by holding a series of potlatches, at which time all his properties, titles, and privileges were passed on to his family.

Although such potlatches were held over an ex-

Illus. 1. Project picture—a Tlingit *box panel.*

tended period of time and made up of eight separate feasts—four mourning feasts followed by four joy feasts—the first mourning feast was the most important. On this occasion, after a period of lying in state, the dead man would be cremated, and then the remains would be carefully collected and stored in a specially carved and decorated burial, or mourning, box.

After a year's mourning, during which time the box was stored in the grave house and ritually brought out and viewed at each of the subsequent mourning feasts, the deceased's goods were given away and the titles and claims were settled.

Finally, the four joy feasts were held, the deceased's remains were either buried in the original box or transferred to another box, and a totem pole was raised.

DESIGN, STRUCTURE, AND TECHNIQUE CONSIDERATIONS

Take a look at the working drawings (Illus. 2) and see how, at a grid scale of three squares to 1″, the half-panel measures 8 × 12″, to make up a complete panel measuring about 12″ high and 16″ wide. Note that, although for this box the grain of the wood runs across the 16″ width of the panel—meaning, horizontally across the design—when you come to buying your wood, you will of course need to ask for a plank, or slab, that is 12″ wide by 16″ long.

Consider the symmetrical arrangement of the design, and how the various stylized motifs have been characteristically cut, worked, and placed. The design is slightly unusual in that many of the motifs—such as the top-central "eyes," the middle-bottom "square," and the left and right "claws"—have been worked with a lowered, flat ground and clean-stepped edge profile.

Finally, having noted the way the design is nicely counterbalanced, with the lowered ground and the positive motifs being more or less of equal weight, modify the size to suit your chosen piece of wood and trace off the design.

TOOLS AND MATERIALS

For this project you need:

• a 1½″-thick slab of wood that's about 12″ wide and 16″ long—the grain must run along the length of the wood, or across the width of the finished panel

• a sheet each of work-out and tracing paper

• a pencil, ruler, and square

• a workbench with a hold-down and/or clamps

• a good selection of gouges, including a shallow-curve straight gouge, a dog-leg chisel, a shallow-curve bent gouge, and a small spoon gouge

• a large straight-bladed knife

• a pack of graded sandpapers

• a small quantity of vegetable oil

• a cloth and a brush for polishing

PREPARING THE WOOD

When you have studied the project picture (Illus. 1) and the working drawings (Illus. 2), and have a clear understanding of exactly how you want the design to be organized, set your slab of wood best-face up on the workbench and check it over for flaws. Ideally, the slab needs to be easy to carve, straight-grained, and free from splits, knots, and stains—it's best to go for a wood such as lime or pencil cedar.

Secure the wood with the bench hold-down and use one of the shallow-curve gouges to bring the surface to a good finish. Bear in mind that in the context of this project, a good surface means a finish that is nicely tooled. Work carefully backwards and forward across the grain until the entire working face looks softly rippled and dappled, with the lines of the little scooped tool running in a well-ordered pattern across the wood.

Having made sure that the wood is square sided, mark the middle of the panel by drawing crossed diagonals, and then draw in the central line (Illus. 3, top left). When this is done, align the tracing with the central line, secure it with tabs of masking tape, and carefully pencil-press-transfer the traced lines through to the wood (Illus. 3, bottom). After you remove the tracing, make sure that the transferred lines are clearly established by going over them with a soft pencil and then shade in the main areas of waste.

OUTLINING AND SETTING IN THE DESIGN

With the panel nicely surfaced, the design clearly established, and the wood held secure with the hold-down or clamp, take a mallet and a shallow-curve straight gouge, and sink a stop-cut (Illus. 4, top left) around the various lowered ground areas—the two

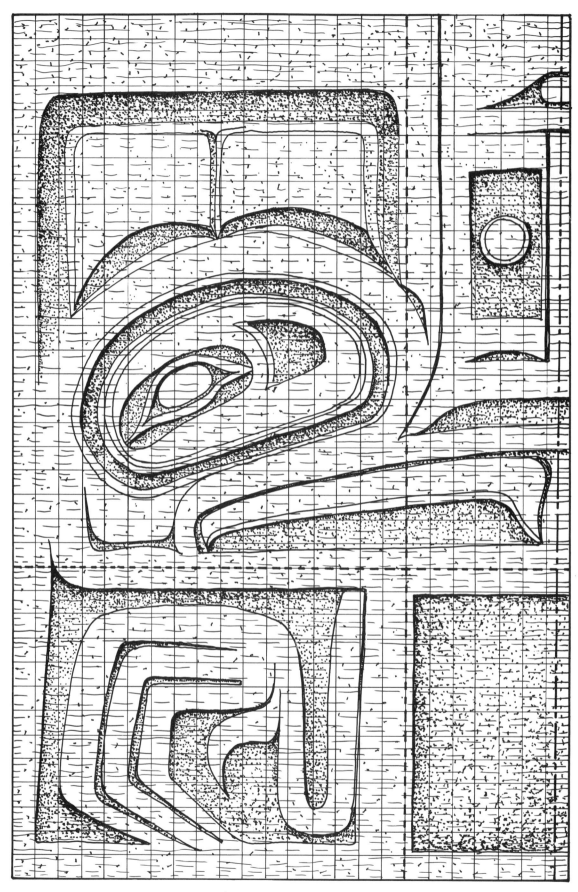

*Illus. 2. Working drawings. The grid scale is three squares
to 1". Note that this drawing only shows a half panel.*

central "eyes," the two "claws," and the bottom-middle square. Work a little to the waste, or ground, side of the drawn line. When this is done, slide the chisel or gouge in at an angle to the stop-cut and remove a V-section sliver of waste (Illus. 4, bottom). Bearing in mind that as you cut around the design you will be working both with and across the grain, hold the tool with both hands, one hand guiding and the other pushing and maneuvering. Work with short, controlled strokes, always being ready to brake and stop short if you feel the tool starting to dig too deep or run away into the grain.

When you have completely outlined these five primary features, then you can start to chop in preparation for wasting and lowering the unwanted ground wood. Take a mallet and gouge, hold the gouge in one hand so that it is upright but leaning slightly over the design, and then work around the inside edge of the V-trench with short, sharp taps of the mallet. Note that when you chop, you will have to change gouges and chisels to suit the constantly changing shape of the drawn profile. Aim to establish a clean, sharp-edged design and to clear the V-section trench down to a depth of a 1/4" (Illus. 4, top right).

LOWERING, OR WASTING, THE GROUND WOOD

When you have set in the design with a crisp-sided trench, then comes the task of lowering or skimming off the waste ground. Take the shallow-curve U-section gouge, and following the incised trench, cut a broad furrow around the entire set-in outline (Illus. 5). When you have established the level, or depth, of the ground, then take the dog-leg chisel and set to work skimming out and lowering the whole ground area (Illus. 5, bottom). Try to leave the lowered ground looking smooth and crisply cut but not so overworked that you can't see the marks left by the tools. Of course, when you come to lowering restricted areas, such as the sharp angles between the "claws," you will have to change the tool to suit the task.

Finally, go over and around the lowered areas, making sure that all the angles are clean and free from tears and rough edges.

MODELLING AND DETAILING

Take a look at the project picture (Illus. 1) and the working drawings (Illus. 2), and see how, apart from the lowered ground areas, the design is made up from

Illus. 3. Top left: Draw crossed diagonals to establish the middle point and central line. Bottom: Align the tracing with the central line, secure it with tabs of masking tape, and pencil-press-transfer the lines through to the wood.

characteristic V-section incisions and details, where the high ground slants and angles in to the depth of the low ground.

From this point on, all you do is chop in on the line of the design with a straight-down stop-cut (Illus. 6, top left), and then slide the gouge in at an angle

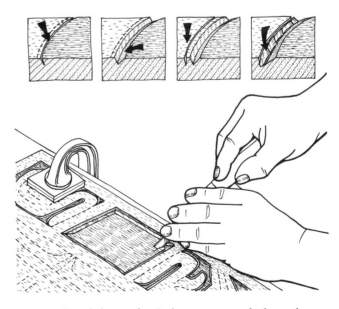

Illus. 4. Top, left to right: Sink a stop-cut a little to the waste side of the drawn line, slide the gouge at an angle to the stop-cut and remove a V-section sliver of waste, cut down on the drawn line, and remove the waste between the drawn line and the trench. Bottom: Slide the gouge in at an angle to the stop-cut to remove a V-section sliver of waste.

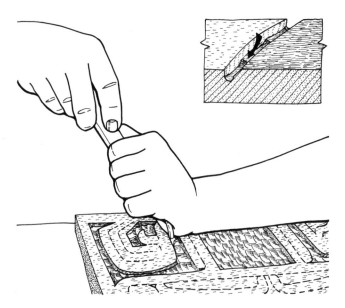

Illus. 5. Top right: Cut a U-section furrow beside the set-in outline. Bottom: Use the dog-leg/spoon chisel to skim and lower the ground area—aim for a smooth, crisp finish.

The only tricky areas are either side of the narrow band, or bridge, of wood that delineates the boat shape of the eye (Illus. 7, top left and right). Bearing in mind that the bridge is short-grained and fragile, mark out the initial stop-cut with the point of a knife rather than a chisel. If you use a knife, there is less chance that you will split away the wood. If necessary, sink a stop-cut in the middle of the area of waste, and then work from the middle to the side with a small spoon gouge, gradually working down and then out until you come to the drawn line.

Finally, use a knife to cut in all the delicate incised lines that run around some of the lowered areas—such as the lines around the "pupils" and those on either side of the "eye" moats. Use a fine-bladed knife, with both hands—one hand guiding and controlling, and the other supplying leverage (Illus. 7, bottom). Note: For greater accuracy, you could use cardboard templates.

FINISHING

Projects like this need to be brought to a good finish. Simply because the forms are so bold, the details so crisp, and the design so minimal, are all the more

to establish the run of the slope and to remove the waste (Illus. 6, top right and bottom). Of course, angles vary and some cuts are deeper than others, but it's still fairly straightforward and uncomplicated.

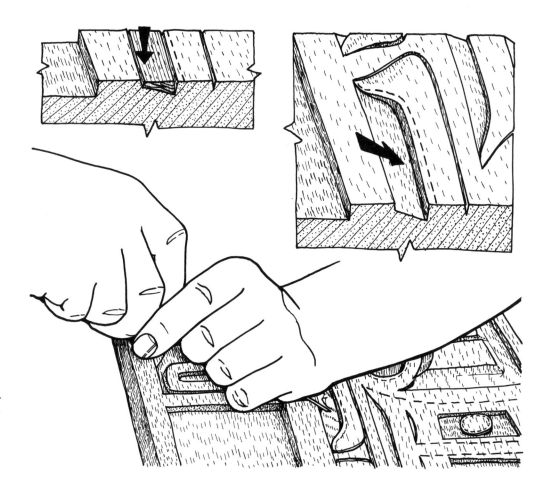

Illus. 6. Top left: Chop in on the line of the design— make a straight-down stop-cut. Top right and bottom: Remove the waste at a slope, or angle, to the face of the workpiece.

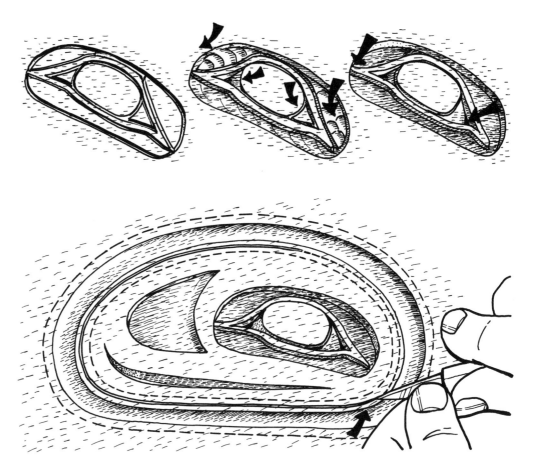

Illus. 7. Top, left to right: Sink the stop-cuts with the point of the knife, scoop away the waste with the 1/16″ spoon gouge, and finish cleaning the angles with the fine-point knife. Bottom: Use both hands to guide and control the knife—make shallow cuts.

reason why the finish needs to be confident and positive. Steps from high to low ground must be crisp, all outlines must be smooth flowing rather than halting and jerky, and the various depressions and angled planes need to be cleanly worked.

Spend time with a knife and the pack of graded sandpapers getting the finish just right. However, we don't mean that you should rub the whole workpiece down, but rather that you should sand carefully selected areas, such as the moats around the eyes and the various high-to-low-ground slopes.

When you consider the workpiece well carved and rubbed down, brush out all the corners and cavities and make sure that the face of the carving is free from dust.

Finally, give the panel a couple of generous coats of vegetable oil, let the oil soak in, and then burnish it to a good finish.

TROUBLESHOOTING AND POSSIBLE MODIFICATIONS

- When you have selected your easy-to-carve, smooth-grained, knot-free wood, leave it in your workshop for a few days prior to carving and let it "settle." If it looks at all unstable and prone to, say, twisting or splitting, then it's best to leave it be for a few months and use another piece of wood.

- If your panel is slightly bowed, then work on the convex face and support the underside with a pad of felt or old carpet.

- A good sharp-edged tool should leave the wood looking smooth and shiny. If the tool leaves the wood looking ragged, then try cutting at a different angle to the working face, cutting at a different angle to the run of the grain, sharpening the tool, or trying a different type of wood.

8
House-Partition Panel (Tlingit)

A panel with "Bear Mother" imagery

Saw, knife, and gouge
Sawn, pierced, lowered, and shallow-relief-carved
Painted, waxed, and burnished

Tlingit villages were a mass of carved-and-painted imagery. There were rows, almost palisades, of totem poles in front of the houses, facing out to the sea, and the buildings themselves were decorated with carved-and-painted images and symbols. Massive, carved posts framed the entrances and the low doorways were cut through a flat, pierced, and painted screen.

Inside the house, there was one huge smoke-filled room, which was divided and subdivided by more screens. Towards the back of the room, a religious and ceremonial area was again divided off by a special carved screen. This screen also had lots of carved-and-painted imagery and a low, pierced doorway that was framed by massive, carved door posts.

Historical accounts describe how the house interiors were an overwhelming profusion of carving, pattern, and color, all of which were given dramatic emphasis from the firelight, which left the far reaches of the rooms in almost total darkness.

This project draws its inspiration from a screen that was once the property of Chief Shakes of Wrangell—the "Brown Bear" is Chief Shakes's clan crest. The screen is about 15 feet high and built from eight planks that have been "sewn" together.

DESIGN, STRUCTURE, AND TECHNIQUE CONSIDERATIONS

Take a look at the working drawing (Illus. 2) and see how, at a scale of one grid square to 1", the screen is about 36" high and 20" wide. This particular screen is a much-reduced miniature, in that it draws inspiration from an original that is well over 14' high. Note that the pierced hole not only of course relates to the doorway in the original, but it also illustrates the Native American "Bear Mother" myth that describes how semihuman cubs entered the world by way of a bear mother. See the human faces of the cubs on the palms of the Bear Mother.

Now, study the various drawings and details, and see how the carving has been reduced to the minimum. Apart from a small amount of dishing and modelling around the eye sockets and cheekbones of the large face and the two small "ear" faces, the design has been achieved by painting and then cutting through the paint, with the unpainted, lowered ground areas giving emphasis to the painted details that are left in high relief. As for color—the lips, eyebrows, and all the other dark areas are painted blue-black and the dotted texture is painted red-brown. All the lowered ground within and around the blue-black and red-brown areas are left the pink-buff color of the natural wood.

When you have studied the structure of the design and decided on the order of work, note the measurements and consider how you might possibly change the scale of the project. For example, you could simplify some of the details and make the panel half its size, or you could make the panel much larger—perhaps using separate planks, as in the original—and then you could change the proportions and use the resultant carving for, say, a door or maybe a room divider. There are any number of exciting possibilities.

Illus. 1. Project picture—a Tlingit *"Bear Mother" house panel.*

Illus. 2. Working drawing. The scale is one grid square to 1".

Once you have decided on the scale, draw the design up to size and make a good tracing. Note how this project is slightly unusual in that the design is painted and blocked in before it is carved.

TOOLS AND MATERIALS

For this project you need:

● a 2″-thick slab of prepared, easy-to-carve wood at about 36 × 20″—the grain needs to run down the length of the wood and the surface needs to be planed

● a pencil, ruler, and square

● a workbench with a vise and large clamps

● a small hand drill and a ½″ drill bit to fit

● a bow saw

● a pad, or keyhole, saw

● a good range of gouges and chisels, including a medium-size spoon chisel, a medium V-section gouge/veiner, and a large shallow-curve spoon gouge

● acrylic paints in blue-black and red-brown

● two soft-haired artist's brushes—a fine-point and a large

● a pack of graded sandpapers

● a can of brown-tinted wax furniture polish

● a cloth and a stiff brush for polishing

SETTING OUT THE DESIGN AND PAINTING

Set your wood down on the workbench and check it over for problems. A 2″-thick plank at 36 × 20″ is quite a hefty slab of wood, so make sure that it is in perfect condition. One or two live knots would be nearly acceptable, and it's likely that such a large plank might be slightly warped, but if the wood shows any signs of splitting, then it has to be rejected.

Square off the ends of the slab, mark the middle by drawing crossed diagonals, and then draw in a central line. When this is done, align the tracing with the central line, hinge the tracing along the top edge with tabs of masking tape, and pencil-press-transfer the traced imagery through to the wood. Make sure that all the transferred lines are clearly and crisply established before removing the tracing—if necessary, go over them with a hard pencil (Illus. 3, top).

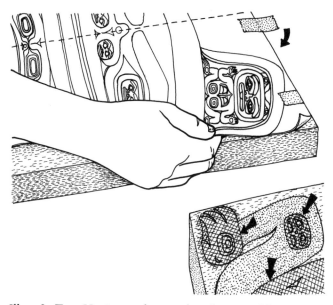

Illus. 3. Top: Having made sure that the central lines are aligned, use masking tape to hinge the tracing on the top edge. Bottom: When you come to painting, be careful that mating red-brown and blue-black areas don't bleed into each other.

Having marked in all the lines that go into making up the design, take the blue-black and red-brown acrylic paints and mix a medium-thin wash of each color. Now, bearing in mind that the colors will lighten somewhat as the paint dries, block in the various design areas. You only need to be especially accurate where the blue-black design touches the red-brown (Illus. 3, bottom). Starting at the top of the panel with the blue-black paint, block in the two little faces, the eyebrows, the eyes, the nostrils, the mouth on the large face, the faces on the Bear Mother's palms, and so on. Don't, in this instance, bother to delineate all the little details and try to paint up to the drawn line, but rather block in the whole area and paint well over the drawn line. For example, when you come to paint the Bear Mother's eyes, don't try to pick out the thin ridge of color that marks out the boat shape of the outer eye, or the little faces that double up as the pupils—just block in the whole eye area. The same goes for the large mouth and nostrils; don't try to pick out the details—just paint in the whole mouth-nose-nostril area as a single unit. And so you continue, working down the panel, blocking in all the painted areas that make up the design.

FRETTING OUT AND PIERCING

When the paint is completely dry, take a close-up look at the workpiece and make sure that the lines of the design are still clearly visible. If they look at all obscured, then realign the tracing paper and rework the design. It's most important that the drawn lines be clearly set out.

Set the slab of wood in the jaws of the muffled vise and set to work with the bow saw, cutting out the design and clearing the waste around the top of the head (Illus. 4, top left). Stopping from time to time

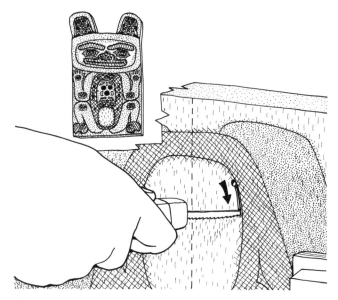

Illus. 4. Top left: Cut away the waste wood from around the top of the head. Bottom: Drill a pilot hole a little to the waste side of the drawn line, and use the pad, or keyhole, saw to clear the waste.

to reposition the workpiece in the vise so that the blade is presented with the line of the best cut, try to cut a little to the waste side of the drawn line. Also, try to hold the saw so that the blade passing through the slab is at 90° to the working face.

Now, having noted how the "door-to-the-world" hole is completely enclosed by wood, drill a pilot hole a little to the waste side of the drawn line and use the pad, or keyhole, saw to clear away the waste (Illus. 4, bottom). Again, you will have to keep repositioning the wood in the vise.

When you have achieved a nicely worked edge profile and a smoothly curved hole, use the riffler files and the graded sandpapers to rub the sawn edges down to a smooth finish. Then take the paint washes and touch up the edges.

LOWERING THE WASTE GROUND

Once you have achieved the painted, fretted, and prepared panel blank, set it face-up on the workbench and secure it with a hold-down and/or clamps. If you

look at the working drawing (Illus. 2), you will see that there are two main lowered ground areas: the outside of the Bear Mother's body (that is, between the body and the edges of the panel) and around the features that make up the face (that is, between the red-brown face band and the inner blue-black features).

Having noted that it is only the unpainted ground areas that need to be lowered and wasted, take the veiner or a small V-section gouge and set in the shape of the various forms and motifs with a precise V-section trench. Several passes will be needed to reach the required depth. Bearing in mind that as you will be cutting both with and across the grain, so you will be presented with all manner of difficulties, hold the tool with both hands, one hand guiding and the other pushing (Illus. 5, bottom). Run the trench around the motifs so that it is about ¼″ deep and a little to the waste side of the drawn line (Illus. 5, top left). Reckon on having about ¹⁄₁₆″ between the drawn line and the edge of the trench. Take one of your medium

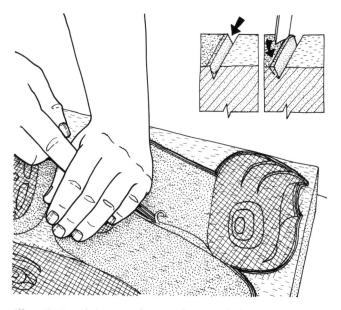

Illus. 5. Top left: Run the trench around the motifs so that it is about ¼″ deep and a little to the waste side of the drawn line. Bottom: Hold the V-section gouge with both hands, one hand guiding and the other pushing. Top right: Use the medium shallow-curve gouge to set in the pencil line.

shallow-curve gouges and work around the design, setting in on the pencil line with an angled-out stop-cut (Illus. 5, top right). If all is well, the narrow sliver of waste between the drawn line and the side of the trench will fall away to reveal the fresh pink-white wood. You will be left with a beautifully cut, crisply painted edge.

Now, having run a V-section trench a little to the waste side of the drawn line and having set in the drawn line, take a spoon chisel and start to lower the waste ground to an overall depth of ¼″ (Illus. 6, top left). When you come to cleaning out the step from the high-relief painted areas to the low ground, change tack slightly and use the knife as well as the gouge. Slice down into the angle with the knife (Illus.

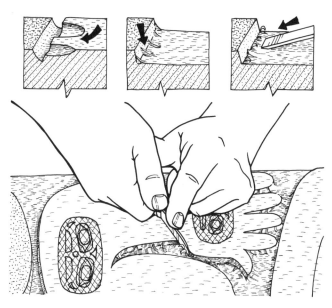

Illus. 6. Top left: Use the spoon chisel to lower the waste ground. Middle-top and bottom: Use both hands to guide the knife—slice down into the angle of the trench. Top right: Clear away the unwanted wood by sliding the chisel across the lowered ground and into the initial knife cut.

6, middle-top and bottom), and then slide the gouge across the lowered ground and into the knife cut (Illus. 6, top right). Try to lower the ground and achieve a step-down that is crisp and square. Once you have lowered the ground area that makes up the main face and the little "ear" faces, then use the tools of your choice to achieve the slight modelling.

MODELLING AND DETAILING

When you have cleared and lowered the main ground areas, then comes the much more tricky task of carving all the inside-color details. Starting with the inside-mouth area, first set in the shape of the mouth with a chisel, and then make a slanting cut from the middle of the mouth and down into the stop-cut so as to remove a little V-section sliver of waste. In this way, you keep cutting out from the mouth's central line and down towards the stop-cut that marks out

the shape of the mouth, until the central line is left as a thin, high ridge (Illus. 7, bottom left).

Take a close-up look at the project picture (Illus. 1) and the working drawing (Illus. 2), and see how, in the main, most of the other details are basically repetitions of the procedures already described. For example, if you look at all the little faces, you will see that the features have been set in and the details created by skimming off the painted surface to reveal the white wood beneath. The only difference is that, instead of then lowering the white wood so as to make a flat level ground, the outer edges of the ground have been sliced in slightly deeper so that the face appears round and convex. The area between the nose tip and the eyebrow looks quite lifelike (Illus. 7, top left). With the moated areas around the little "island" motifs on the belly and feet, the painted surface is cut away, and then the white ground is lowered and shaped so that the middle of the moat is just slightly concave (Illus. 7, bottom).

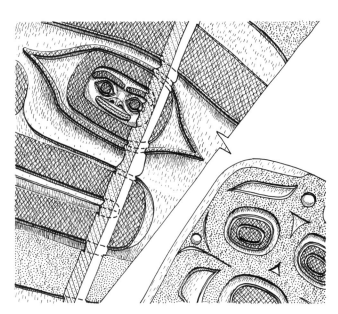

Illus. 7. Bottom left: Cut out from each side of the mouth's central line, until it is left as a thin high-relief ridge. Top left: Model the little faces so that they have raised cheeks and hollow areas under the eyebrows and around the eyes and the nose. Aim for lifelike features. Bottom right: The little "islands" on the belly need to be worked with concave "moats."

If you study the details, you will see that apart from some slight modelling to the white ground, all the carving procedures are more or less the same. Of course, some areas need to be cut in with incised lines, and you will have to chop and change tools to fit the demands of the job at hand, but from this point on it's pretty straightforward.

FINISHING

When you have achieved what you consider to be a good carving, dust off all the cavities and have a stand-back look at the sum-total carving. Consider how you might make improvements. Could you, for example, make some minor adjustments by highlighting an edge or detail with paint, or could you make a moat deeper, or a cut wider? It's best to look at the piece over a period of days and then to make modifications, if you see fit. Note how, in the belly area, the blue-black lines are painted within the natural wood areas so as to make an inner "frame" (Illus. 7).

Finally, give the workpiece the lightest rubbing down just to break through the paint on selected edges, remove all the dust, apply a couple of generous coats of tinted furniture wax, and burnish the surface to a good finish.

TROUBLESHOOTING AND POSSIBLE MODIFICATIONS

- If you decide to make the panel much larger, then you will need to build yourself a screen by butt-jointing a number of planks together. It is best to have the planks dry-jointed and secured at the back with slotted, screwed horizontal members—this allows for movement.
- As the wood is painted first and then cut and carved, care should be taken not to damage or soil the painted surface while the work is in progress. You could cover painted areas with a clean cloth.
- If the wood appears to be very absorbent, then seal it with a clear polyvinyl-acetate wash just prior to painting.
- If you mess up a detail, then consider levelling, re-painting, and then recarving the problem area.
- The gouge, chisel, or knife should slice through the painted surface smoothly and crisply to reveal the white, unpainted wood. If, on the other hand, the cut edge looks blurred or ragged, then the wood is still damp after painting, the tool needs resharpening, or you have chosen an unsuitable piece of wood.
- Where red paint meets black, score a line just prior to painting. The scored lined will serve as a "stop" when painting and a stop-cut when carving.

9
Bear Rattle (*Haida*)

A shaman's ceremonial dance and curing rattle

Saw, gouge, and knife
Sawn, shaped, hollow-carved, and shallow-relief-carved
Painted, waxed, and burnished

Bearing in mind that the rattle was considered to be an important part of the shaman's ceremonial equipment, a *Haida* shaman would have needed specific rattles for specific occasions. He might well have had a whale rattle for predicting the return of whales, a rattle for finding lost and wandering souls, a salmon rattle for catching salmon, a rattle for predicting the outcome of battles, and so on. Of course, each type of rattle was shaped, carved, detailed, and painted with related forms, designs, and motifs.

For example, the salmon rattle was usually shaped like a salmon, pierced, and painted, with maybe an enclosed figure of the shaman and/or a small salmon visible through the piercing. The killer-whale rattle was characteristically carved so as to show an adult whale, with a small whale's face peering out from a half-open mouth. There were bear rattles, beaver rattles, eagle rattles, and so on, all carved with related imagery.

From rattle to rattle, the reverse face might be worked with a mirror image of the front or with a meaningful symbol, or even, as with this project, be left plain.

Generally speaking, rattles were carved in the round, with the surface being decorated with stylized symbols and motifs. Usually the form was split into two halves, hollow-carved, with noisemakers—pebbles or bones—placed in the cavity, and then sewn together with leather thongs.

DESIGN, STRUCTURE, AND TECHNIQUE CONSIDERATIONS

Study the working drawings (Illus. 2 and 3) and see how at a scale of four grid squares to 1″, the rattle is about 9″ high and 5″ in diameter. Note how it is very nearly globular in form, with the nose being boldly three-dimensional, while the rest of the low-relief design is stylized and incised and wraps around the form.

The animal form is almost certainly a bear or bear cub. The bear was considered to be an important clan and spiritual figure, and so consequently all manner of carvings were worked with bear imagery.

This *Haida* rattle illustrates how, characteristically, there is an overlap between animal and human imagery. Apart from the rounded bearlike nose, or snout, and the two stylized bearlike ears, this particular face is nearly identical to carvings of human masks.

The clear-cut, crisply worked eyes, eyebrows, ears, and mouth are characteristic of the mid-to-late nineteenth-century *Haida* style.

As for color—the mouth, the tongue, the bulge around the nostrils, and the bridge shape at the top of the ears are painted a bright vermilion red; the eyebrows, the irises of the eyes and the thin eyelids are painted a dark cobalt blue; while the main area of the face is given a thin wash of copper-oxide green.

See how the handle springs out of the front of the rattle. Think of the front of the rattle as being a deep

Illus. 1. Project picture—a Haida *shaman's bear rattle.*

Illus. 2. Working drawing of the front view and section.
The scale is four grid squares to 1″. Note the pebble shaker.

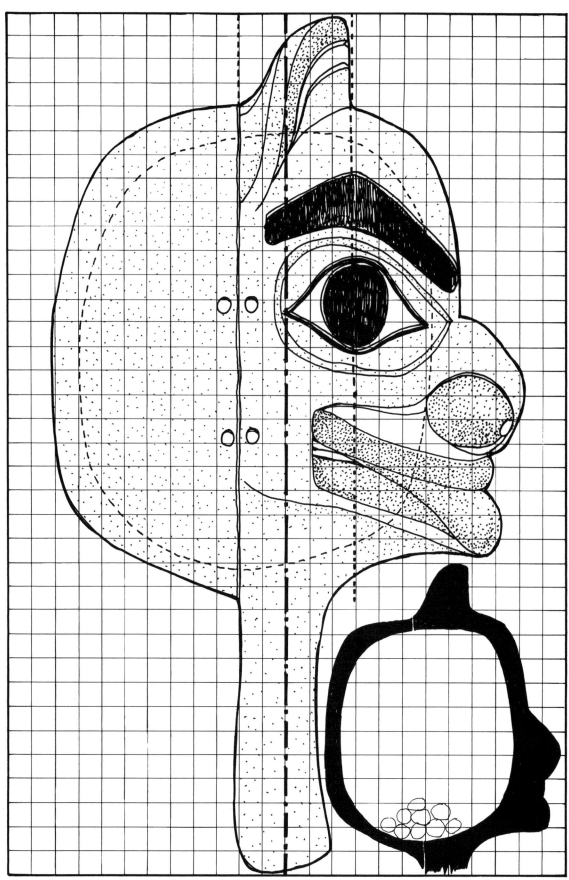

Illus. 3. Working drawing of the side view and section. The scale is four grid squares to 1". Note the join and the lace holes.

spoonlike shape, with the back of the rattle being a much shallower, lidded addition.

When you come to roughing out the basic form, it's best to work it from a single piece—meaning, rough out the overall ball-on-handle form and then use a saw to cut away the back.

TOOLS AND MATERIALS

For this project you need:

• a piece of easy-to-carve, straight-grained wood that's about 6 × 6″ square and 10″ long—you could use a traditional wood such as red cedar

• a pencil, ruler, and work-out paper

• a pair of compasses

• a small straight saw

• a workbench with a vise

• a hold-down type of clamp

• a couple of hooked, or crooked, knives—one with a gentle curve and the other with a tight spoon-carving hook

• a good selection of gouges, including a shallow curve, a small deep U-curve, a medium spoon-shaped gouge, and a small flat chisel

• a pack of graded sandpapers

• a small awl

• artist's watercolor paints in vermilion red, dark cobalt blue, black, and green oxide

• a couple of artist's brushes—a broad and a fine-point

• nine small pebbles

• a couple of leather-thong bootlaces

• a can of clear beeswax

SETTING OUT THE DESIGN AND CLEARING AWAY THE WASTE

When you have studied the working drawings (Illus. 2 and 3) and the other illustrations, and have a clear understanding of how the project needs to be worked, take your block of wood and check it over for possible faults and problems. Reject any wood that appears to

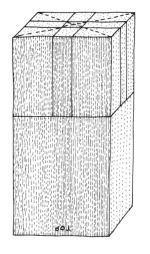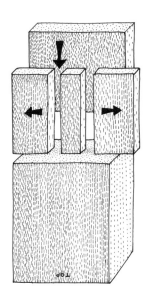

Illus. 4. Left: Draw lines across the end of the wood to establish the overall dimensions of the handle. Right: The 1 × 1″ square handle should stand out from the 5 × 5 × 6″ square block.

be stained, split, knotty, twisted, or in any way less than perfect.

Set the wood out on the work surface and check it for size. You need a 5 × 5″ square section of wood that's 10″ long, with the grain running along its length.

Now take the pencil and ruler and set out the various measurements that go into making up the design. First find the middle point in the ends by setting each 5 × 5″ end out with crossed diagonals. When this is done, mark the ends of the wood "top" and "bottom." Next, with the wood still flat down on the bench, and the top end to your right, measure 4″ from the bottom and use the square to run a line right around the wood. The 10″-long block should now be divided along its length into two pieces, one at 4″ and the other at 6″.

Now, with the wood set bottom-up on the bench, step off each of the four 5″ sides with the measurements of 2″, 1″, and 2″. Make sure that the 1″ step-off always occurs at the middle of each side. If you now link step-off points by drawing lines across the end of the wood, the end should be set out with naughts and crosses or a tick-tack-toe type of grid. Extend the ends of the lines down the wood to meet the 6″ head-handle line (Illus. 4, left).

Bearing in mind that you want to cut down into the wood to a depth of no more than 2″, set the wood in the vise or up against a bench hook, and run the saw right around the block, turning and repositioning the wood as you go. When this is done, secure the block of wood bottom-up in the vise, and saw down through the lines of the tick-tack-toe grid. If all is well, the waste should fall away as four pieces and you should be left with a 1 × 1″ square stump or handle, sticking straight up from a 5 × 5 × 6″ square block (Illus. 4, right).

ROUGHING OUT

With the square section for the handle now secured down in the jaws of the vise, set the compasses to a radius of 2½″, and scribe a 5″-diameter circle on the top end of the block. Use a pencil and ruler to draw tangents to the circle—diagonal crossover lines—so that the wood is set out with an octagon. Take the saw and clear away the corners of waste so that you are left with the octagonal shape (Illus. 5, left).

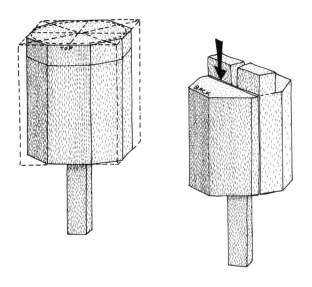

Illus. 5. Left: Take the saw and clear away the corners of waste. The resultant shape should be octagonal. Right: Cut away what will be the back half of the rattle.

With the wood still secured handle-down in the vise, take a pencil and emphasize one of the crossed diagonals. With the rough octagonal shape now visually halved by a line, take the pencil and mark the line "central line" and the areas on either side "front face" and "back head." Now measure from the central line ¾″ to the front and ½″ to the back, and draw lines parallel to the central line. Halve the resultant 1¼″-wide strip along its length and mark in a ½″-wide area that runs from the front of the head through to the back. If you now measure a little under an inch down from the top of the wood and run a line right around the four side faces, you will have marked out

and established the two columns that need to be set out for the bear's ears. When this is done, use the saw to cut away the pieces of waste from in front and behind the ears.

Finally, take the straight saw and run it behind the ears and down through the wood, so as to cut away what will be the back half of the rattle (Illus. 5, right). It's most important that you saw down behind the ears rather than in front, so double-check with the working drawings and with your various measurements before you make a cut. If all is well, the final cut down behind the ears should run down through the wood and come out just to the back of the 1″ square handle.

CARVING

With the bulk of the waste cut away, the basic form roughed out, and the bear rattle split into two halves, take another look at the working drawings (Illus. 2 and 3) and see how the wood needs to be cut and carved. See how the back half of the rattle needs to be worked until it is smooth and gourdlike, whereas the front piece and handle need to be carved in the round, modelled, and detailed with shallow-relief motifs.

Clamp the front piece with the sawn face down on the workbench, and mark in the main details that make up the features. Mark in a central line from between the ears to the chin, the position of the chin, the position and breadth of the nose, the position of the eyes, the slant of the ears, and so on. When this is done, take the mallet and one of the larger shallow U-section gouges and start to clear away some of the waste (Illus. 6, bottom).

Ideally, the form needs to flow in smooth, confident lines, up from the smooth, rounded handle, under the chin, over and around the cheekbones, over one ear, down between the ears, over the other ear, and so on, down to the other side of the handle. Once you have established the round head form, then you can begin to lower and shape the area above and beside the nose. Cutting across, or at an angle to, the grain, carve and shape the forehead, the eye area, and the cheeks. Don't try to remove the waste in great chunks; it's much better to go for lots of little slices. And so you continue removing small slivers of waste, all the while trying to shape the total profile and to achieve the beautifully rounded form.

Once you have cleared away the bulk of the cheek and forehead waste, then comes the tricky business

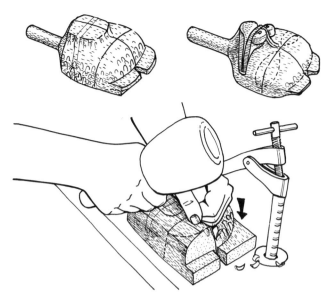

Illus. 6. Bottom: Take a mallet and one of the large shallow-curve U-section gouges and clear away the primary waste. Top, left to right: Stages in modelling the nose, tongue, and lips.

of shaping and modelling the nose, lips, tongue, and chin. There is no single easy way to carve such details. However, you might think of these raised features as being like a cluster of rocks on the beach. You can't see the rocks when the tide is up, but when the tide slowly goes out—then the rocks gradually begin to appear as small individual shapes above the water level. The rocks were there all the time, but you only see them when the water level goes down. And so it is with carving. You could think of the high round features as being hidden away just below the surface of the wood. It is your task as a carver to lower the concealing layers of waste wood little by little, until the form is revealed. However, this is no easy task, because if you chop down in one great thrust, then you will undoubtedly cut into, say, the nose or chin.

The process involves cutting down a layer, looking at the working drawings, using the pencil to reestablish the lines of the form, cutting away another layer, and so on. When you think you have lowered the wood around, say, the nose, check with the side profile, and then take a smaller gouge, or maybe even one of the knives, and start shaping, modelling, and rounding the convex and concave curves that make up the nostrils (Illus. 6, top—left to right).

Once you have cut and modelled the large forms—the nose, lips, tongue, ears, and forehead—then you can cut in the shallow-relief-carved details that make up this particular design. So, starting with, say, the outer eye socket and the inner eye, trace off these

details from your master design or working drawing, and then adjust them to fit around the shape. When this is done, pencil-press-transfer the details through to a sheet of thin cardboard. Do this for the outer eye socket and the inner eye, and cut out the shapes so that you have two templates. Now use the templates to draw the designs in on the actual workpiece. Hold the cardboard shapes in place, adjust them to fit the curve of the wood, and then draw around them with a soft pencil (Illus. 7, top left).

Now, starting with the line of the outer eye socket, take the tool of your choice (you might use a knife or a gouge) and set in the line to a depth of about 1/8″ (Illus. 7, bottom right). Take a good look at the project picture (Illus. 1) and the details and see how the various cuts need to be angled. Now, using either a crooked knife or a small shallow-curve gouge, begin to lower the wood within the socket. Again, don't try to remove the wood in one great sweep; just settle for lots of little-by-little skimming strokes. When you have lowered the wood, redraw the eye and begin to model between the outer-socket line (Illus. 7, top right) and the eye—meaning, the beautiful almond shape of the eye. Repeat the procedure between the line of the almond-shaped inner eye and the round pupil. Work in exactly the same way, only this time be extra careful that you don't chop into the thin ridge of wood that makes up the shape of the almond eye. Remove the waste so that the narrow band of high-relief wood angles up from a wide base (Illus. 7,

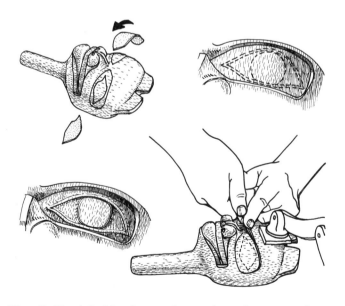

Illus. 7. Top left: Use the template to draw the curves of the eye socket. Bottom right: Set the line in to a depth of about 1/8″. Top right: Lower the wood within the socket. Bottom left: Model the eye so as to leave a narrow band of high-relief wood that delineates the shape.

93

bottom left). This buttressing gives the wood strength and prevents short-grain crumbling without spoiling the design. Continue working backwards and forward across the wood, lowering the surface, cutting in details with V-cut, incised lines, and so on.

SHAPING THE BACK AND CARVING OUT THE HOLLOW

When you consider the front of the head finished, take the two halves of the rattle, set them together sawn face to sawn face, and pencil around the finished front half so as to transfer the profile through to the sawn face of the back half (Illus. 8, top—left and right). Use the saw, gouge, and knife to swiftly cut the back half of the rattle to shape. When this is done, take the two halves a piece at a time, drill pilot holes to establish the depth of the dishing, or hollow, and then set them on your lap and use the crooked knives to scoop out the inner waste (Illus. 8, bottom). Again, work with lots of small scooping strokes, all the while maneuvering both the wood and the knife so as to make the most efficient cuts. It's all fairly safe and straightforward, as long as you hold the knife so that the long handle is braced by your thumb, and you work with a small, arm-braced, wrist-rocking scooping movement. Aim to hollow-carve the two forms until the walls are about ¼ to ½" thick. Don't try to work into the back of the nose or the chin; just settle for a dishlike hollow.

Once the carving is finished, use the awl to bore the eight cord holes; then go over the whole workpiece with the finest crooked knife, trimming and skimming the surface to a good tooled finish.

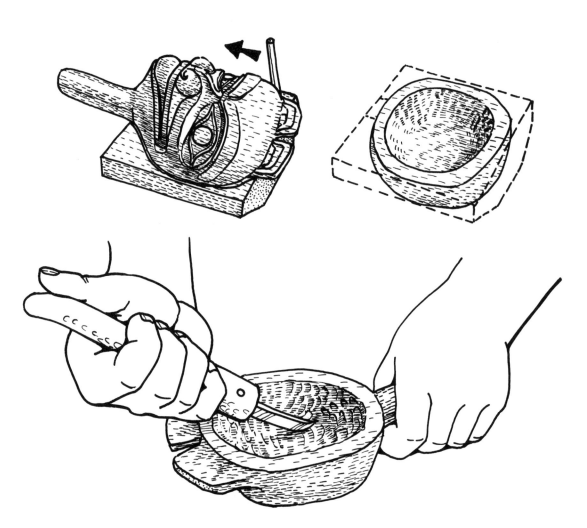

Illus. 8. Top left and right: Pencil around the finished half so as to transfer the profile through to the back. Then use the saw and knife to swiftly cut the back to shape. Bottom: Use the crooked knife to scoop out the inner waste.

PAINTING AND FINISHING

Clear away all the clutter and debris, and make sure that the working area and the workpiece are completely free from dust. Set out your paints and brushes so that they are comfortably close at hand, and pin up the working drawings so that they are out of harm's way and yet in clear view. When this is done, start by mixing washes of each color—you need a thickish wash of red and blue-black and a thin, watery wash of green.

Beginning with the main ground areas—meaning, the forehead, the cheeks, the chin, the handle, and the back of the head—take the green wash and apply a couple of thin coats. Don't lay the paint on so thickly that you can't see the grain; aim for an even wash rather than a thick cover. On the other hand, when it comes to painting the blue-black eyebrows, eyes, and eye rims, and the red areas—the tops of the ears, the lips, the tongue, and the nostrils—make sure that you do block out the character of the wood and that the profile lines are hard-edged and well-established. Now take the fine-point brush and the blue-black paint and block in the eye pupils and the fine line that goes around the eyes. If everything works out right, the inner "whites" of the eyes, the middle area of the ears, the narrow strip between the lips, the main ground area, and the nostril holes should all be left unpainted.

When the paint is dry, take the very finest sandpaper and give the whole workpiece a swift rubbing down. Rub through the paint on the main "wear" areas—the end of the nose, the tongue, the tips of the ears, and so on. Aim for an old, used, and much-handled look.

Finally, pop the nine little pebbles in the rattle, secure the two halves with the leather thongs, apply a generous coat of wax, and burnish the surface to a smooth, shiny finish.

TROUBLESHOOTING AND POSSIBLE MODIFICATIONS

- If you are at all worried about how a particular detail ought to look, then it's best to make a model with clay or Plasticine—it's a very good way of visualizing the whole piece.
- Traditionally, this rattle might well have been cut and worked from green wood. Certainly green wood is easier to carve, but, on the other hand, it's more likely to twist and warp as it dries.
- If, when you are carving, you come across an unexpected problem with, say, a hidden knot or cavity, then be prepared to adjust the design, or, in extreme cases, to even start over again.
- If your hands feel sore after a few minutes' work, then protect them from the main pressure points with Band-Aids.
- In carving the delicate details of the nostrils, eyes, and mouth, keep the cuts tight and controlled, use both hands to control the tool, and watch out for fragile short-grain areas. Also, be careful that you don't lever the tool against a fragile detail.
- Save the wood cut off from around the handle for smaller projects, such as the charm in Project 15.

10
Knife Handle (Tlingit)

A handle for a fighting knife

Carving and whittling knives
Waxed and burnished

When the Native Americans of the Pacific Northwest waged war against a neighboring tribe, clan, or individual, they didn't necessarily resort to arms. Of course, there were occasions when battles were fought and lives were lost, but more often than not disputes were worked out through dance and mime, a shaman intermediary, ritual insults, or negotiation and payment. For example, one clan might shame another at a potlatch, or a vigorous war of words might be waged, with one tribe offering challenges, making threats, and generally being insulting. Or then again, the antagonist might employ a shaman to plant a "disease" object in the enemy.

However, if all else failed, the Indians would go to war with every intention of killing. Such physical conflicts ranged from massive hand-to-hand battles, with hundreds of warriors bloodily fighting it out with clubs, knives, and spears, to the more stealthy, undercover-of-darkness, man-to-man, kill-and-run approach. A shaman would be consulted as to the best time and place for an attack. If the signs were good, the antagonist would lie in wait on such and such a propitious day and hour and then ritualistically put his victim to death with a special knife or club. Such a weapon had to be carved and decorated with meaningful supernatural designs and motifs, as has this knife.

DESIGN, STRUCTURE, AND TECHNIQUE CONSIDERATIONS

Study the project picture (Illus. 1) and the working drawings (Illus. 2), and see how, at a scale of four grid squares to 1", the knife handle measures about 7½ to 8" long and a little under 3" wide at its widest point. Take a close-up look at the carved details and see how the characteristic *Tlingit* bear's head motif has been modified for this fighting knife to make it suitably fearsome and aggressive. In addition, the bulbous, head-shaped pommel and the long, rather delicate shaft of the handle make for a firm, stable, non-slip grip.

When you come to putting the knife together, slide the flat blade tang-up into the slotted handle and hold it in place with a twine binding.

We have smoothed out potential design and carving problems for this project by making a full-size Plasticine maquette.

TOOLS AND MATERIALS

For this project you need:

- a piece of close-grained, knot-free 3 × 2" wood that's 8" long—it's best to use an easy-to-cut wood such as a Virginian pencil cedar

- a pencil, ruler, and work-out paper

- a coping saw or fretsaw

- a good selection of knives—we used a crooked knife, two small penknives, and a scalpel and/or a fine-bladed knife

- a block of Plasticine

- a pack of graded sandpaper

- a can of beeswax polish, a brush, and a cloth

SETTING OUT THE FORM AND ROUGHING OUT THE SHAFT

Take your chosen piece of wood and give it a last checking over, just to make sure that it is free from such wood-carving nasties as splits and dead knots. If all is well, measure 3″ down the 8″ length of wood

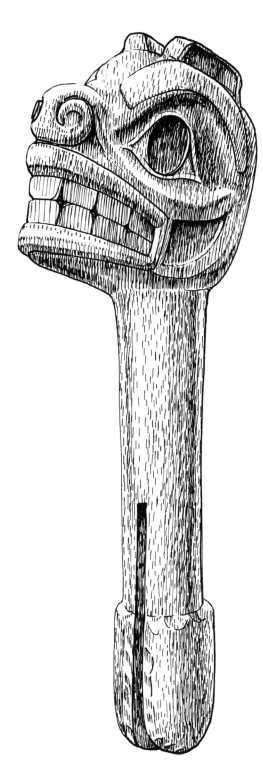

Illus. 1. Project picture—a Tlingit fighting-knife handle.

and run a pencil line right around the 3 × 2″ section. Draw central lines down all four long faces, measure and mark in the width of the handle shaft, and cross-hatch the areas of waste that need to be cut away (Illus. 3, left). When this is done, take the 3″ head—that is, the pommel end of the handle—in one hand and your crooked knife or chosen "wasting" knife in the other, and begin carving the handle shaft to size (Illus. 3, right). Noting that the bear's head in profile is turned a little bit to one side, cut the shaft down to a slightly oval form that's good to hold. Aim for a form that measures about an inch in diameter at its narrowest point.

MAKING THE PLASTICINE MAQUETTE

Now put the wood aside and start building the maquette, or model. It's best to mould the Plasticine over the end of a 4″ length of 1″ broomstick dowel. With one eye on the working drawings (Illus. 2), use a knife and/or a modelling stick to model all the details that make up the design. Consider the tilt of the bear's head and take into account how the mouth is angular and aggressively thrusting forward. Note such details as how the shaft flows smoothly and stemlike into the head and how the eyes are deep-set and tilted, and then model the Plasticine accordingly.

The good thing about building a maquette is that you can make as many mistakes as you like. There's no problem if the eyes are too small, if you cut away too much material, or if you completely mess it up—all you do is stick a wad of Plasticine back on the maquette and start over again. And, of course, along the way you will iron out potential problems and be able to finalize the design.

Once you have achieved what you consider to be a good image, put the maquette within view but out of harm's way and clear the work surface for carving.

SETTING OUT THE DESIGN AND MAKING YOUR FIRST CUTS

Having first made a good clear working drawing (Illus. 2) and a maquette, trace off the design of the bear's head and then pencil-press-transfer the main profile lines through to the four faces of the wood (Illus. 4, top left). Take a medium-size knife and start cutting away the main areas of waste. At this stage, don't try to carve out any details; just aim to block out the main forms. Clear away the waste from under the

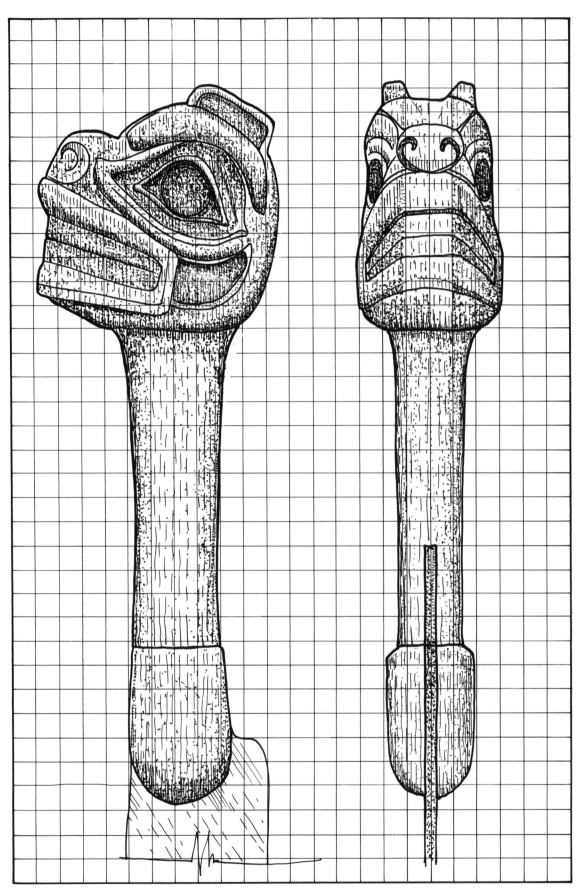

Illus. 2. Working drawings—side and front views. The scale is four squares to 1". Note the blade slot.

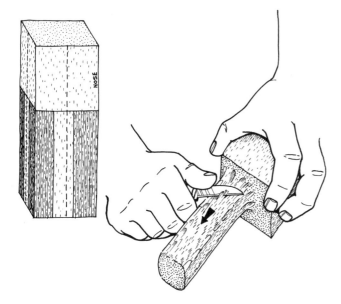

Illus. 3. Left: Measure and mark in on the wood the position of the pommel and grip. Right: Hold the pommel end of the wood and carve the grip to size.

chin, the back of the head, above the nose, and between the ears (Illus. 4, bottom). When this is done, refer to the working drawings (Illus. 2), the maquette, and the tracings, and pencil in the main details (Illus. 5, top left). Now take up the workpiece and the knife, and run stop-cuts around the wood at what you consider to be primary points (Illus. 5, top right). You might make stop-cuts around the base of the ears, across the bridge of the nose, or snout, above and below each lip, between the upper lip and the lower

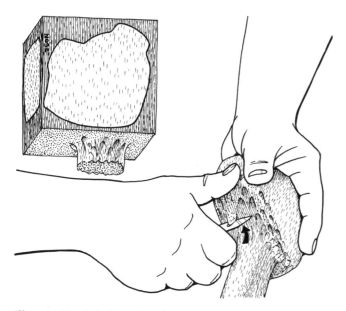

Illus. 4. Top left: Pencil in the main profile lines. Bottom: Clear away the waste from under the chin.

ridge of the outer eye socket, under the jaw, and so on. Relating closely to the working drawings (Illus. 2) and the maquette, cut down into the wood to a depth of about 1/16 to 1/8″.

Start with, say, the four main stop-cuts that go into making up the mouth. Above and below the top lip and the bottom lip, chop in at an angle on each side of the stop-cuts so as to cut a V-section trench or incised line (Illus. 5, bottom). When you come to the area inside the mouth—that is, below the top lip and above the bottom lip—repeatedly deepen the stop-cut and the width of the incision until you reach the lower level of the bear's teeth (Illus. 6, top left). Continue in this manner, working backwards and forward over the bear's head, adjusting and deeping the width and depth of the stop-cuts, until you can almost see the shape and form emerging from the wood.

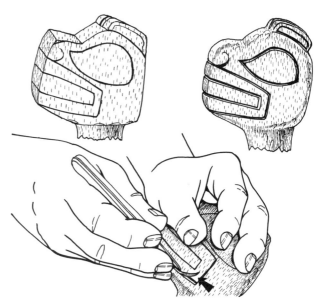

Illus. 5. Top left: Pencil in the main design lines. Top right: Run stop-cuts around the primary features. Bottom: Chop in at an angle on each side of the stop-cuts so as to cut a V-section trench.

CUTTING IN THE DETAILS AND MODELLING THE FORM

Having further studied the working drawings (Illus. 2) and the maquette and having reestablished the lines of the design, take the scalpel or a small fine-bladed knife and start to curve and lower the forms into the stop-cuts. For example, with the area inside the mouth, once you have established the depth of the teeth by sinking the stop-cuts, then you can start

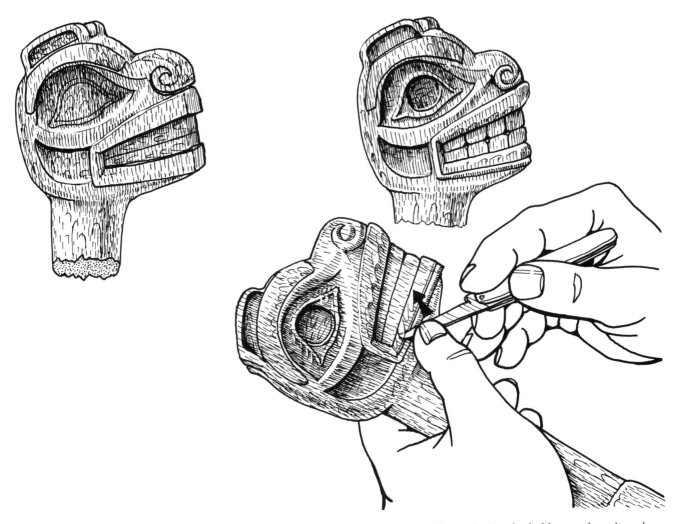

Illus. 6. Top left: Repeatedly deepen the stop-cut and widen the incision until you reach the lower level of the teeth, ears, eyes, and cheeks. Top right: Redraw the fine details of the design and continue to model to obtain the subtle

shapes. Bottom: Shape the lips by holding and guiding the knife with one hand, while at the same time applying leverage by pushing with the thumb of the other hand.

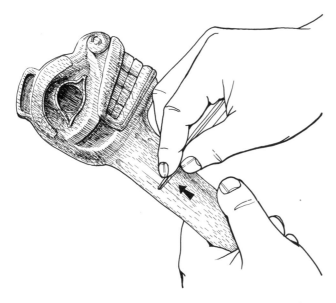

Illus. 7. Hold the blade between your thumb and forefinger and go over the surface with a firm, dragging action.

to clear the inside-mouth waste, while at the same time shaping the lips. Bearing in mind that the lips are well-defined and yet subtle, clear away the waste with cautious paring strokes. When you reach the level of the teeth, change tack slightly and shape the lips by holding and guiding the knife with one hand, while at the same time supplying leverage by pushing it with the thumb of the other (Illus. 6, bottom). Now continue carving all the large, broad forms and planes.

To recap the carving procedure—establish the depth with a stop-cut, deepen and widen the stop-cut or areas between stop-cuts to clear away the waste, and carve and shape over and down into the stop-cuts to achieve the main broad forms. Of course, as you get closer and closer to the envisaged form, you will have to be more cautious and take smaller cuts.

Finally, when you consider the carving finished, hone the scalpel or knife to a razor-sharp edge and go over the carving, using the blade much as you would use a scraper. In other words, hold the blade between your thumb and forefinger and go over the surface with a tight, firm, dragging movement. Work from high to low areas and with or across the grain, removing whiskers of wood and cutting down some of the coarser tool marks (Illus. 7).

FINISHING

When you have completed the bear's head and brought it to a good finish with the edge of the scalpel blade, return to the handle-to-head area and trim the wood down so that the head runs into the handle in a smooth, curved gradation. Along the way, spend time trying the handle out for size and grip. If it feels a bit thick or is in any way rough or awkward, then be prepared to modify it.

When you come to fitting the blade (these blades can be purchased at a specialist shop, or you could use an old kitchen knife), use the coping saw to cut the tang slot. Don't strive for too tight of a fit, which could split the handle, but rather go for an easy-friction push-fit. Use a waxed-linen twine to bind the handle.

Finally, rub the workpiece down with the finest-grade sandpaper, just to remove any whiskers of grain, brush off the dust, apply a couple of coats of beeswax, and burnish the wood to a smooth finish.

TROUBLESHOOTING AND POSSIBLE MODIFICATIONS

- With a project of this size and character, most of the cuts are made with the knife being braced and controlled with a levering or pushing action of the thumb.
- If the wood cuts ragged or rough, then it is coarse-grained, knotty, or damp, or your knife needs to be sharpened.
- If, after sharpening your knife, the wood still cuts ragged, try changing your angle or direction of cut. It may be that you are cutting into end grain or slicing into the wood at an unsuitable angle.
- Don't be tempted to overuse the sandpaper—sandpaper tends to blur the image and reduce the power and tension of the tool marks. Use fine-grade sandpaper and concentrate your efforts on the broad, undecorated areas of the carving.
- When you come to carving the top lip and the delicate ridges of high-relief wood around the eyes, watch out for areas of fragile short grain—go at it nice and easy and don't be tempted to lever or force the tool.

11
Whorl (Salish)

A spindle whorl used for spinning fibres

Saw, knife, and small gouge
Fretted, pierced, relief-carved, incised, and chip-carved
Waxed and burnished

Although the *Salish* Indians commonly adorned themselves with all manner of beads and bracelets, they wore very little in the way of clothes. In fine weather the men went completely naked, while the women wore nothing more than small aprons. This is not to say that they didn't know how to make textiles—they were in fact very accomplished weavers—but, in the main, they reserved their weavings for special social and ceremonial occasions.

These special items of prestige clothing—capes, women's aprons, and blankets—were made from a mixture of crushed cedar bark, dog hair, and goat wool. And as with all the other daily activities, the spinners and weavers believed that supernatural beings were able to help or hinder them in their work. Therefore, spindle whorls were nearly always decorated with images, designs, and motifs that represented friendly, helpful spirits.

In use, the *Salish* whorl, a small plate-sized disc, is slid down over the spindle stick, wedged into position, and then spun like a child's spinning top. The dual role of the whorl is to provide momentum to the spin and to prevent the buildup of yarn from sliding down the spindle stick.

DESIGN, STRUCTURE, AND TECHNIQUE CONSIDERATIONS

Study the project picture (Illus. 1) and the working drawings (Illus. 2) and see how, at a scale of four grid squares to 1″, the whorl disc is about 5″ in diameter and about 3/4″ thick. Take a close-up look at the

design and see how it is carved in shallow relief—that is, the motifs stand up in relief while the surrounding ground has been lowered. Note also how the small details within the overall design are either incised, chip-carved, or lowered. For example, the large crescent shapes around the central stick hole are incised, the triangular infill on the ear is lowered, and most of the details on the bird's wing and the fish are chip-carved. Although the overall ground has been lowered so that the main motif stands up about 1/8 to 1/4″ higher than the ground, nevertheless, within the design many of the chip-carved pockets are cut well down into the body of the wood.

Most *Salish* whorls of this size, type, and period are characterized by being relatively modest and stylized, with the motifs being worked and modified so that they fit the circle.

TOOLS AND MATERIALS

For this project you need:

- a square 5½ × 5½″ piece of heavy, close-grained wood that's about 3/4″ thick—it's best to use a wood such as box or American cherry

- a pencil, ruler, and work-out paper

- a compass

- a hand drill with a 1/2″-diameter bit

- a coping saw or fretsaw

- a crooked knife

*Illus. 1. Project picture—a
Salish spinning whorl.*

- a small fine-bladed knife—we used a scalpel
- a pack of graded sandpaper
- a can of clear beeswax polish

SETTING OUT THE DESIGN

When you have studied the project picture (Illus. 1) and the working drawings (Illus. 2), draw the design up to size and make a clear pencil tracing. Establish the middle of the 5½ × 5½" square piece of wood by drawing crossed diagonals. Fix the compass to a radius of 2½" and set the wood out with a 5"-diameter circle (Illus. 3, top right).

CUTTING OUT THE PROFILE AND BASIC SHAPING

Secure the wood in the vise and use the saw to cut out the circle. When you are sawing, try to cut a little to the waste side of the drawn line and to hold the saw so that the blade passes through the wood at right angles to the working face (Illus. 3, bottom). You will naturally have to change both the wood in the vise and your angle of approach so that the saw blade is always presented with the line of the best cut. When you have cleared away the waste outside the circle, run the ½"-diameter drill bit through the middle of the circle and bore out the stick hole.

Now, with the wood in one hand, the crooked knife in the other, and with your lap protected with a heavy apron, set to work cutting out the basic form (Illus. 4). Aim for a smooth, round-edged pill or puck profile. Run the knife around the circle and cut away the sharp corners—do this on both sides of the disc. Having cut away the two corner edges and having achieved a mitre, or angled, edge to the disc, repeat the procedure, only this time make finer cuts and cut away the sharp corners of the four resultant flatter angles. And so you continue—turning and cutting, turning and cutting, all the while getting closer and closer to the

Illus. 2. Working drawings. The scale is four grid squares to 1". Note the section.

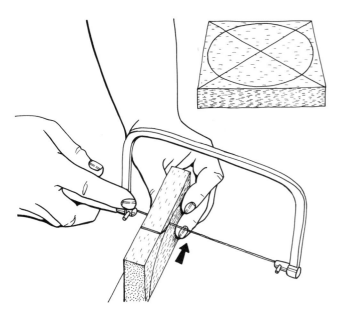

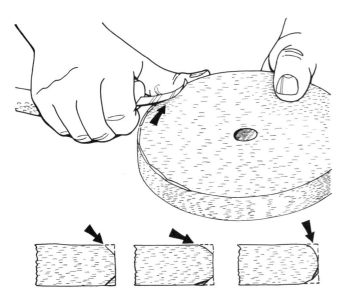

Illus. 3. Top right: Fix the compass to a radius of 2½" and set the wood out with a 5"-diameter circle. Bottom: Secure the wood in the vise and use the coping saw to cut out the circle.

envisaged round-edged form (Illus. 4, bottom—left to right).

When you come to shaping the ½"-diameter hole in the middle of the disc, use the same approach of gradually cutting away the angles, only this time use a small knife and work with a twisting apple-coring action.

Finally, rub the workpiece down with the finest-grade sandpaper until it is smooth to the touch.

Illus. 4. Top: Cut a smooth, round-edged pill profile. Bottom, left to right: Repeatedly cut away the sharp corners until the edge is smooth and curved.

CARVING THE DETAILS

Once you have cut and worked the round-edged section, pencil in the back of the tracing, and then secure the tracing to the best face of the wood and pencil-press-transfer the lines of the design. Pencil in the main outline or profile and make sure that all the details are clear and well set out. Having shaded in all the areas outside the design that need to be lowered and wasted (Illus. 5, top right), take a sharp-pointed knife and cut in the main profile lines to a stop-cut depth of about ⅛" (Illus. 5, left). Run the knife at an angle to the initial stop-cut and remove a V-section sliver of waste. Now take the crooked knife, hold it at a flat angle to the face of the wood, and then lower

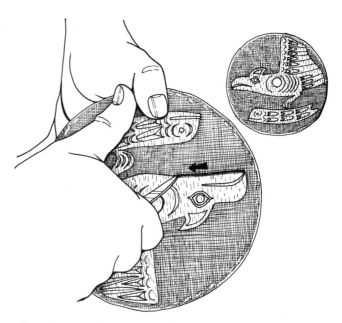

Illus. 5. Top right: Transfer the design through to the wood and shade in the areas that need to be lowered. Left: Use a sharp knife to cut in the stop-cut lines to a depth of about ⅛".

the waste with careful skimming or shaving cuts. Work across and/or at an angle to the grain, all the while cutting in from the edge of the circle and in towards the stop-cut. In this manner, continue removing the waste and lowering the wood, all the while making sure that the blade of the knife stops short at the stop-cut (Illus. 6, top). When you have lowered the entire area outside the design to a depth of about ⅛ to ¼", reestablish the curved section at the edge of the disc as well as the smooth finish.

Take a small knife—it's best to use either a fine-bladed penknife or a scalpel—and cut in all the incised lines that make up the design. Each incised line or

V-section cut needs to be worked with three strokes (Illus. 6, bottom—left to right). First you make an initial straight-down cut into the wood to establish the depth; then you make two more cuts, one at each side and at an angle to the first. Continue working backwards and forward over the workpiece, removing all the V-section, incised cuts.

Now you can start to cut in all the round-ended, boatlike details. If you look at the design close-up, you will see that there are six such details on the fish and nine towards the front of the bird's wing. One shape at a time, start by running the point of the knife around the two long, curved sides and establishing two stop-cuts (Illus. 7, top right and middle left). Work around and down one side and then around and down the other. Cut down into the wood to a depth of about 1/8″. When this is done, position the knife blade on the central line and slide the blade down at an angle towards one of the two stop-cuts. Do this on both sides so that the central line is left standing ridgelike in high relief.

Take another look at the working drawings and see how there is a little triangular pocket at one end of the boat shape. Take the knife and set in the triangle with three straight-down stop-cuts. Have the three cuts running from the middle of the triangle to the points of the angles (Illus. 7, middle right). Now set the blade of the knife on one of the sides of the triangle and slide the point down towards the middle so as to remove a little pocket of wood (Illus. 7, bottom left). Do this on all three sides of the triangle. You should now be left with a little triangular depression, or pocket, that looks a bit like an upside-down pyramid. When you have worked one chip-carved boat shape, then you move on to the next, and so on. This sounds more complicated than it actually is, but if you have any doubts, it's best take a scrap of smooth-grained wood and make a trial run. The secret of success is to use a knot-free, easy-to-carve wood and a thin-bladed, razor-sharp knife.

FINISHING

When you have lowered the ground, cut in the incised lines, worked the chip-carved details, and generally taken the design as far as you want it to go, then it is time to stand back and be critical. Ask yourself, Are the cuts positive and crisp? Are the forms con-

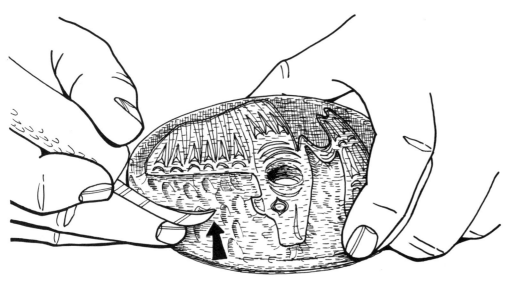

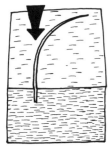 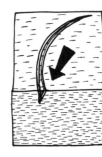 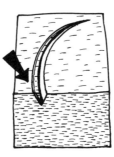 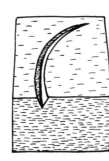

Illus. 6. Top: Working at an angle to the grain, cut in from the edge towards the stop-cut and lower the background area. Bottom, left to right: Make the initial straight-down cut, and then angle the knife in at each side of the cut so as to make a V-section trench.

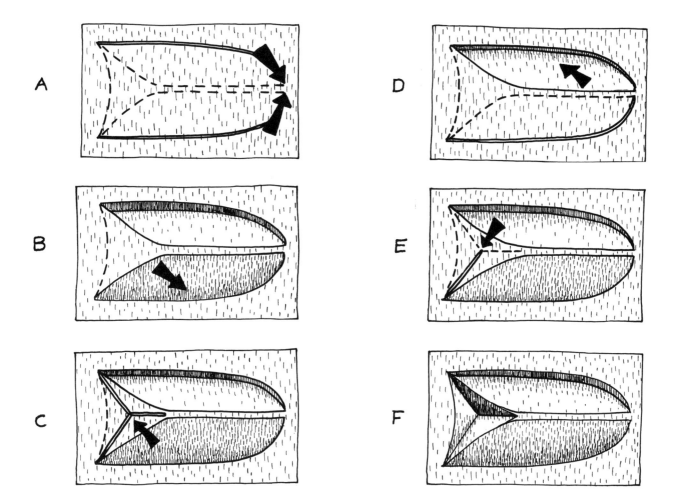

Illus. 7. Left to right and top to bottom: Cutting the scales. (A) Run the knife around the two long sides to establish stop-cuts. (B) Make one angled cut from the middle of the motif and down into the stop-cuts. (C) Repeat this on the other side of the motif. (D) Make a stop-cut deep into the middle of the small triangle and up and out to the point of the angle. (E) Repeat this with all three angles. (F) Remove three little pockets of waste by sliding the blade down towards the middle of the triangle and in to the depth of the initial stop-cut.

fident? Does the imagery fit the shape of the whorl? and so on.

If you are satisfied with the piece, take a scrap of fine-grade sandpaper and rub the work down to a good finish. Don't blur the details; just rub off some of the sharp edges and remove the end-grain whiskers.

Finally, brush away all the dust and debris, apply a couple of coats of beeswax polish, and burnish the wood to a high-shine finish.

TROUBLESHOOTING AND POSSIBLE MODIFICATIONS

- When you are roughing out the basic disc shape of the whorl, most of the cuts need to be made with a simple paring action of the knife. This is how the carving action goes: Turn the wood so that the knife is presented with the area of the next cut, brace your thumb against the workpiece and lever the knife along the wood, reposition the wood, take another cut with the knife, and so on.

- The secret of chip carving is having a bland, straight-grained, knot-free wood and a very sharp knife. The working action should be a continuous process of cutting and honing.

- If by chance, when you are lowering the ground, the knife slips and the blade runs into high-plateau wood, it's certainly unfortunate, but with a free-interpretation design like this, it is possible to adjust the design to accommodate your mistake.

- In many ways this project is deceptively simple, so don't lose sight of the fact that it requires careful planning and that the knife cuts need to be sure and clean.

12
Thunderbird Mask (*Kwakiutl*)

A helmetlike mask with feathered horns that was worn during the sacred *Tseteka* winter season

Saw, chisel, gouge, and knife
Sawn, constructed, deep-carved, and detailed
Painted, waxed, and burnished

For the *Kwakiutl* Indians, all things in nature—rocks, water, trees, animals, the sun, the moon, and the stars—were possessed by spiritual forces and powers. They saw these spirits as supernatural beings that lived in all the deep, dark, and inaccessible corners of their everyday world. There was a horrific Cannibal-Spirit-at-the-North-End-of-the-World who lived in the mountains and who, dripping with blood, flew shrieking and screaming across the skies. There was a Wild-Woman-of-the-Woods spirit who delighted in eating little children. And there was a truly monstrous cannibal spirit called Crooked-Beak-of-Heaven who pecked and crushed men's heads and fed on their brains and eyeballs. The *Kwakiutl* Indians had spirits and supernatural beings to match and counterbalance all human activities.

There was no doubting the existence of these beings—their presence could be heard in the wind, seen in the torrential rivers, observed when trees moved, and felt when there were rock falls. As far as the Indians were concerned, these spirits were beings of real flesh and blood.

On a slightly different plane from these everyday spirits were the totem, or mythical, spirits, whose existence could only be guessed at and whose whereabouts were more mysterious. One such supernatural force, or totem spirit, was the Thunderbird, a huge birdlike being who lived in the skies and who kept lightning bolts as companions. It was the giant Thunderbird who was responsible for all the violent thunderstorms that were so common along the Northwest coast. Because the Thunderbird was so powerful, his

imagery was frequently used for clan and crest motifs. To use a Thunderbird symbol was in some way to become endowed with supernatural powers that had to do with thunder, lightning, and rain.

DESIGN, STRUCTURE, AND TECHNIQUE CONSIDERATIONS

Take a good look at the project picture (Illus. 1) and the working drawings (Illus. 2), and see how, at a grid scale of one square to 1″, the overall Thunderbird mask, complete with horns, is about 20″ long, 17″ high, and 15″ wide at its widest point. Without the additions, the beaked head is much smaller—at 20″ long, 12″ high, and 12″ wide.

The flared, V-shaped form sits on the head like a helmet, with the two fretted and pierced feathered horns pinned and pegged to each side of the flared "V." Note also how the little crest at the top is more than decorative in that it doubles up as a brace, or support, at the top of the head. The crest in turn is held in place by two little bridge strips that span the "V."

Now, take a close-up look at the project picture (Illus. 1), and see how the grain runs along the length of the Thunderbird's head—that is, from the back to the beak—whereas with the horns, the grain angles up from the head and more or less runs along the length of the primary struts.

The original mask that inspired this project was decorated with a fringed mane of feathers and grass.

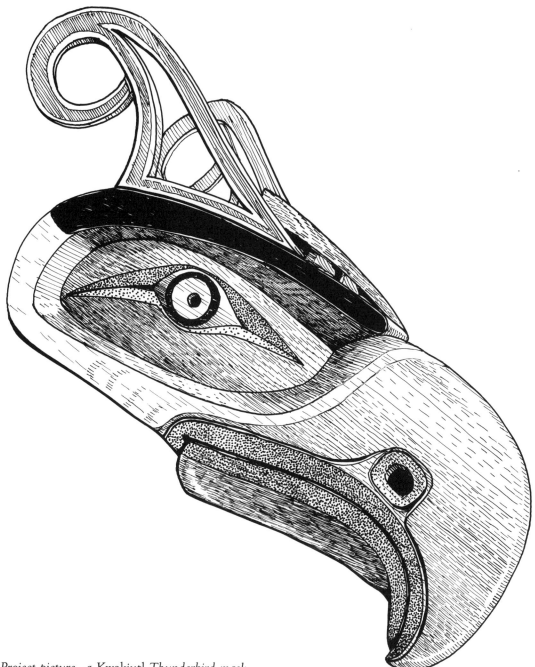

Illus. 1. Project picture—a Kwakiutl Thunderbird mask.

In addition, the eyebrows were inlaid with brass and the lower half of the beak was hinged.

TOOLS AND MATERIALS

For this project you need:

• a 20″ long, 12 × 12″ square block of straight-grained, knot-free, easy-to-carve wood—you might try true cedar or perhaps pencil cedar

• two pieces of ½″-thick prepared wood at about 8 × 12″ for the horns and the other built-up additions

• a pencil and ruler

• a sheet each of tracing and work-out paper to the fit of the wood

• a bow saw

• a small pin hammer

• a handful of panel pins—it's best if they are between ½ and ¾″ long and made of brass

• a fretsaw or piercing saw

• a workbench fitted with a vise, a good selection of large clamps, and a hold-down

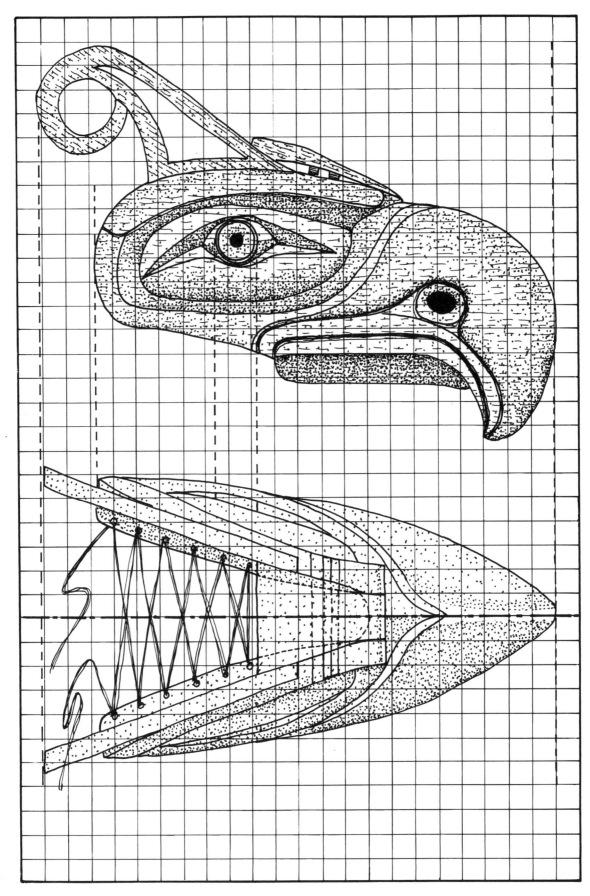

Illus. 2. Working drawings—side and plan views. The grid scale is one square to 1″. Note the lacing detail.

- a hand drill with a selection of drill bits

- a good range of gouges and chisels

- a selection of knives

- a pack of graded sandpapers

- a small amount of white polyvinyl-acetate adhesive

- acrylic paints in blue, red, and white

- two soft-haired paint brushes—a fine-point and a broad

- a can of wax polish

- a polishing brush and cloth

TRANSFERRING THE DESIGN AND SAWING OUT THE BLANK

Set your chosen block of wood down on the workbench and check it over for possible problems. Since it's a large section, there might be a few small, yet acceptable end cracks. However, as you will be cutting deep into the wood and almost dividing the block into two parts across its width, the wood really needs to be in the best possible condition. Be on your guard against dead knots and large areas of twisted grain. As a general rule of thumb, the straighter the grain, the easier the work.

Establish the middle by drawing crossed diagonals and run a central line around the wood. Trace off the side profile and pencil-press-transfer the traced design through to the wood (Illus. 3, top left). Make sure that the lines are clearly established by going over them with a soft pencil. Secure the wood in the vise and use the large bow saw to rough out the profile and to clear away the waste. Don't try for a precise cut; it's much better in this instance to settle for a cut that's about ¼″ to the waste side of the drawn line (Illus. 3, top right).

When you have roughed out the side profile, take a good look at the plan view, and then use your eye,

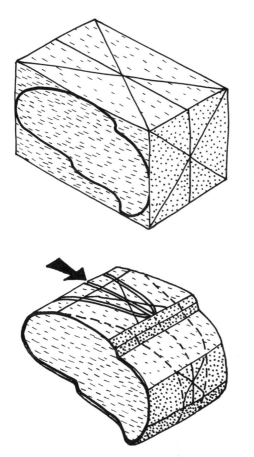

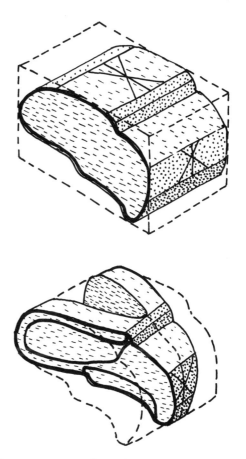

Illus. 3. Top left: Transfer the side profile through to the wood and mark in the various central lines. Top right: Work a little to the waste side of the drawn line and cut out the profile. Bottom left: Cut away the V-section waste in back of the head by making a pilot central-line cut and

then cutting on either side of the initial cut. Draw in the shape of the beak. Bottom right: Cut away the waste wood on either side of the beak and draw in the lines of the main design.

what remains of the central line, and the tracing paper to transfer the view through to what is now a sawn and contoured face.

Allowing a good margin for error, secure the wood in the vise and again use the bow saw to clear away the waste. Pay particular attention to the middle of the V-area—make three cuts, one on the central line, and one on each side to angle in to meet at the "V." Try to run the sawn line in a smooth curve around the bottom of the "V" (Illus. 3, bottom left).

Now, reestablish the central line on the beak, draw in the wedge shape of the beak, and use the bow saw to remove the waste on either side (Illus. 3, bottom right).

CARVING THE FORM

When you have removed the bulk of the waste, check with the project picture (Illus. 1) and the working drawings (Illus. 2) and then use your pencil to reestablish the lines of the design. Don't draw in every last detail; just go for the big, bold forms (Illus. 3, bottom right). When this is done, secure the wood side-down on the workbench, using one of the wedge-shaped pieces of waste to prop the wood up, and set to work with one of your shallow-curve straight gouges, clearing away the sharp-edged waste (Illus. 4, right). Work systematically around one side-face, and then flip the wood over and carve the other side-face in like manner.

Again, don't, at this stage, attempt to cut in secondary details such as the eye sockets and the nostrils; just target cutting away the waste and carving the primary form. Continue this way, working backwards and forward over the workpiece, all the while making smaller and smaller cuts, and working towards a smooth, rounded form and a delicate, tooled finish. Spend time getting the beak just right—the underside of the beak needs to slope and step under the upper curve—and don't skimp on what needs to be a full, generous, rounded shape (Illus. 4, top left).

MODELLING THE DETAILS

When you have achieved the full, rounded primary form, refresh your eye by studying the project picture (Illus. 1) and the working drawings (Illus. 2), and then press-transfer the surface imagery through to the wood. Draw in the shape of the eye socket and the

eyeball, the position of the eye and nostril holes, and the shape of the beak "lips."

Now take the mallet and one of your small shallow-curve straight gouges and set in the bottom-of-moat line of the eye with a ¼"-deep stop-cut. When this is done, set a medium-width shallow-curve gouge between the outer-socket line and the bottom-of-moat

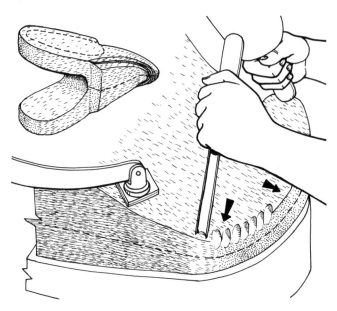

Illus. 4. Right: With the work supported on one of the pieces of waste, use the shallow-curve straight gouge and the mallet to round off the beak. Top left: Note how, under the overhang of the beak, the underside profile slopes and steps.

line, and start making deep, slanting scoops down in towards the stop-cut (Illus. 5, top left). Work once around the outer-socket line, and then repeat the procedure with the eye-socket line, only this time work from the outer ring of the eyeball and out towards the stop-cut (Illus. 5, top right). Work around and around from the middle to the side, and then from the side to the middle, all the while deepening the stop-cut and cutting down at an angle towards the stop-cut until you reach the desired level. When you come to carving the front of the eye socket, modify the procedure to take into account the beautiful, sharp valley that runs up and over the top of the beak. And, of course, when you have carved the eye socket on one side of the form, you have to flip the wood over and cut the other eye the same way.

When you have carved the sockets, draw in the long boat shape that makes up the eyelids and the circle for the eyeball. Take one of the knives and set in the six stop-cuts that mark out the deep valleys around the eye and between the lids. Set the blade down on the top-lid line and slide it down into the long, deep stop-cut so as to slice out a long, triangular nick of waste (Illus. 5, bottom left). Each pocket, or slit, on the sides of the eye is made up from three such triangular chip-carved pockets. Repeat the procedure on all three sides that make up each pocket—on the bottom-lid line, on the top-lid line, and then on the line of the eyeball (Illus. 5, bottom right). Work to the left of the eye and then to the right, and then flip the wood over and repeat the procedure with the other eye. Run the various individual cuts into each other so that the eye looks like a smooth ball that is partially contained by the eyelids.

When you have detailed the eye, finalize the position of the eye and nostril holes and then bore them out with the drill. Use, say, a ¼" bit for the pupils and a ½" bit for the nostrils. Work the drilled nostril hole with the gouge and knife until the face of the workpiece runs in a smooth curve down into the hole. And so you continue—cutting the little V-section trenches that set out the shape of the beak, cutting the incised line that runs around the nostrils, cleaning up the little curve over the bridge of the beak, and shaping the underside of the lower beak.

FITTING AND FIXING

Take a look at the working drawings (Illus. 2) and see how the feathered horns are fretted additions that are glued and pinned onto the flared arms of the large V-shape. See, also, how for the mask to become a

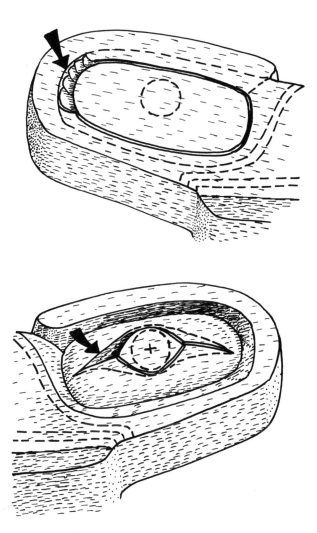

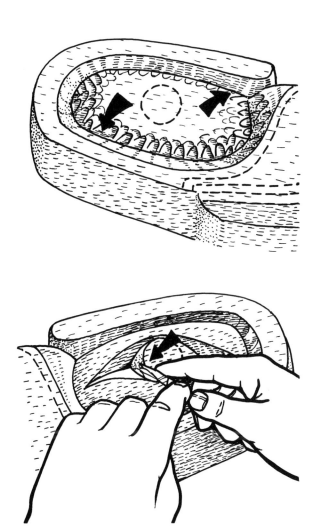

Illus. 5. Top left: Use the shallow-curve gouge to remove the waste between the outer and inner bottom-of-moat lines. Top right: When modelling the curved eye socket, carve out towards the stop-cut. Bottom left: After making the stop-cuts, use the knife to slice away the triangular

shape—set the blade down on the top-lid line and then slide it at an angle into the long, deep stop-cut. Bottom right: When you come to carving the rounded, sloping sides of the eyeball, hold the knife in one hand and use the index finger of the other hand to guide and steady it.

113

helmet, it is necessary to drill and lace the top and the back of the form to make a support for the head.

Trace off the shape of the feathered horns, pencil-press-transfer the traced lines through to the face of

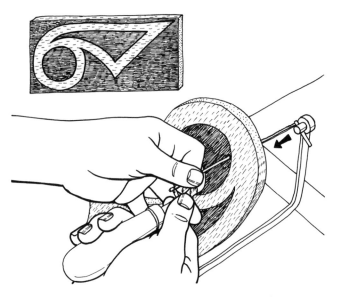

Illus. 6. Top left: Transfer the traced details of the feathered horns through to the wood and shade in the areas of waste. Bottom: Pass the blade through the pilot hole and ease the tension by pressing the saw frame against the bench.

the thin wood, and shade in the areas of waste (Illus. 6, top left). Support the wood in the vise and use the fretsaw or piercing saw to cut out the design. Be sure to cut on the waste side of the drawn line and to hold the saw so that the cut edge is at right angles to the working face. Now take the drill and a ⅛″-diameter bit, and run pilot holes through the enclosed "windows" that make up the design. There are two such areas on each horn—an almost-round shape and a long, hook-ended triangle. This is the order of work for the enclosed areas: Unhitch the saw blade, pass it through the pilot hole, hitch up the blade, run the saw around the window (Illus. 6, bottom), unhitch the blade, and then go on to the next hole. Use a scrap of sandpaper to rub the sawn edges down to a smooth, slightly rounded finish.

Having noted how the holes for the lace run along the top inside edge of the V-shape at about ¾ to 1″ apart, take the drill and a ⅛″ bit and run holes through the corner of the top edge. Ideally, the holes need to run at an angle of about 45° so that they are set back about ¼″ from the edge of the wood (Illus. 7, top left). When this is done, shape and fit the bottom edge of the feathered horns so that it meets the top of the curved brow; then glue and pin them in place on the top edge so that they are set back slightly from the lace holes.

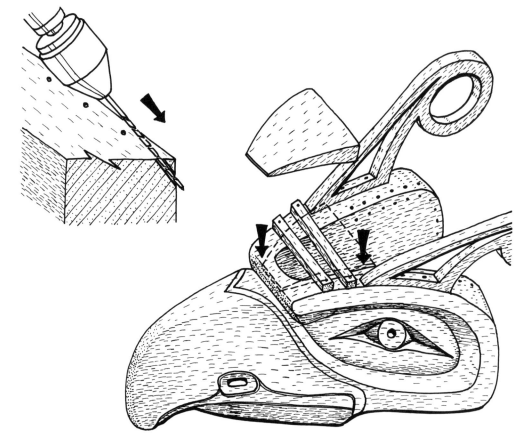

Illus. 7. Top left: Run the holes at an angle of 45° through the top to the inside edge of the mask. Bottom: Attach the tapered, wedge-shaped piece of wood on the bridge of the beak and between the feathered horns.

114

Study the details of the working drawings and see how the V-shaped part of the mask—that is, the bit between the eye ridge and the horns—is roofed over by a central crest piece that is supported by two small bridge strips. Cut a couple of thin strips to size, and glue and pin them in position. Now, having noted that the little crest-roof piece runs from the bridge of the nose right through to the feathered horns, cut a piece of tapered, wedge-shaped wood to fit (Illus. 7, bottom).

PAINTING AND FINISHING

When you consider the mask well carved and fitted, and you have brought all the details to a good, crisp conclusion, use a fine-bladed knife and the graded sandpaper to bring the overall workpiece to a good finish. Concentrate your efforts on the eyes, the sweep of the hooked beak, and the delicate incised lines that set out the shape of the mouth and the nostril holes.

Now, wipe away the dust and move the workpiece to the area that you have set aside for painting. You need to use three colors—blue for an allover base, or ground, coat; red for the mouth "lips" and the boat-shaped areas around the eyes; and white for the eye-balls, the sweeping line around the bottom and front of the cheek, the top of the beak, the nostril holes, and the small edge details of the horns.

Mix a thin wash of blue and give the whole work-piece a couple of allover coats. Don't lay on the paint in big, thick daubs—ideally, the grain texture should show through the paint. When the base coat is completely dry, take a scrap of fine-grade sandpaper and rub the surfaces down so as to break through the paint at "wear" areas.

Bring out the mouth and the eyes with red, and trail in the white edge striping on the horns and other white areas. Finally, when the paint is dry, rub the workpiece down again, brush away the dust, apply a generous coat of wax, and burnish the wood to a good finish.

TROUBLESHOOTING AND POSSIBLE MODIFICATIONS

- If you have any doubts at all as to how the mask fits the head, or how the wood needs to be carved and worked, then use a lump of Plasticine to make a small maquette.
- If you want to speed up the project, then you could use a band saw to achieve the initial form and to clear the bulk of the waste.
- If you would rather not "roof" the top of the mask with strips of wood and lacing, you could modify the details by working the mask interior as an up-side-down bowl that fits the shape of your head.
- This project draws its inspiration from a mask that has a workable hinged lower beak. If you are interested in such an approach, turn to Project 16 for guidance.

13
Moon Mask (Tlingit)

A shaman's mask representing the moon

Saw, gouge, and knife
Roughed out, deeply carved, incised, hollowed, and detailed
Painted, waxed, and burnished

The *Tlingit* Indians carved masks of unsurpassed beauty and quality. Most individual tribe members, both men and women, at some time or other, had worn a carved, painted, and crest-decorated mask. However, within the *Tlingit* tribe, the finest masks were worn by the shamans.

The shaman inherited, owned, and used a great many masks, which he would use when he wanted to represent and personify his spiritual guides and helpers.

The shaman would help individuals with all manner of personal problems—birth, sickness, witchcraft, and death. But his primary task was to provide good fortune and succor to the whole community by calling upon various guardian spirits for help and advice.

Of all the ceremonies, the midwinter full-moon dances and rituals were considered to be the most important. Wearing a suitable costume and mask that represented the genial, nonaggressive spirit of the full moon, the shaman would appear and assume his role as a medium. At some point in the ceremony, he would go into a trance and make contact with the moon spirits. It was his task to interpret the moon spirits' guidance, and to pass the advice, predictions, and warnings on to the chief and his people.

DESIGN, STRUCTURE, AND TECHNIQUE CONSIDERATIONS

Take a look at the project picture (Illus. 1) and the working drawings (Illus. 2 and 3), and see how, at a grid scale of five squares to 2″, the mask is about 10″ wide, 12″ high, and 4 to 5″ deep. Note how the moon

has been given human characteristics. The mask is round and surrounded by a corona, and has a slightly sinister expression, suggesting that the moon spirit is powerful and yet somewhat emotionally removed. Consider how the carver has indicated such human attributes by working the eyes, for example, so that the pupils are hooded, slightly divergent, and mysterious. Note, also, the downward slant of the rather cruel, full-lipped mouth.

Study the various views and details, and see how the eyes and mouth are pierced, while the eyebrows, nose, nostrils, and lips are characteristically carved and stylized. Finally, note how, although the various features have been flattened and modified so that the total mask fits into a shallow dome, there is an illusion of depth.

TOOLS AND MATERIALS

For this project you need:

● a slab of easy-to-carve wood at about 12 × 12 × 5″—such as lime, cherry, or sycamore

● a pencil and ruler

● a sheet each of work-out and tracing paper

● a pair of scissors and a sheet of thin cardboard

● a workbench with a vise

● a bench hold-down

● a bow saw, or better still, the use of a band saw

● a mallet

Illus. 1. Project picture—a Tlingit *shaman's moon mask.*

- a good selection of gouges, including both a small and a large shallow-curve front-bent gouge, both a small and a large spoon or spade gouge, a flat-curve chisel, and a deep V-section gouge

- a selection of knives, including a crooked knife, a small penknife, and a scalpel

- a small hand drill with a ⅛″ bit

- a pack of graded sandpapers

- a couple of brushes—a broad and a fine-point

- acrylic paints in crimson, black, white, and blue

- a can of clear furniture wax

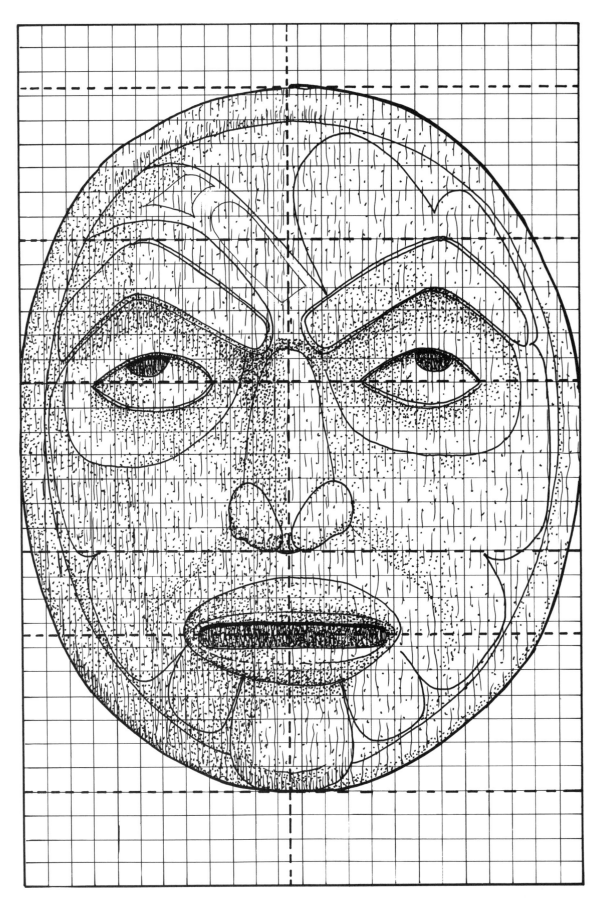

Illus. 2. Working drawing—front view. The grid scale is five squares to 2".

118

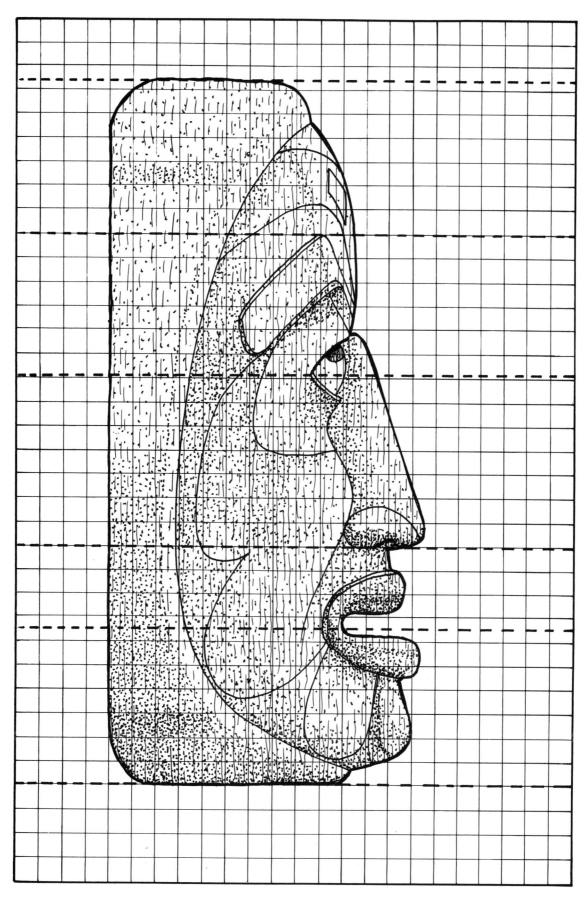

*Illus 3. Working drawing—side view. The grid scale is five
squares to 2".*

SETTING OUT THE WOOD AND CLEARING THE ROUGH

When you have studied the working drawings (Illus. 2 and 3), considered various options, and selected your wood, clear the workbench of clutter and arrange all your tools so that they are comfortably close at hand. Set your block of wood down flat on the workbench and spend time making sure that it is free from faults. Of course, you can't do much about hidden cavities and cracks that develop once the carving is under way, but you can at least make sure that the surface of the wood is free from splits, stains, and loose knots.

With a square side of the wood set face-up on the workbench, locate the middle by drawing crossed diagonals. Taking bearings from the sides of the slab and from the central point, draw in crossed top-to-bottom and side-to-side central lines. Now, having made sure that the head-to-chin central line runs in the direction of the grain, and remembering that the finished mask needs to be about 12″ high and 10″ wide, draw in the outer limits of the large, oval corona that frames the face (Illus. 4, top right). Using the various crossed lines as a guide grid, make sure that the form is as symmetrical as possible. When this is done, use the bow or band saw to clear away the waste (Illus. 4, left and bottom).

When you have achieved a straight-sided, oval-shaped blank, secure the wood with the hold-down

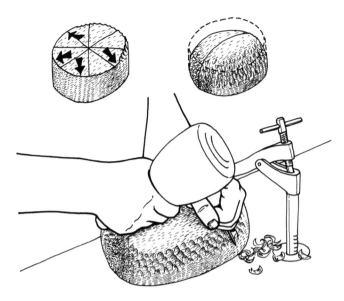

Illus. 5. Top left: Work from the middle to the side and across the grain. Top right and bottom: Use the mallet and a deep U-section gouge to clear the waste. Work from the middle to the side, aiming for a smooth-tooled mound.

and set to work cutting back the top edge. Take a look at the working drawings and see how the workpiece is shaped like a mound. With the mallet and a deep U-section gouge, work around and around the top edge of the oval. Work from the middle to the side, holding the chisel at a low angle, and reducing the waste by removing shell-like scallops (Illus. 5, top left). Continue around and around, and backwards and forward, until the workpiece is a low-curved, smooth-tooled mound (Illus. 5, top right and bottom).

SETTING OUT THE DESIGN

When you have roughed out the mound, take another look at the details (Illus. 3) and see how, in profile view, the various high-relief features all fit comfortably within the mound. With the top of the nose being the high summit and the curve of the bottom lip being the secondary peak, the profile then steps down with the chin, the top lip, the forehead, and the cheeks.

When you have a clear picture of how the finished mask relates to the wood, draw in the main guideline grid—the central line and the horizontal lines that run across the top of the eyebrows, through the eyes, under the nose, and through the mouth (Illus. 6, top center). With the aid of tracing paper, calipers, and dividers, lightly sketch in on the wood all the primary features that make up the design. When this is done, draw the various motifs out on thin cardboard and

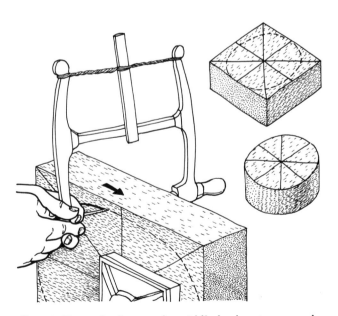

Illus. 4. Top right: Locate the middle by drawing crossed diagonals and then draw in the top-to-bottom and side-to-side central lines and the outer limits of the oval corona. Left and bottom: Use the bow saw to clear away the waste.

cut out the profiles to make templates. There's no need to repeat identical motifs—all you need is the mouth and one eye and one eyebrow.

Bearing in mind that the shape and position of the features are likely to shift and change as you cut into the wood, set the templates down on the design sketched on the surface of the mound and draw out more definite images (Illus. 6, top right and bottom).

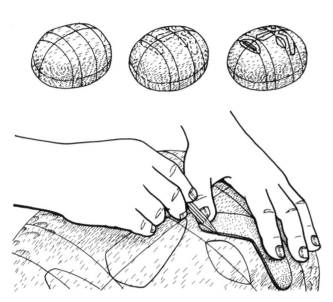

Illus. 6. Top left: Draw in the main guidelines—the central line and the horizontal lines that run across the top of the eyebrows, through the eyes, under the nose, and through the mouth. Top middle: Sketch in all the primary features. Top right and bottom: Use the templates to draw in the eyebrows and lips.

SETTING IN THE DESIGN AND CLEARING THE WASTE

When you have transferred the motifs through to the wood, take the mallet and a small shallow-curve gouge and carefully set in the design with stop-cuts. Don't, in the first instance, cut too deep; just settle for about ⅛". For example, set in stop-cuts around the eyebrows, the mouth, and the outer limits of the column that makes up the nose.

Having set in the stop-cuts, clear and lower the wood. First slice in at an angle to the initial cut so as to remove a V-section sliver of waste; then skim off the wood to the waste side of the V-section trench so as to leave the raised motif (Illus. 7, top left to right). Lower the ground using repeated short-stroke cuts. Thus, you continue by repeatedly chopping in a stop-cut, slicing out the V-section trench, and then

lowering the waste ground, until the various primary motifs are left as plateaus and the areas between the features are hollowed out to the required depth.

As you are working, you will have to refer to the project picture and the working drawings, comparing one partially worked detail with and against another. Carving is a continuous process of cutting away waste wood, reestablishing the form and/or the position of the form, comparing the position and shape of one detail with and against another, and then, in the light of these comparisons and fresh references, readjusting the direction, depth, and weight of subsequent cuts. But of course this process needs to be undertaken with care and in the certain knowledge that there is a finite amount of wood. There will always come a point when you will have to call a halt to the carving. For example, you can readjust the position and the shape of the eyes against the nose and/or the eyebrows, but if you cut too deep, then there's no going back. This is all the more reason why you need to keep standing back from the work to assess your progress. If necessary, leave the work be and come back to it the next day.

MODELLING THE FORMS

Bearing in mind that carving is not a process of taking one detail to completion and then moving on to the

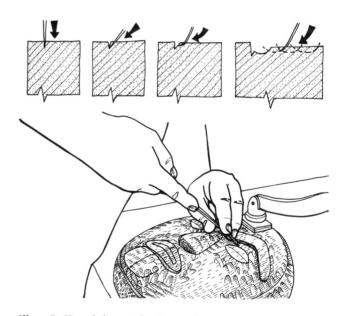

Illus. 7. Top, left to right: Set in the stop-cut, remove a V-section sliver of waste, scoop out to the waste side of the trench, and remove the waste with long, scooping strokes. Bottom: Use the small shallow-curve gouge to carefully cut back the sharp edges, the stepped angles below the eyebrow, and the surrounding ground.

next but rather a continuous process of moving backwards and forward over the work—still, somewhere along the line, you will need to start the final modelling. Beginning with, say, the stylized eyebrows, take a close-up look at the details, and see how you need to constantly change the direction of the cut to suit the run of the grain. For example, on the top edge of the eyebrow you need to work from the end to the middle, whereas on the bottom edge you need to cut from the middle to the end. Having noted the run of the grain, use a small shallow-curve gouge to carefully cut back the sharp edges and to clean up the stepped angle between the eyebrow and the surrounding ground (Illus. 7, bottom).

When you come to the lips, start by setting in the line between the lips with a row of punched points and then use the drill and a 1/8"-diameter bit to clear out the waste inside the mouth. Run the drill in as far as it will go (Illus. 8, top). Having worked a row of holes, take one of the small shallow-curve gouges and set to work cutting the rounded shape that makes up the lips (Illus. 8, bottom). Having noted that because of the run of the grain, you have to work the outside lips from the side to the middle and the inside

lips from the middle to the side, carefully pare away the waste on the edge of the plateau until the lips are round, plump, and slightly undercut.

And so you continue, working the shallow moats around the eyes, drilling out the pupils, undercutting the inside lids, scooping out the nostrils, shaping the cheekbones, cutting in the crease, or furrow, that sets out the width of the corona around the mask, and so on.

Finally, turn the mask over so that it is face down, support it on a cushion of old rags, and use the scoop and spoon gouges to clear out the waste inside the mask (refer to Project 1 or 2). Work from the side of the rim to the middle, and be extra careful when you are working the holes through the eyes and mouth.

PAINTING AND FINISHING

When you consider the carving finished, take the graded sandpapers and, being careful not to blur the details or obliterate the marks left by the gouges, rub the surface down to a smooth finish. Pay particular attention to the eyebrows, nostrils, and lips—try to

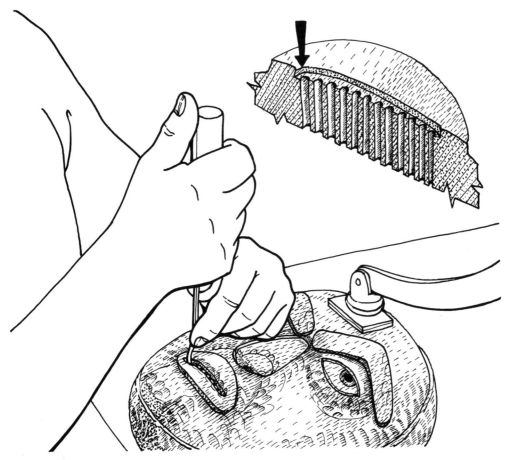

Illus. 8. Top: Use the drill and the 1/8" bit to clear the inside-mouth waste. Work a row of holes through the wood. Bottom: Use the small shallow-curve gouge to model the full roundness of the lips.

leave them very smooth. Brush off all the dust and debris and then retreat to the area that you have set aside for painting.

Having noted how the lips, nostrils, corona, and eye rims are painted red, the eyebrows and the inner eye rim are painted black, and the decorative crest motif is painted blue, mix the acrylic paints with water until you have thin washes. Allowing for paint bleed, carefully block in all the colors that go into making up the design. Strive for thin, transparent washes rather than solid colors.

When the paints are completely dry, take the finest sandpaper and cut through the colors at the main "wear" points: the nose ridge, the point of the chin, the lips, and the cheeks.

Finally, apply several generous coats of wax, let it soak into the wood, and then burnish the mask to a dull-sheen finish.

TROUBLESHOOTING AND POSSIBLE MODIFICATIONS

- When you are modelling the delicate details—the lips, nose, and eyebrows—be extra careful that you don't split off areas of fragile grain.

- It's most important that your tools are razor sharp—every five minutes or so, spend time honing the tool to a good edge.

- Be careful when you are scooping out the nostrils that you don't lever the shaft of the tool on the fragile rim. It's much better to use a small front-bent spoon gouge and to work with a scooping, twisting action.

- When you are painting with a wash, you have to allow for the paint bleeding and running along the grain of the wood. Therefore, it's a good idea to leave a narrow margin between the paint line and the edge of the area that is to be painted. For maximum control, paint the edge of the design first—pull the brush towards your body while constantly turning the work so as to paint from the inside to the edge. Once this has been done, you can block in the remaining area to be painted.

- If, by chance, the paint does bleed and run, let it dry and then rub the paint back with a scrap of fine sandpaper.

- If you are going to hang this mask on the wall, and there's no reason why you shouldn't, leave it solid, except for the eye and mouth holes.

14
Chest Panel (*Haida*)

A chest panel with crest and clan imagery

Saw, knife, mallet, and gouge
Carved in deep relief with inlay
Waxed and burnished

The Native Americans' most common article of furniture was the chest. In the homes of northern *Haida* Indians, the various screened-off areas were literally piled high with carved-and-painted chests, boxes, trays, and containers. Doubling up as seats, tables, and places of safekeeping, the cedar chest was used to store just about everything, from dried foods, small personal possessions and clothes to valuable ceremonial regalia.

Chests containing important religious or ceremonial items were stored in special areas that could only be ventured into by secret-society members. The ordinary, everyday storage chests, on the other hand, were conveniently positioned around the communal living area or stored away in the rafters, piled one on top of another.

In most instances, the function of a chest could be almost instantly recognized by its carved-and-painted decoration. And, of course, the more important the chest, the more complex and involved the construction, the carving, and the decoration.

In terms of technique, Native American chests can be divided into two basic categories: those made from separate slabs, or boards, in much the same way as, say, eighteenth- and nineteenth-century American and European dower chests, and those that were made all of a piece from massive, long, wooden planks.

The latter are uniquely interesting in that single planks were kerf-cut at the corners, and then steamed and folded at the kerfs so as to form the four wrap-around sides of the chest. The base was pegged, grooved, and sewn into position at a later stage. The chests that resulted were watertight, and used traditionally for holding such liquid commodities as hot water for cooking and the precious candlefish oil that was used for food dips and general food preservation.

DESIGN, STRUCTURE, AND TECHNIQUE CONSIDERATIONS

Take a look at the project picture (Illus. 1) and the working drawings (Illus. 2), and see how, at two grid squares to 1″, the panel measures about 18″ high and 12″ wide. Note how the carving is monolithic, in that it has been cut and worked from a single 2½″-thick slab of wood.

See how the relief carving is, at least in terms of chests, slightly unusual in that not only is it somewhat realistic in design and deeply carved, but it is also inlaid with pieces of abalone shell and sea-snail shells. The forms appear to have more in common with the deeper carving of the *Haida* totem poles and masks than with the stylized, incised, and painted work that characterizes most of their chests.

Study the details and consider how the designs have been lowered and rounded to suggest three-dimensional realism. Note how although the bearlike animal forms have been worked so that they are set stylistically one within the other, the bulging fullness of the forms—the cheeks, the lips, the belly, and such—create a sense of realism. Consider how the animal forms have been squared up so that they fit within the allotted ground area.

Bear in mind that this project requires that you use a good range of wood-carving tools—everything from

124

Illus. 1. Project picture—a Haida *chest panel with crest and* clan imagery.

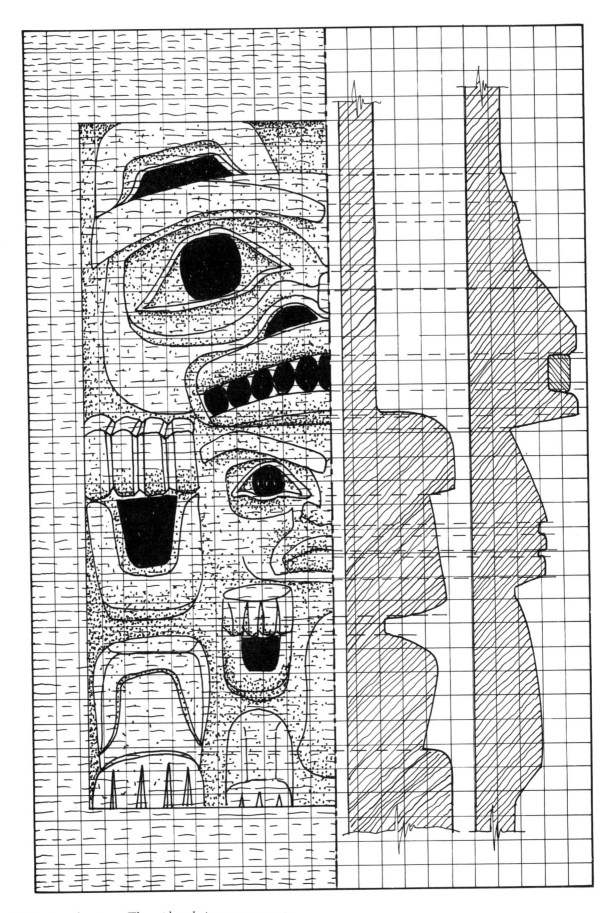

*Illus. 2. Working drawings. The grid scale is two squares to
1". Note the two sections and the depths of cut.*

a straight chisel and crooked knife to a spoon gouge and a mallet.

Finally, note the various inlaid details and consider your options. Can you get abalone or snail shells from a supplier? Or are you going to use easier-to-find material such as old pearl buttons or mother-of-pearl from a fish shop? This requires some thought.

TOOLS AND MATERIALS

For this project you need:

• a slab of 2½″-thick wood at about 12″ wide and 18″ high, which allows for an all-around border margin—it's best to use a traditional wood such as straight-grained Northwest coast cedar

• a pencil and ruler

• a roll of masking tape

• a sheet each of work-out and tracing paper

• a block of Plasticine

• a good number of carving gouges, including a shallow-curve straight gouge, a deep U-section spoon gouge, and a small V-section gouge

• a mallet

• a selection of knives

• a workbench

• a hold-down

• flat inlay material, such as abalone shell, mother-of-pearl, and old pearl buttons

• a piercing saw

• a bird's mouth/V-mouth sawing table and clamp

• a double-tube resin adhesive

• a can of wax

• a stiff polishing brush

MAKING A MAQUETTE AND SETTING OUT THE DESIGN

When you have studied the design, considered all the options, and familiarized yourself with the overall project, sit down with a pencil and work-out paper and draw the design up to scale. When this is done, take your block of Plasticine and start to build a scale-size working model, or maquette. Consider the way

the various forms are squared up with the slab and left as plateaus. That is to say, see how the primary features—the faces, knees, and hands—have been fitted into an all-square grid and then carved so that they are left at various levels within the thickness of the wood. Note the way the design has been broken down into 10 main plateau areas: the large face that takes up the top third of the panel, the four large hand and knee-foot areas, the smaller central face, and the four small hand and feet details of the smaller figure. Consider all these features and then mould the Plasticine accordingly. When the model is finished, place it within view and prepare your work surface for carving.

Having studied the drawings and the various details, and worked out potential difficulties by making the maquette, trace off the master design and pencil-press-transfer the lines of the design through to the best face of the slab of wood. Finally, establish all the top-surface details and shade in all the areas that need to be lowered (Illus. 3, left).

SETTING IN THE DESIGN AND ESTABLISHING THE PRIMARY PLANES AND FORMS

Secure the wood to the bench with the hold-down clamp, and then use the mallet and a selection of

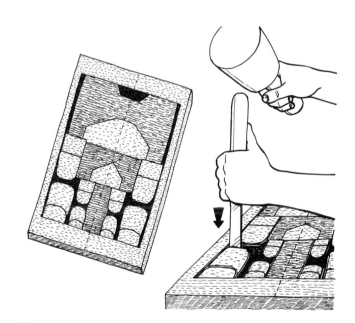

Illus. 3. Left: Shade in all the areas that need to be lowered, using the darkest shading for the deepest areas. Right: Chop straight down into the wood to a depth of about ¼″. It's best, while working these first cuts, to steady the gouge by holding it down low on its shaft.

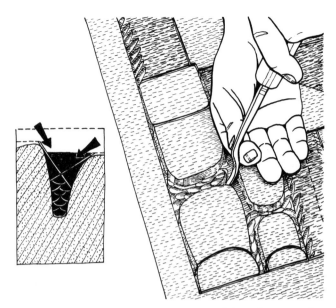

Illus. 4. Right: Scoop out the waste wood from between the set-in features. Left: A cross section showing the right-angled sides and the gradual stages of lowering.

straight, deep-curved, and shallow-curved gouges to set in the lines of the design. Being watchful that you cut a little to the waste side of the drawn line, hold and support the gouge down low on its shaft to provide good control, and set in stop-cuts around the 10 hand and leg plateaus. In the first instance, chop straight down into the wood to a depth of about ¼″ (Illus. 3, right). Repeat the procedure and set in the design-border line—meaning, the line between the design and the border margin. Be careful, when you are setting in the line between the ears, hands, and feet, and the border, that you stay on the drawn line.

When you have set in the main design areas or plateaus to a depth of about ¼″, then comes the pleasurable task of lowering the primary areas of waste. Using a selection of shallow-curve, back-bent spoon- and spade-type gouges, start scooping out the waste between the various set-in features (Illus. 4, right). Being extra careful to stay well clear of the two faces and the belly, cut both across and at an angle to the grain, where possible, so as to lower the waste down to the level of the initial stop-cut.

If you now look at the working drawings (Illus. 2), you will see that there are two distinct types of lowered waste areas. There are the rapid fall-away areas, such as between the palm and the knee, where the sides of the sinking are almost at right angles to the working face, and there are secondary-level areas, such as the belly, where the bed of the lowered waste area becomes in itself a carved feature. With this in mind, be careful when you are lowering the waste, that you

don't cut into secondary details. It's a good idea to keep referring to the working drawings and reassessing your progress.

When you are lowering the waste around the ears, at the top of the knuckles, between the two heads, between the large hands and the small face, and between the small hands, be ready to change your tool to one of a different size or shape, and to alter your technique.

When you come to lowering the belly area, be aware that although it is set lower than the surrounding hand and knee plateaus, the peak of the belly is only about ¼″ lower than these plateaus. Therefore, work out from the middle of the belly so that the hill-like form runs down in a smooth curve into the various surrounding stop-cuts (Illus. 5, top). Work so that you create a sharp-angled moated area.

Now, continue lowering the areas of waste and shaping the hill-like forms that make up the two main faces. Note that with the main face, the snout feature peaks almost at the surface of the wood (Illus. 5, bottom).

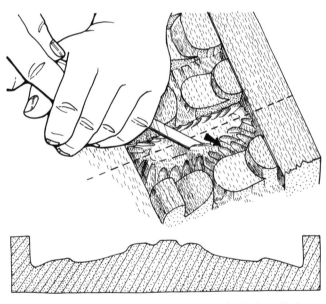

Illus. 5. Top: Work from the middle of the belly, all the while gradually lowering the hill-like form. Bottom: Cross section of the main face—see how the nose, or snout, peaks near the surface of the wood.

CARVING THE DETAILS

Take a look at the working drawings (Illus. 2) and details, and note how, although the raised areas—the faces, hands, and knees—have been carved in deep, seminaturalistic relief, the details within these primary features have only been surface-carved in stylized shallow relief. For example, even though the fingers and palms can be recognized as such, they are nevertheless no more than stylized interpretations of what we know to be fingers and palms (Illus. 6, left). The same goes for the toes, knees, lips, and the other details—they are no more than stylized forms that have been incised and shallow-relief-carved.

When you come to carving the four fingers and knuckles, first use a small skew-bladed knife to sink stop-cuts down between each finger (Illus. 6, top right), and then use a straight-bladed knife to carve the shape of the fingers by deepening and widening the stop-cuts (Illus. 6, bottom right). Repeat the procedure with the palms, knees, and toes.

Before you start to carve the eyebrows, take a close-up look at the drawings, noting their smooth surface and how they are stepped up from the main level of the forehead. Use your tracing to establish the shape of eyes and eyebrows, making sure that they are symmetrically placed. When this is done, use a knife with a sharp point to set in the shape of the eyebrow to a depth of about 1/8″. Next, take a shallow-curve, front-bent spoon gouge or even a dog-leg spade gouge, and

skim off and lower the area of wood around the eyebrow until you are down to the level of the stop-cut. Now continue setting in and lowering all the details that make up the design.

SETTING IN THE INLAY AND FINISHING

When you consider the carving finished, clear the work surface of clutter and set out your chosen inlay material, the piercing saw, the bird's mouth sawing table, and the double-tube resin glue. Now, having noted all the areas that need to be decorated—the ears, eyes, nostrils, teeth, and palms—take a small, flat spade type of gouge and go over the areas, making sure that they are crisply edged and level-bedded.

Take the inlay material and start to fit and place the various pieces. Aiming as much as possible to have large single pieces, especially for the eyes and the individual teeth, use the piercing saw to cut the inlay to a good fit (Illus. 7, top). Take a dry run to make sure that the inlay mosaic fits the allotted areas, and then, when you are happy with the overall fit, carefully

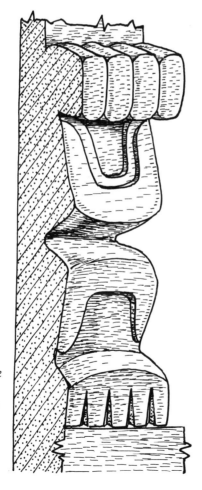

Illus. 6. Left: Detail of the fingers, palms, knees, and toes. Top right: Carving the fingers—first sink stop-cuts between the fingers. Bottom right: Holding a straight knife at an angle, slice down and widen the initial cuts.

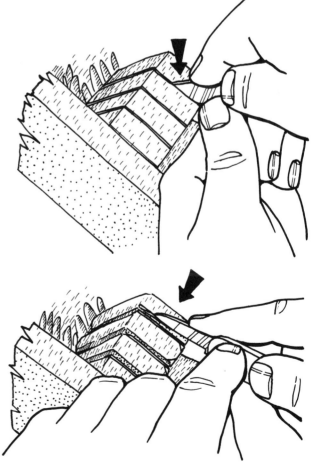

129

remove the inlay pieces and set them out—still in order—on your original tracing. Mix enough double-tube glue for one detail, say, for one of the eyes; then spread the glue over the cavity and carefully set the inlay piece into position (Illus. 7, bottom). Follow this process with all the inlay areas in the design.

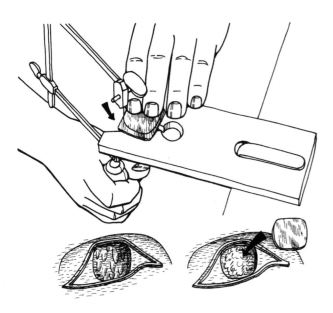

Illus. 7. Top: Use the piercing saw to cut the inlay pieces to a good fit. Bottom: Clear out the sockets, spread glue in the cavity, and set the inlay into position.

When the glue is dry, trim up all the edges and cavities with the point of a knife, and rub the whole workpiece down with a piece of medium-fine sandpaper. Finally, wipe away the dust with a cloth dampened with turpentine, apply a generous coat of clear wax, and use the stiff brush to burnish the surface to a high-shine finish.

TROUBLESHOOTING AND POSSIBLE MODIFICATIONS

- When you are working a large slab-wood project of this character, spend extra time making sure that the wood is free from faults and flaws. Avoid wood that appears to be split, sappy, stained, unseasoned, and knotty. Be warned—if the wood is unseasoned, then it is likely to warp and split.

- Spend time making sure that the tools are sharp. Ten minutes or so spent bringing them to a good edge could well save you hours of sweat and frustration.

- If you are using a high-speed grinder to sharpen the gouges, watch out that you don't overheat them and burn the edges. It would be better to grind away the rough with the grinder and then to bring the gouges to a fine edge with a stone and slip.

- If you are unable to obtain inlay material, then settle for painting the details.

15
Shaman's Necklace Charm
(Haida)

A charm worn suspended from a neck ring alongside
other charms and amulets

Saw and knife
Fretted, pierced, shallow-incised, and shallow-relief-carved
Waxed and burnished

The Indians believed that spirits and supernatural
beings were present in all things—in the trees, in the
rocks, in the water, in every aspect of daily life. They
were always on the lookout for friendly spirits or at
least spirits who might be persuaded to protect them
from evil spirits.

In their search for supernatural power and protection, it was often necessary for them to undergo a
rigorous, ritualized regime of bathing in icy water and
of going without food and sleep. When the seeker was
in a semiconscious trance state, if he had what he
thought was a supernatural experience or encounter,
he would consider his spiritual quest successful.

Of course, certain individuals were more in touch
with the spirits than others—and these were the shamans. Young men who were perceived as having special shamanistic powers were expected to undergo a
lengthy period of training to develop their gifts. A
shaman's search for spirit contact through ritual dep-
rivation would be intense and would last for several
years.

In many tribes, once a shaman's training was over,
his status was publicly announced, and from then on
he wore a special beaded charm necklace as a badge
of office or insignia. Typically, a shaman's necklace,
or neck ring, might be made of leather and sinew,
trimmed with a fringe of delicate bone head scratchers
and nose pins, and further decorated with special
charms and amulets.

DESIGN, STRUCTURE, AND TECHNIQUE CONSIDERATIONS

Take a look at the project picture (Illus. 1) and the
working drawings (Illus. 2), and see how, at a scale
of eight grid squares to 1″, the charm measures about
3″ long, 1½″ wide at its widest point, and ⅜″ thick.
Note how the overall stylized double-fish form—
thought to be a salmon—is smooth and rounded,
while the design lines are no more than small, stepped,
and incised shallow-worked cuts.

Let your eyes run slowly, from the tail to the mouth,
over the project. Observe all the details that make up
the rather soft and subtle design. See how the three
incised circles give emphasis to the otherwise blank
tail area, while the pierced hole and the slender bridge
between the tip of the tail and the body give tension
to what would otherwise be a rather stolid form. See
how the incised fish-eating-fish imagery fits very nicely
into the single-fish profile. Note the way, just below
the stepped feature that sets the head apart from the
body, the characteristic U-shaped motif is used here
to set out the shape of the salmon's gills. All in all,
the design is delicately understated.

Although the overall fish form appears at first sight
to be carved in the round, you can see that it is really
no more than a round-edged profile with a small
amount of incised work cut into the surface. However,

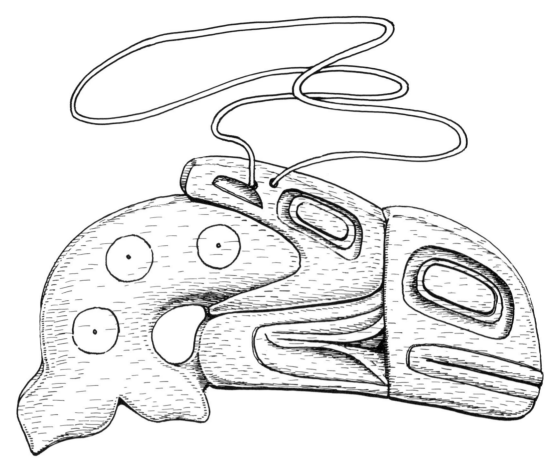

Illus. 1. Project picture—a Haida *shaman's charm and amulet.*

we don't mean to minimize the piece, but just to say that it is more straightforward than might be expected. Certainly, you do have to cut out the fish profile, round up the edges of the profile, and work the design on both sides of the wood, but it is still a straightforward piece of incised-pattern work.

TOOLS AND MATERIAL

For this project you need:

- a small ½″-thick remnant at about 3 × 1½″—it's best to go for a smooth, tight-grained, pale wood such as box or pear

- a pencil and ruler

- a small hand drill with ⅛″ and ³⁄₁₆″ drill bits to fit

- a fine-bladed saw with a pack of blades—it's best to use either a fretsaw or a piercing saw

- a bench with a vise

- a selection of small fine-point knives—we used a small penknife and a scalpel

- a pack of graded sandpapers

- a can of clear beeswax polish and a cloth

SETTING OUT THE DESIGN

When you have spent time carefully considering the project picture (Illus. 1) and the working drawings (Illus. 2), and you have a good understanding of all the implications of working a project of this size and character, finalize your drawing of the design and take a tracing. Check that your wood is free from faults, and then pencil-press-transfer all the lines of the traced design through to the working face of both sides of the wood (Illus. 3, top left).

Now, set out all your tools, pin the working drawings up so that they are in view, and clear the workbench.

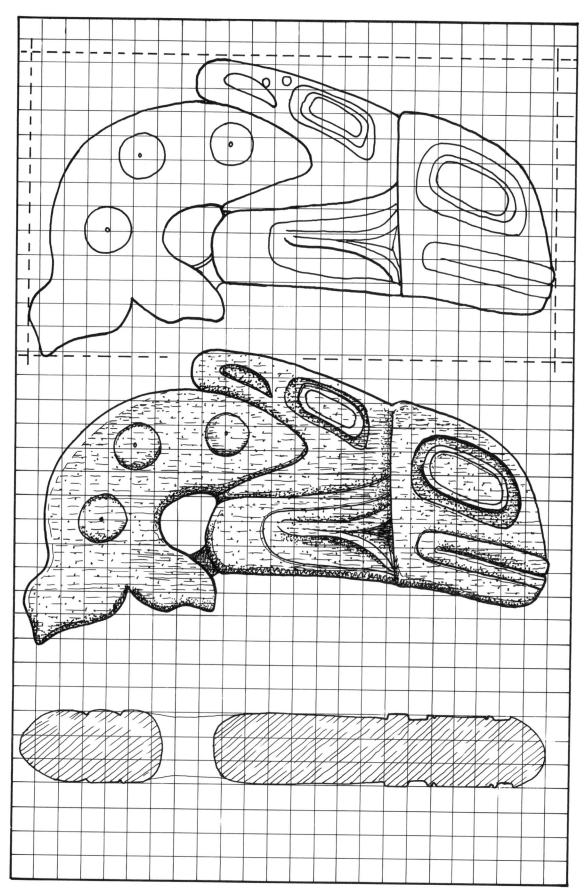

*Illus. 2. Working drawing. The grid scale is eight squares to
1". Note the primary profile lines and the cross-section detail.*

133

CUTTING OUT THE PROFILE

When you have achieved a good, clear profile line, shade in the areas that need to be cut away and secure the wood in the jaws of the vise. Now take your chosen saw and cut away the areas of waste.

When you are sawing, keep the blade at 90° to the working face of the wood and only cut on the waste side of the drawn line (Illus. 3, bottom). And so you continue, repositioning the wood in the vise and changing the speed and direction of the saw stroke, so that the blade is always presented with the line of the next cut. Saw with a steady, even stroke, speeding up at tight corners and keeping the blade square with the work.

It's all pretty easy and straightforward. However, when you come to the small tight angles of the tail—meaning, the angle, or point, where the cut rapidly changes direction—you will have to speed up as you approach the angle, and mark time to establish the point of the angle and to make room with the twisting saw blade. The trick is to always keep the saw blade moving. Be warned—if you try to change the direction of the cut while the saw is at a standstill, then you will undoubtedly break the blade. If you are a beginner, it would be best to go through a trial run before starting the project, and to always have a spare pack of blades.

CUTTING THE WINDOW AND ROUGHING OUT

Establish the position of the window—meaning, the enclosed hole near the curve of the tail—and then take the drill and run a 3/16″ pilot hole through the window area (Illus. 4, top right). Unhitch the saw blade from its frame, pass it through the drilled hole, and rehitch the blade by pushing the saw frame against the edge of the bench (Illus. 4, bottom left). Now retension the blade and set to work fretting out the hole. Just as you did when you were sawing out the profile, work at a steady and even pace, making sure that the blade passes through the wood at right angles to the working face, and trying to keep both the wood and the saw on the move so that the blade is always presented with the line of the best cut. Be very careful when you come to the slender, relatively fragile bridge of short-grained wood between the tail and the body—go at it slow and easy. Now take the 1/8″ drill and work the two cord holes.

Having cut out the profile and the pierced window,

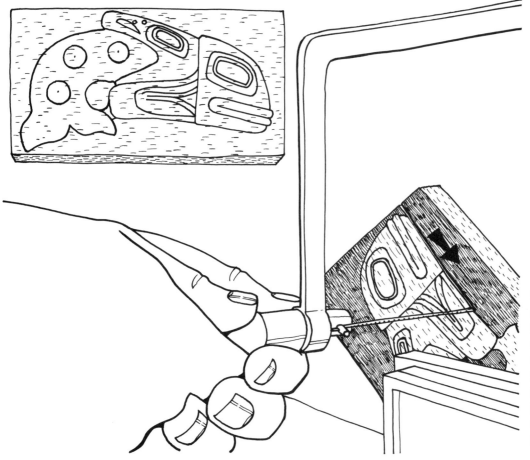

Illus. 3. Top left: Press-transfer the traced design through to the working face of the wood. Bottom: Keep to the waste side of the drawn line and hold the saw so that the blade passes through the wood at right angles to the working face.

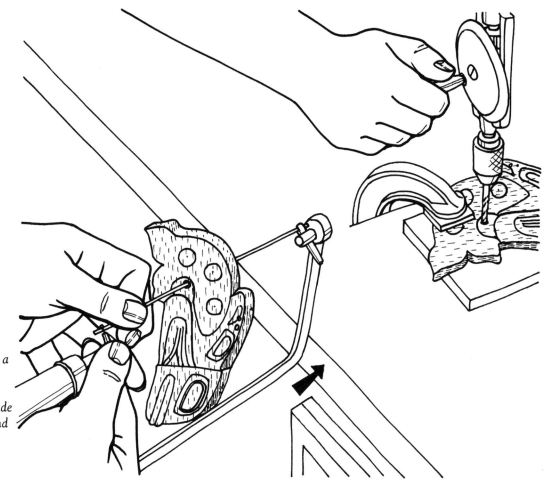

Illus. 4. Top right: Drill a pilot hole through the "window" of waste. Bottom left: Pass the blade through the pilot hole and rehitch the blade by pressing the saw frame against the bench.

take the workpiece in one hand and your chosen knife in the other, and proceed to pare away all the sharp-edged corners. Much as you might peel an apple, work with a thumb-braced paring cut. In other words, if you are right-handed, hold the workpiece in your left hand, and slowly pare away in a counterclockwise direction around the profile (Illus. 5, top left). Working small can sometimes be a bit tricky, but the thumb-braced paring action allows for maximum knife leverage and control.

When you have pared off the bulk of the waste on both sides of the wood, then change to a thumb-pushing action—that is, push the blade of the knife with the thumb of the hand that's holding the wood (Illus. 5, bottom right).

Finally, take your sharpest knife or scalpel and shave the whittled edges down so that they are smooth and rounded.

SETTING IN THE PRIMARY STOP-CUT LINES

Take a look at the project picture (Illus. 1) and the working drawings (Illus. 2), and see how the four main areas, or forms, are set out by three primary stop-cut lines. These are the main line that divides the head from the body, a line that runs from the pierced hole through to the head, and a line that simultaneously divides the tail from the rest of the body and defines the shape of the secondary tail-swallowing mouth. Of course, these lines occur on both sides of the charm.

Now, reestablish the main dividing lines with a pencil so that they are clearly defined. If necessary, use the tracing paper to reestablish the design. Next, take the penknife and cut the lines in to a stop-cut depth of between $3/32$ and $1/8"$. For example, with the line around the head, sink the blade down into the wood and then run the line right around the head—that is, across one flat working face, around the edge, across the other flat face, and then around the other edge to your starting point. Repeat this procedure with all the main stop-cut lines (Illus. 6, top).

Take a close-up look at the working drawings and see how the main lines have been variously stepped and rounded. For example, with the area immediately behind the head, the line has been angled, chopped in, and lowered, so that there appears to be a step up from the body to the head (Illus. 6, bottom). Take

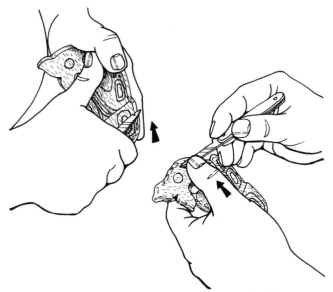

the knife, hold the workpiece so that the head is pointing away from you, and then slide the blade at an angle down and into the head-body stop-cut. Work right around the wood, cutting out small slivers of waste. Continue until all the main stop-cut lines have been stepped and/or rounded.

CUTTING THE INCISED MOTIFS

When you have defined the main forms, take a pencil and reestablish all the motifs—the eyes, the mouth, the nostrils, and the three circles. All the motifs are made up from V-section cuts of various widths and depths. That is to say, if you make a cut straight down into the wood, and then slide the knife at an angle into this cut, thereby removing a thin slice of wood (Illus. 7, top), you will finish up with a smooth slope or an angled plane. By doing this repeatedly and at carefully selected angles, it is possible to shape all the various V-sections that go into making up the design. In many ways the technique is similar to chip carving,

Illus. 5. Top left: Hold the work in one hand and carve with a thumb-controlled apple-paring action, cutting away the sharp edges. Bottom right: For maximum control, push the blade of the knife with the thumb of the hand that's holding the wood.

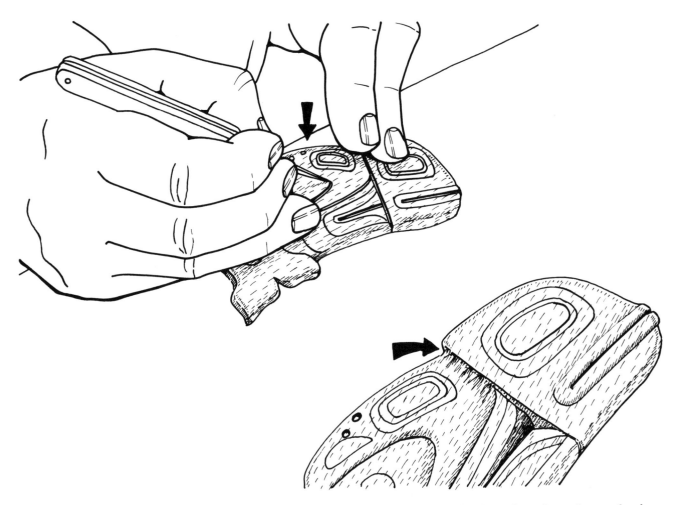

Illus. 6. With the work well supported on the bench, cut down into the wood and make the primary stop-cuts.

Bottom: On this detail, see how the surface angles down into the head-body stop-cut.

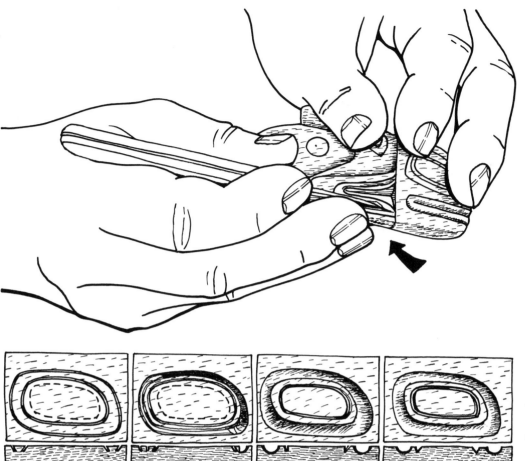

Illus. 7. Top: Slide the knife at an angle and into the stop-cut and remove a thin slice of waste. Bottom, left to right: These are the stages in carving the eye motif: Make the primary side-of-moat stop-cuts, clear the waste, make the inside-eye stop-cut, and broaden the eye cut slightly so as to make a V-section trench.

the only difference being that instead of repeatedly chopping into the wood to remove single chips, you slide the knife blade around and into stop-cuts to remove thin curls of wood.

When you come to cutting the shallow trench around the eye and the thin, incised cut around the pupil, you do have to watch out that you don't damage the sharp lines and the areas of fragile short grain (Illus. 7, bottom—left to right). With a small carving of this character, you will find that the lowered areas should never need to be cut in deeper than about $1/8''$.

When you have what you consider to be a fair carving, repeat the procedure on the other side of the wood; then give the whole workpiece a swift rubdown with the finest grade of sandpaper, and use the point of the scalpel to bring all the details to a crisp sharp-edged finish. Finally, give the workpiece a generous waxing and burnish it to a high-shine finish.

TROUBLESHOOTING AND POSSIBLE MODIFICATIONS

- When your workpiece is in the vise, watch out that you don't crush the wood. It's a good idea to place a couple of pieces of smooth, clean scrap between the jaws of the vise and your work.
- When you are considering working a small, finely detailed carving of this character, it is vital that you choose your wood with care. Avoid wood that appears to be stained, cracked, or knotty.
- Always have your working drawings and perhaps some photographs in view; then you won't lose touch with the subject.
- If you decide to use box wood, avoid Central American or West Indian varieties because they are liable to split. It's best to use slow-growing English or European box.

137

16
Dance Mask (Tsimshian)

An articulated mythical character mask worn during dance dramas

Saw, knife, gouge, and drill
Fretted, deep-carved, pierced, and constructed
Painted and waxed

Several months of the *Tsimshian* year were traditionally given over to sacred rituals and ceremonies. Having labored throughout the summer and the autumn to build up supplies of smoked and dried fish, eulachon oil, dried fruit, and berries, the *Tsimshians* retired to their well-stocked houses to spend the winter months acting out dance dramas.

During this supernatural season, they dropped their normal names and ranks and took on religious and secret-society identities. Each society mounted huge, spectacular dance dramas to demonstrate its traditional legends and myths.

It was during these dramatic reenactments that the Indians wore special articulated dance masks. Such masks were used to depict and express events that had to do with the spiritual status of the group. A mask might be used to show a spirit or person dying, in which case the eyes and mouth would open and close. A mask might show the various stages of a person's human-to-spirit metamorphosis by projecting an image that was part human and part spirit. Or a set of masks might be used to demonstrate the different stages in a person's life: being born, before marriage, getting married, having children, old age, dying, and being dead.

The common feature among all these masks is that they were capable, in some way or other, of being swiftly and dramatically altered in form or character. From mask to mask, the eyes might open and close, the teeth might be removable, the front of the mask might open out to reveal an inner face or creature, the top of the mask might open out so as to transform the imagery, and so on. Articulated masks were used in the dance dramas to express changes in mood and/or physical form and character.

The original mask that inspired this project had articulated eyes—open, closed, and "dying"—and several jaw changes. It was wonderfully complex and beautifully carved.

DESIGN, STRUCTURE, AND TECHNIQUE CONSIDERATIONS

Take a look at the project picture (Illus. 1) and the working drawings (Illus. 3 and 4), and see how at a scale of three grid squares to 1", the mask is about 8" wide, 8" deep from the back of the head through to the nose, and 8" high from the top of the head down to the chin. Take a look at the detail drawing (Illus. 2) and see how, at a scale of approximately one grid square to 1", by way of a simple pull-string, see-saw mechanism, the articulated bottom jaw can be lowered to reveal the teeth. See how the prongs are pivot-hinged at the sides so that the jaw fits over the teeth.

If you like the overall shape and form of the carving, but would prefer the mouth to be fixed open or closed, or the eyes to be capable of opening and closing, there's no reason why you can't make these modifications. The same goes for the size of the mask—if you want to make it smaller or larger, then all you do is modify the scale accordingly.

Note the way the main body of the mask needs to be worked from a 9 × 9 × 9″ block of wood, with the grain running through the wood from crown to

Illus. 1. Project picture—a Tsimshian *dance-drama character mask.*

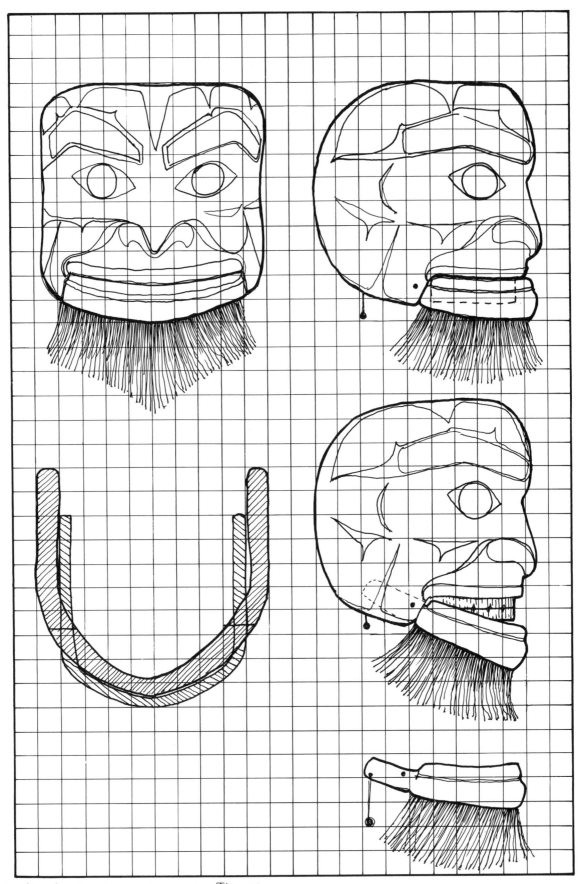

Illus. 2. Working drawing—front and side views. The grid scale is three squares to 1". Note the articulated-jaw details.

140

*Illus. 3. Working drawing—painting grid, front view. The
grid scale is about three squares to 2″.*

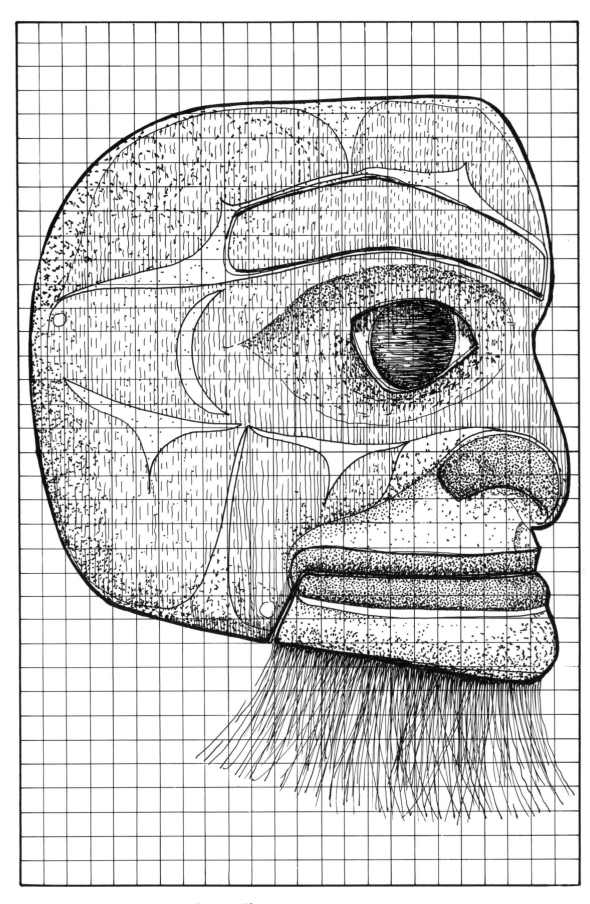

*Illus. 4. Working drawing—painting grid, side view. The
grid scale is about three squares to 2".*

142

chin. Consider, also, how, because of the depth of the mask from the front to the back, the project involves not only band- or bow-saw work but also some deep-gouge carving. This is not to say that the project is particularly complicated, but only that it does require that you use a good range of tools. However, fitting the articulated lower jaw is more than a bit tricky, although the process itself is not difficult to understand.

Now, when you have a clear picture in your mind's eye of how the project needs to be worked and put together, sit down with a sketch pad and draw up all the profiles, sections, and details.

TOOLS AND MATERIALS

For this project you need:

• a block of wood at about 9 × 9 × 9"—it's best to use an easy-to-carve wood such as lime, pencil cedar, or maybe even a fruit wood like apple

• a 9 × 2" slab of wood at 9" in length for the lower jaw—it's best to have the grain running from the chin through to the back of the head

• a large bow saw or band saw—one with a 9" depth of cut

• a large block of Plasticine

• a workbench and hold-down

• a pencil and ruler

• a good selection of carving gouges

• a crooked knife and a scalpel

• a small hand drill with a ¼" bit to fit

• acrylic paints—red-ocher for the lips, nostrils, and "dashes," and blue-black for the overall motif and between the teeth

• a couple of brushes—a broad and fine-point

• a hank of natural raffia—for the beard

BUILDING THE MAQUETTE

Study the project picture (Illus. 1) and the various working drawings (Illus. 2–4) and make sketches and notes. When you have a clear idea of how the block of wood needs to be worked and how the lower jaw needs to fit snug over the teeth, take the Plasticine and build a maquette, or working model. Aim to have the model about half size—that is, about 4 × 4 ×

4". Establish the thickness of the mask, the depth of the waste inside, the face, the set of the teeth, the shape of the lower jaw, and the fit of the pivot mechanism (Illus. 5, left). The pivot is particularly important, so spend time getting it just right. If necessary, whittle a jaw-prong-to-cheek detail to sort out any problems.

Once you have achieved what you consider to be a well-worked maquette, use a ruler and a pin to set it out with a one square to 1" grid (Illus. 5, bottom).

MARKING OUT THE WOOD AND CLEARING THE ROUGH

Having made a maquette, put it in view but out of harm's way, and start to mark out the wood. Take the 9 × 9 × 9" block, and with the grain running from the crown down to the chin, mark out the inside-face waste (Illus. 6, top left). When this is done, use the bow or band saw to clear the inside waste (Illus. 6, bottom). It's best to split the waste by sawing straight through from the back of the head, and then to remove it in two halves.

When you have worked the long bridge shape that goes to make up the inside mask, check with your working drawings and with the model, and then mark the wood out with the front and side outside-face profiles (Illus. 6, top right). Again, use your chosen saw to clear away the waste. Aim for a wraparound, bridgelike shape that is about 3" thick at the front of the face and 2 to 2½" thick at the sides.

Study the working drawings. Note how the sides of the mask are relatively featureless, whereas the front is quite deeply carved, with the eyes, the bridge of the nose, the nose, the upper lip, and the teeth all being worked in more or less naturalistic, all-around relief. Being very careful not to force the blade into the end grain, take the crooked knife and clear some of the waste from the inside cheeks and the sides of the head (Illus. 7, top). Gradually scoop away the inside-mask waste from the cheeks and temples, until the bridgelike shape fits over your face. Allow for plenty of room in the inside-jaw area for the jaw mechanism.

CARVING AND MODELLING THE FEATURES

Having carefully studied the maquette and the working drawings, use a pencil, ruler, tracing paper, and dividers to draw in the grid and to step off the various measurements that go into making up the front of

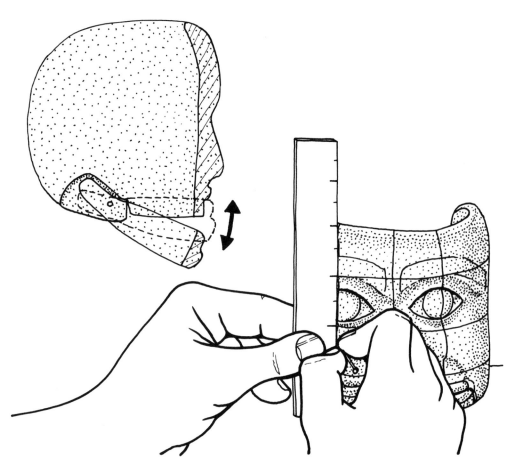

Illus. 5. Left: Establish the thickness of the mask walls, the depth of the inside waste, and the fit of the jaw pivot. Bottom: Use a rule and a pin to set the surface of the maquette out with a grid at one square to 1".

the mask. Draw in the line that runs through the eyes and the bridge of the nose, the line that marks out the drop of the nose, and the two lines that define the distance between the nose and the top lip, the thickness of the top lip, and the depth of the teeth. Run these lines parallel to each other, and across, around, and at right angles to the front-central line. Likewise, draw in lines to establish the middle of the eyes, the breadth of the nose, the width of the mouth, and so on. Then mark in all the other features that go into making up the face (Illus. 7, bottom). Remember to allow for the small strip of waste under the teeth.

Having marked in the primary features, and bearing in mind that the position of the details will change to some extent as you cut into the thickness of the wood, use the hold-down to secure the workpiece to the bench. Use a straight chisel to set in the lines of the primary features with stop-cuts. Don't cut too deep—about ⅛ to ¼″ will do just fine. Now, starting with, say, the line that sets out the position of the bridge of the nose, take a shallow-curve scoop gouge and cut down at an angle into the initial stop-cut. Aim to lower the wood to a depth of about ¼″. Repeat

this procedure until you have roughed out the main forms.

When you have set in the position and shape of the primary features, then comes the pleasurable task of modelling the details. Using the crooked knife and one or more gouges, and starting with, say, the nose, gradually deepen the stop-cuts and lower the waste. Noting the run of the grain, and being aware that the end of the nose will become increasingly short-grained and fragile, work from the tip and bridge of the nose down and out towards the eye sockets, the cheeks, and the top lip (Illus. 8, bottom). Move backwards and forward over the workpiece, all the while lowering the waste, redefining stop-cuts, and modelling details. And so you continue—cutting away an area of waste here, redefining a detail there, working two areas so that they relate to each other, and so on. For example, you might slice in each side of the nose with a stop-cut and then leave the nose in high relief by lowering the waste area to the sides of the nose (Illus. 8, top—left to right). Bear in mind, as you are working, that carving is not so much a process of completing a single detail and then moving on to the next, but rather one of working the whole piece, all the while checking off various details or features against one another. In this way, layers of waste are gradually removed and lowered, so as to leave the design features standing in high relief. It's as if the nose, eyes, and cheeks are waiting, just below the surface of the wood, for you to peel away the concealing layers.

At this stage, don't be too concerned about completing the top lip, but do take the curved band that makes up the teeth to completion.

FITTING, ATTACHING, AND CARVING THE ARTICULATED JAW

When you have finished carving the upper part of the face, including the teeth, refresh your eye by taking another look at the working drawings and the maquette. See how the lower-jaw piece curves around the teeth, how the grain runs from the chin to the back of the head, and how the ends of the jaw are cut and stepped, fitted inside the cheeks, and then pivot-fixed. When you have a good understanding of how the various details relate to each other, set the 9 × 2″ piece of 9″ long wood out on the workbench and pencil in the faces—"top" and "front." When this is

done, set the mask down on the wood so that the curve of the teeth is centrally placed, and then take a pencil and use the teeth as a template to draw the curve (Illus. 9, top left). Allowing for the long pivot prongs that fit inside the mask, and with the teeth curve now transferred through to the top face of the wood, use your chosen saw to clear away the waste (Illus. 9, top right).

Bearing in mind that the short-grained area at the front of the jaw is relatively fragile, take the knife and whittle away at the jaw-prongs and the inside-cheek areas, until the jaw and the teeth come together in a good fit (Illus. 9, bottom left). When you have achieved a good fit, strap the jaw in place with transparent tape and drill the two pivot holes. Make sure that the holes are set in line and on the same axis. Ideally, you ought to be able to push a length of dowel through one hole, across the width of the mask, and out the other hole. Having drilled well-aligned holes through the cheeks and jaw prongs, cut short lengths of dowel, trim them to a loose fit in the jaws and a tight fit in the cheeks, dab a little glue in the holes in the cheeks, and tap them home (Illus. 9, bottom right).

When you have pivoted the jaw, remove the trans-

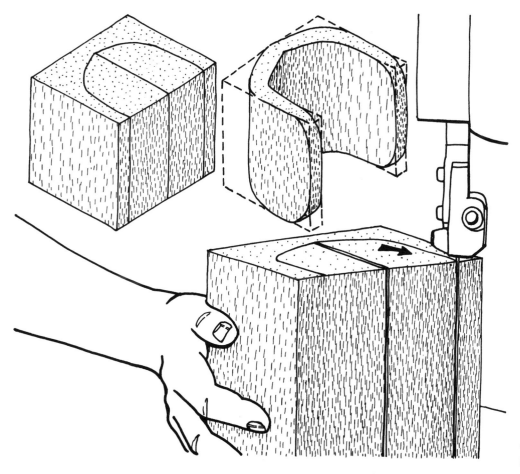

Illus. 6. Top left: Mark out the inside-face waste on the 9 × 9 × 9″ block. Top right: The outside-face waste removed. Bottom: Saw a pilot cut straight through from the back of the head to the inside front; then saw around the inside so as to remove the two pieces of waste.

parent tape strapping so that the jaw hangs loose. If necessary, ease the wood around the pivots so that the jaw opens and closes smoothly. When this is done, use the tools of your choice to carve and shape the outside-jaw profile. Strive to have the lips running in a continuous, smooth curve around the corners of the mouth. Now continue shaping the lower jaw and the lips, until the two pieces of wood relate to each other and look to be part of a whole. If all is well, when the mouth is closed, the side profile of the forehead, nose, and upper lip should run smoothly and convincingly down to the bottom lip and chin.

Finally, fit a pull string to one of the jaw prongs, cut in the incised lines around the eyebrows, detail the eyes and the nostrils, use a scalpel to clean out all the crannies and generally take the carving to a good clean finish.

FINISHING

When you have what you consider to be a well-worked mask, use the sandpaper to rub it down to a good, smooth finish, paying particular attention to the nostrils and the lips. Now use a soft pencil to draw in the outline shape of the ground areas to be painted

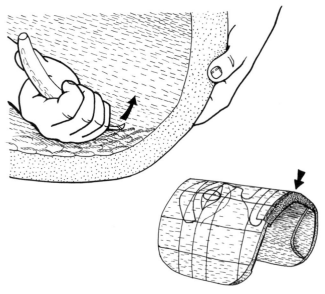

Illus. 7. Top: Use the crooked knife to clear the waste from inside the cheeks and from the sides of the head. Bottom: Draw the grid and the main features onto the mask, and then shade in the small area of waste just underneath the teeth.

blue-black. Mix a quantity of blue-black paint to a good, nonrunny consistency, and carefully block in the areas, aiming for clean-cut edges and smooth, confident lines. Paint the outlines first—turn the work

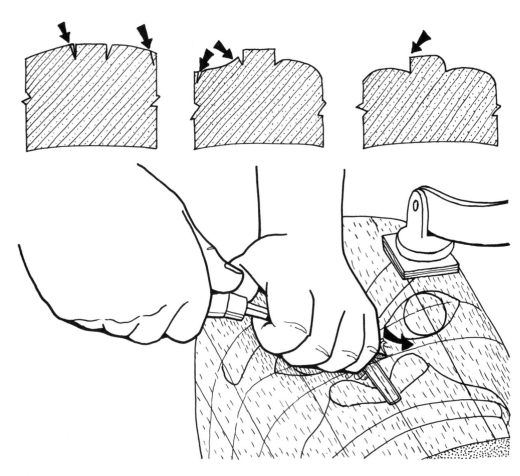

Illus. 8. Bottom: Work from the bridge of the nose and out and down towards the eyes and the cheek. Top, left to right: Lower the wood around the nostril area.

146

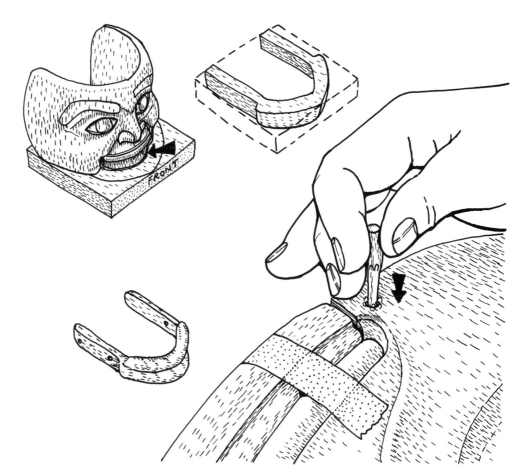

Illus. 9. Top left: Using the carved mask as a template, draw around the teeth for the fit of the jaw. Top right: Allowing for the long pivot prongs, use a saw to clear away the waste. Bottom left: Whittle the jaw to a good fit. Bottom right: Trim the dowels to a loose fit in the jaw holes and a tight fit in the cheek holes; then dab a little glue in the cheek holes and tap the dowels home.

so that the brush is to the right of the drawn line and being pulled towards you. Once the outline is complete, fill in the shape and then go on to the next area. When the main blue-black ground areas are dry, mix the red-ocher, and paint in the lips, the nostrils, and all the dashes.

Finally, when the paint is dry, wax the whole workpiece, burnish it to a matt-sheen finish, and attach the beard to the inside rim of the jaw.

TROUBLESHOOTING AND POSSIBLE MODIFICATIONS

- If you can't find a block of wood at 9 × 9 × 9″, then you could laminate three 3″ thicknesses.

- If you don't have a band or bow saw, consider removing the inside-mask waste with a large scoop gouge.

- When you are cutting the bottom jaw prongs to fit, don't try to remove the waste in one great thrust; it's much better to remove the waste little by little, all the while fitting and refitting to test for size.

- Regarding painting, mix the acrylic paint to a non-runny consistency, and allow for a certain amount of grain bleed when you come to painting up against a line.

- If the mask is to be worn, then a strap should be attached to go behind the head, and "hair" should be added to cover the top of the head.

17
Totemic Clan Crest (Tlingit)

A wall-mounted plaque

Saw, gouge, and knife
Shaped, relief-carved, and incised
Painted, waxed, and burnished

Native American clans consisted of families or households who were (or at least believed they were) descended from a common mythical or legendary ancestor. Within a single clan, there might well be smaller, secondary clans. For instance, within the *Tlingit* tribe, there were not only two primary clans who were related by traditional ties—the Ravens and the Wolves—but within these two main groups, there were also smaller clans whose members were more closely related by blood. The clan groupings and family bonds were made even more complex as a result of whether or not the clan belonged to the northern tribes who traced descent through the mothers, or the southern tribes who traced descent through the fathers.

Each clan—the Eagles, the Ravens, the Wolves, the Killer-Whales, and so on—was entitled to privileges based upon myths or legends that told of their connection with certain supernatural beings known as totems. And so it was that each clan had a specially carved-and-painted badge or crest that proclaimed that its members were entitled to certain ancestral privileges. In much the same way as the coat of arms on, say, a medieval knight's shield or banner told of his descent from various other families and groups, his allegiances, and maybe even his name through pictorial imagery, so a Native American's totemic crest or heraldic badge told of his physical and spiritual rights, his properties, and his entitlements.

DESIGN, STRUCTURE, AND TECHNIQUE CONSIDERATIONS

Take a look at the working drawings (Illus. 2) and see how, at a scale of three grid squares to 2″, the salmon crest, the crest of the *Tlingit-Kut* clan, is about 24″ long, 6½″ wide at its widest point, and 2″ thick. Note the way the overall form of the crest is no more than a stylized profile that has been partially relief-carved, rounded at the edges, and then surface-decorated with characteristically *Tlingit* designs and motifs.

See how the relatively flat surface has been washed with blue paint, whereas the "hand" motif, the "M"-details on the fins, the six circles, and the U-shaped "cheek" have been left the pink color of the wood. Note, also, how a couple of selected deep-relief areas, such as the large, long eye under the dorsal fin and the smaller eye towards the tail, have been blocked in with a light blue.

Along the length of the salmon, note the full array of symbols: the human hand to the left of the dorsal fin, the various U-forms that double as stylized fins, scales, and nostrils, the cheek design to the left of the mouth, and of course the primary and secondary "eye" motifs.

Consider how the carving can be broken down into three basic techniques: rounding the sawn form with

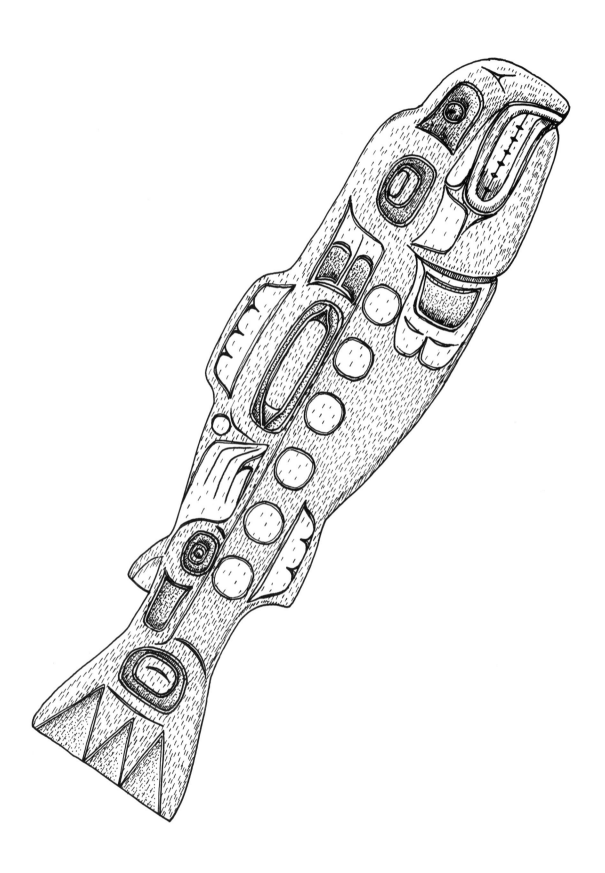

Illus. 1. Project picture—a Tlingit totemic clan crest.

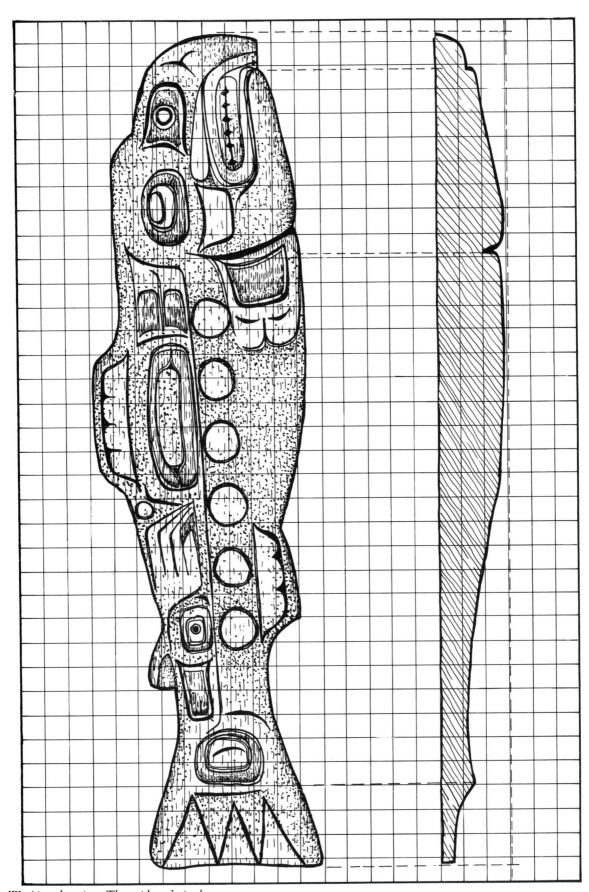

Illus. 2. Working drawing. The grid scale is three squares to 2". Note the section with the flat back and the contoured profile.

a large section U-gouge to achieve the basic profile, working the relatively realistic mouth and lips with a small gouge and knife, and lastly using a spoon gouge and knife to cut the motifs.

TOOLS AND MATERIALS

For this project you need:

• a slab of smooth-grained, knot-free plank wood, such as Virginian pencil cedar (not a true cedar), at about 26″ long, 8½″ wide, and 2″ thick—this allows for wastage

• a pencil and ruler

• a sheet each of work-out paper and tracing paper, to fit the size of the wood

• a large coping saw, or a bow saw, or better still the use of a band saw

• a hold-down clamp

• medium- and light-blue watercolor paints

• a couple of soft-haired watercolor brushes—a broad and a fine-point

• a carver's mallet

• a selection of knives—we used a penknife, a heavy craft knife, and a scalpel

• a good selection of wood-carving gouges, including a large U-section gouge; a small, almost flat U-section gouge; and a small, deep spoon gouge

• a pack of graded sandpapers

• a can of beeswax

• a stiff brush and a cloth for polishing

SETTING OUT THE DESIGN

When you have studied the project picture (Illus. 1), the working drawings (Illus. 2), and the details, make a good, clear tracing of the design and pin up all the master drawings. Now take the 2″-thick slab of wood and check it over for possible faults and flaws. Ideally, the wood needs to be a clear pink color, well-seasoned, straight-grained, dry, and free from knots, splits, stains, and mould. You can't do better than using a good piece of Virginian pencil cedar. Reject wood that appears to be mildewy, sappy, yellow, or at all slimy to touch. If need be, use a penknife to check the wood for density and working quality. You should be able

to cut a curl of wood away without the fibres crumbling or cracking—the cut surface should look pink and shiny.

If all is well, secure the tracing to what you consider to be the best face of the slab, and pencil-press-transfer the traced design outline through to the wood. Remove the tracing and go over the transferred profile line with a pencil, aiming to make it single, clear, and positive (Illus. 3, top right).

CUTTING THE PROFILE AND CARVING THE FORM

Having established the profile line, take your chosen saw and clear away the waste. Work a little to the waste side of the drawn line (Illus. 3, bottom left) and try to achieve a clean-cut sawn edge that is at right angles to the working face.

Use the hold-down to secure the salmon profile right-side up on the workbench, making sure that the wood is stable and firm. If necessary, support the workpiece on a pad of felt or newspaper. Now take a look at Illus. 1 and 2, and the top of Illus. 4, and see how the salmon is full and rounded along the top of the head and towards the mouth, is much less rounded on the back and on top of the dorsal fin, and tapers and flattens towards the end of the tail. Having studied these details and forms, take the mallet and a U-section gouge and start to clear away the waste around the profile edge (Illus. 4, bottom). This is the process: Step in about ½″ from the edge of the profile, position the wood and the gouge so that you are cutting from the middle to the side (that is, from the middle ground towards the edge of the wood), hold the gouge so that it is set at an angle of about 45°, decide whether or not you are going to have the chisel braced with your thumb above or below the handle, and then tap down with the mallet so as to cut away the sharp angle. Continue working around and around the profile, all the while chopping off scoops of waste and striving towards what you consider to be a good face-to-edge contour. When this is done, take a flatter tool and cut the upper surface of the salmon down to a well-considered thickness. For instance, reduce the thickness of the wood as you work down towards the tail. Then variously carve, scrape, and sand the entire surface of the workpiece down to a good, smooth finish.

When you have achieved a nicely curved and smooth profile, stop for awhile and look at the project picture and the working drawings and consider how the mouth is the only part of the design that is in any

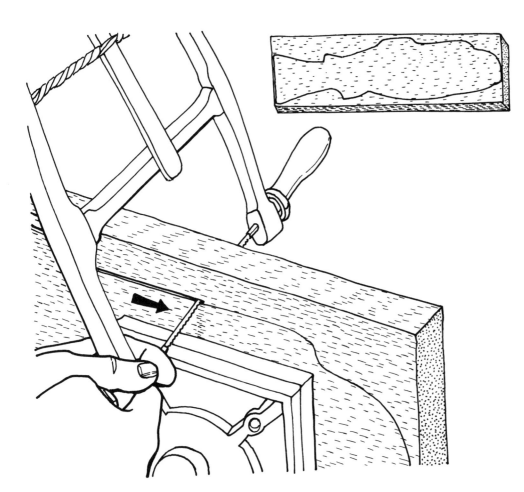

Illus. 3. Top right: Go over the transferred line with a pencil, aiming to achieve a single, clear, positive line. Bottom left: Work to the waste side of the drawn line and saw out the profile.

way realistically carved. Of course, the profile is recognizably salmon shaped, but only in a stylized, abstract sense. The mouth, on the other hand, is much more of a realistic interpretation of a mouth (although not necessarily a salmon's mouth), in that the teeth are at one level, the lips are full and are raised from the teeth, the face is stepped down from the lips, and so on. When you have a clear picture of just how the imagery needs to be worked, cut your tracing to fit the fish profile, tape it in position over the contoured form, and then pencil-press-transfer the traced lines through to the surface of the wood.

Set the shape of the lips in to a depth of about ⅛ to ¼" on the outside of the lips (Illus. 5, right), and about ½" on the inside—that is, from the front of the mouth, around the top of the upper lips, around the bottom of the lower lip, inside the mouth and along the top of the lower lip, and then around the underside of the upper lip to the starting point. Try to stay within the full, rich curves. Once you have set in the shape of the mouth, then use a knife and a flat-curve spoon gouge to lower the inside-mouth area (Illus. 5, top left). Working from the middle to the side—that is, from the inside-mouth area towards the inside-lip area—chop down towards the set-in stop-cut so as to

remove scooped chips of waste. Work all around the inside-lip area with a series of scooping chops until you reach the lower "teeth" level. When this is done,

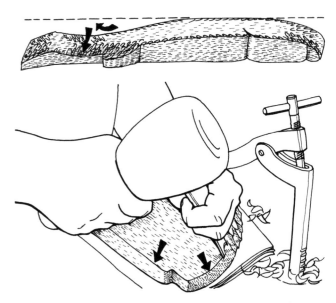

Illus. 4. Top: The side profile showing the areas to be lowered and tapered. Bottom: Use the mallet and a U-section gouge to clear away the waste.

152

clear the waste from inside the mouth so as to lower and level the "teeth" area.

Finally, cut in the line where the teeth meet and whittle out the six little nicks between the teeth. Lower the cheek and nose so that the lips are raised, and then use the small shallow-curve gouge to model the curved profile of the lips (Illus. 5, bottom left).

PAINTING AND CARVING THE MOTIF DETAILS

When you have carved and shaped the mouth, take a look at the project picture and the working drawings, and see how the rest of the design is made up, in the main, from a series of characteristically stylized motifs. Note that the imagery is either painted blue or left the natural pink color of the wood.

Once you have a clear understanding of how the various motifs need to be worked, mix a wash of medium-blue paint, note the areas that need to be left unpainted, and then give the workpiece a couple of coats (Illus. 6, top).

When the paint is dry, use the tracing to reestablish the lines of the design (Illus. 6, bottom). Note the various motifs: the three "eyes," a human hand, several "U"-shapes, several "cheeks," and a good number of secondary fill-ins. If you can carve an "eye," then the rest should all come easy.

Take a close-up look at the main "eye" and consider how it is made up from three components: a central plateau, a lowered-and-trenched moated area around the plateau, and two incised, thin V-section trenches on either side of the moat. Now take a sharp, fine-bladed knife and set in the thin line at either side of what will be the moated area. Set the lines in with a 1/8"-deep stop-cut (Illus. 7, top left). When this is done, angle in on either side of the stop-cut so as to remove a V-section sliver of waste. Aim to work the V-section line so that it is no more than about 3/16" deep and 1/8" wide. Try to keep the top width of the cut looking crisp, positive, and parallel with the sides of the moat.

Take a small, almost flat shallow-curve gouge, and set in a stop-cut to define the width and depth of the moated area around the eye. Set this stop-cut to a depth of about 1/4" and angled in slightly. Be very careful that you don't undercut the moat sides. When you have established the width and depth of the moat,

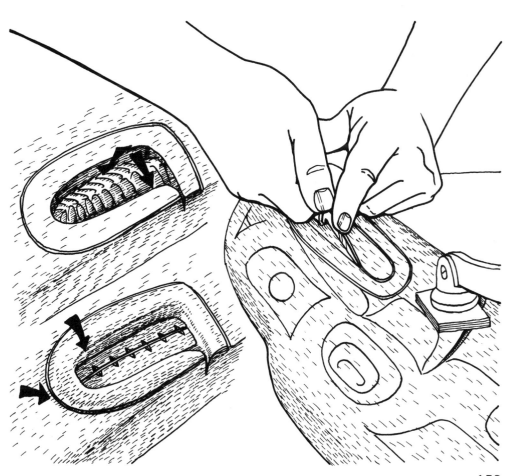

Illus. 5. Right: Hold the knife steady with both hands and set in the stop-cuts around the mouth. Top left: Working from the middle to the side, use the spoon gouge to lower the inside-mouth area. Bottom left: Lower the cheek and nose so that the lips are raised, and then model the curve of the lips.

153

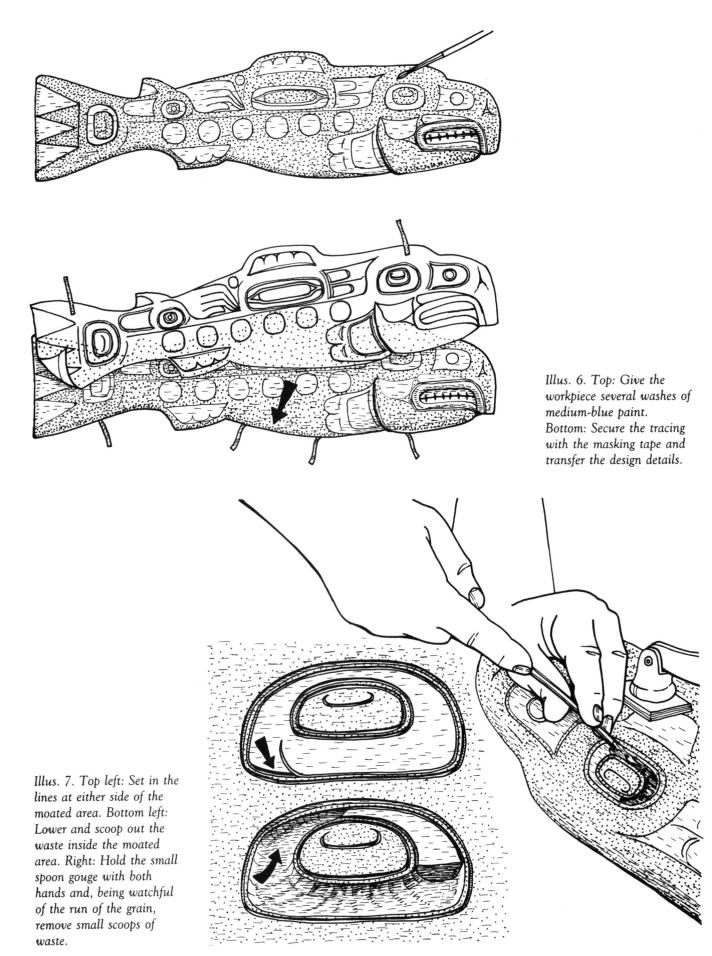

Illus. 6. Top: Give the workpiece several washes of medium-blue paint.
Bottom: Secure the tracing with the masking tape and transfer the design details.

Illus. 7. Top left: Set in the lines at either side of the moated area. Bottom left: Lower and scoop out the waste inside the moated area. Right: Hold the small spoon gouge with both hands and, being watchful of the run of the grain, remove small scoops of waste.

take a small spoon gouge and start to clear away the waste (Illus. 7, right). Being watchful of the run of the grain and the relatively fragile central plateau area, lower and scoop out the waste to the depth of the stop-cut. Strive to leave the moated area looking clean cut with smooth sides, and the wood running in a crisp curve from the walls of the sides down into the base.

Continue working all the other sinkings, shallow depressions, and incised lines that go into making up the design. When you consider the detailing to be finished, mix a little light-blue wash and block in the various moats around the eye and the nostril holes.

Finally, when the paint is crisp and dry, swiftly rub the whole workpiece down with fine sandpaper, apply a generous coat of wax, and use the stiff brush and the cloth to burnish the wood to a dull-sheen finish.

TROUBLESHOOTING AND POSSIBLE MODIFICATIONS

- When you are working the moats around the eyes, you will have no choice but to cut both with and across the run of the grain. Make sure that your tools are razor-sharp and only remove the thinnest whiskers of waste.

- When you are painting, it's best to aim for thin washes rather than heavy layers of paint. Ideally, the grain should show through.

- In rubbing down the workpiece, use fine sandpaper and be careful not to blur the edges. Try to leave the imagery looking fresh and crisp.

- As the workpiece is partially painted before the carving is finished, you might consider keeping it clean by covering it with a piece of fine cheesecloth.

18
Carved-and-Painted
House Board (Tlingit)

An interior board showing ancestry and social position

Saw, knife, and gouge
Sawn to shape, tool-textured, incised, and lowered
Painted, waxed, and burnished

Within the *Tlingit* tribe, when a man inherited titles from his family or his wife's family, he had to proclaim his lineage, ancestry, and accompanying privileges not only by setting up totem poles but also by having his clan crests carved and painted on all his possessions. Therefore, just about everything that he owned—from the totem poles, door posts, and walls of his house, down to the smallest utilitarian boxes and food bowls—were decorated and embellished in one way or another with totem figures and crests.

Of all the objects decorated with crests, the interior clan-crest boards were perhaps the most beautiful and the most important. Standing about 8 or 9 feet high, four such boards (two at each end of the house) would be attached to the massive wooden posts that supported the main roof beams. In much the same way as European armorial banners and shields showed with stylized imagery and motifs the glories and status of the family, so these boards illustrated all the legends and stories that related the history of the Native American clan and family.

From board to board, the carved-and-painted crests and motifs might illustrate how an ancestor was carried off by the Killer-Whale spirit, how he made an alliance with Great Bear, or how he was taken away by Migrating Wolf, and so on.

Within the *Tlingit* tribe, the mythical stories and their accompanying privileges were passed down from generation to generation. A family's mythical or legendary status, as set out on the four house boards, was as important, if not more so, than material wealth.

DESIGN, STRUCTURE, AND TECHNIQUE CONSIDERATIONS

Take a look at the project picture (Illus. 1) and the working drawing (Illus. 2), and see how, at a scale of approximately two grid squares to 1″, the board measures 11″ wide and 17″ high. The slab needs to be at least 1¾″ thick. Rather than involving the complexity of images that made up the original board, this project consists of a single, relatively straightforward figure motif.

Consider how the design is composed of a lowered ground and a high-relief surface. The resulting counterbalance between low and high ground characterizes *Tlingit* carvings of this nature. However, the design is particularly exciting in the way all the rather delicate details come together to make a sum-total image that is both subtle and strikingly powerful. Look, for example, at the central torso area and note how the characteristic "banding" has been achieved with a series of carefully placed cuts and incised lines.

All in all, the project is probably one of the most difficult in the book. It's not that the techniques are difficult—in fact, the carving stages are relatively simple—but that the design needs to be set in and carved with careful precision.

To achieve a good measure of success, the design should be symmetrically set out, well defined, crisply executed, and nicely finished.

Illus. 1. Project picture—a Tlingit *clan board.*

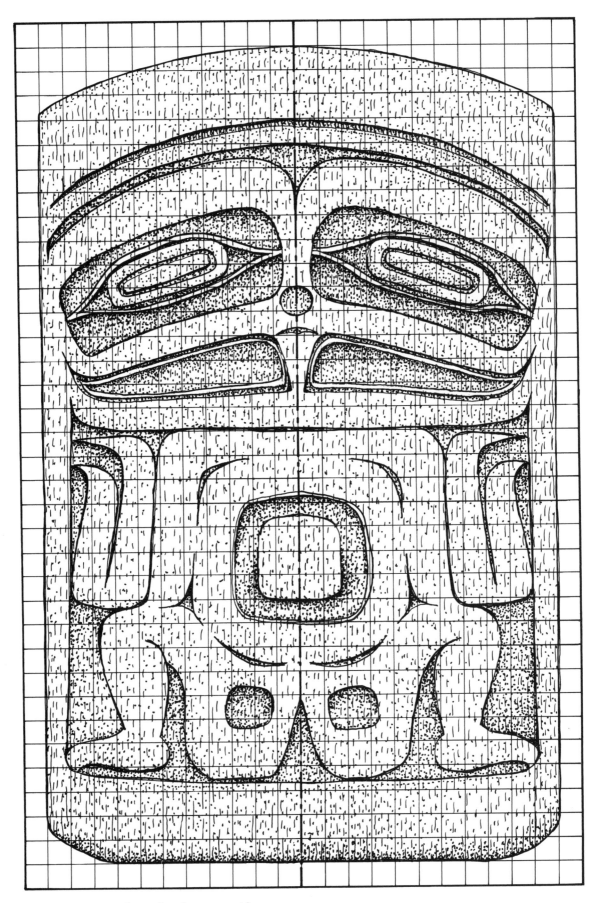

Illus. 2. Working drawing. The grid scale is two grid squares to 1".

158

TOOLS AND MATERIALS

For this project you need:

● a slab of 1¾"-thick, easy-to-carve wood at 12 × 18"—this allows for wastage

● a pencil and ruler

● a set square

● a sheet each of work-out and tracing paper

● a cord and a stick of chalk—for marking the central line

● a large coping saw or the use of a band saw

● a bench fitted with a vise and a hold-down

● a good selection of chisels and gouges

● a couple of knives—such as a penknife and a scalpel

● a pack of graded sandpapers

● acrylic paints in red, black, and light blue

● a couple of brushes—a broad and a fine-point

● furniture wax, a brush, and a cloth

CUTTING THE SLAB AND TOOLING THE SURFACE

Having carefully studied the project picture (Illus. 1) and the working drawing (Illus. 2), draw the design up to full size and take a good clear tracing. Make sure that the wood is in good condition and then use the pencil, ruler, and square to set out the slab at 11" in width and 17" in length. When this is done, establish the middle of the slab by drawing crossed diagonals, and then use this point to set the slab out with a central line. Use a pencil and ruler to run the line right around the slab. Align the tracing with the central line, secure it with four tabs of masking tape, and then pencil-press-transfer the profile line through to the working face of the wood.

When you have established a profile line, secure the wood in the jaws of the vise and use the coping or band saw to clear away the small amount of waste. Make sure that you cut slightly to the waste side of the drawn line, and that the blade runs through the slab thickness at right angles to the working face. If you doubt your ability in using the coping saw or band saw, then opt for using a tenon saw for the straight cuts and a combination of a small straight saw and a gouge to shape the curves.

With the profile nicely cut out, take a knife and cut small V-notch registration marks in the middle of

the front and back edges (Illus. 3, top left). Use a hold-down to secure the wood best-face up on the workbench and then take the medium shallow-curve straight gouge and start to cut away the machine-sawn texture (Illus. 3, right). Now, being very careful that you cut at a slight angle to the grain, and being watchful that you don't let the gouge run too deeply into the wood, work backwards and forward over the workpiece so as to give it a gently rippled or dappled texture. When you come to the sawn edge of the slab, first cut away the sharp angle, and then run the rippled texture down in a smooth, easy curve over the slab thickness.

Take a piece of fine-graded sandpaper, support it in the palm of your open hand, and then give the tooled rippling a swift rubdown so as to create a soft-undulating, smooth-to-the-touch finish. Now run the cord across the working face and locate it in the two central-line registration notches (Illus. 4, top right). Give the cord a good chalking, and then pull it taut and snap it down on the workpiece so as to mark in the central line (Illus. 4, bottom). Finally, remove the cord and go over the chalk line with a pencil.

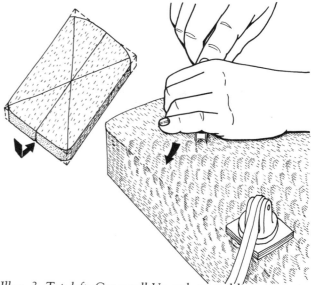

Illus. 3. Top left: Cut small V-notch central-line registration marks in the middle of the front and back edges. Right: Use a medium shallow-curve straight gouge to cut away the machine-sawn surface.

MARKING OUT AND SETTING IN THE DESIGN

Realign the tracing with the central line, secure it in place with the tabs of masking tape (Illus. 5, top left), and pencil-press-transfer the lines of the design through to the wood. Remove the tracing and make

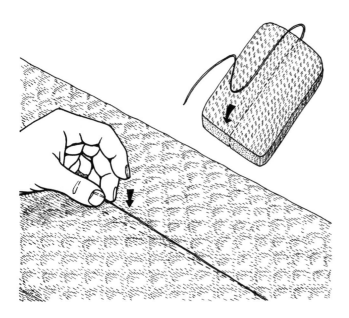

Illus. 4. Top right: Run the well-chalked cord across the face of the board and locate it in the two central-line registration notches. Bottom: Pull the chalk taut and twang it down on the workface so as to mark in the central line.

sure that the transferred lines are crisp and clearly set out—if need be, go over them with a hard pencil.

Having noted how a good part of the design needs to be lowered or wasted, take a soft pencil and go over the transferred design and shade in all the areas that need to be cut away (Illus. 5, top right). Bearing in mind that with a carving of this character it's most important for the images to be symmetrical and crisp, make a special point of seeing that the various curves and angles are perfectly placed and sharply defined in relationship to each other and to the central line.

If you take a good look at the project picture (Illus. 1) and the working drawing (Illus. 2), you will see how, from motif to motif, the edges of the ground are either sharp-cornered, as with the areas around the main "body," curved and dished, as with the eyes and the central-body moat, or angled and varied in depth, as with the small, incised cuts within the body area.

With the workpiece held secure with the hold-down, take the small, sharp-angled V-section parting tool and set in the lines of the design. That is to say,

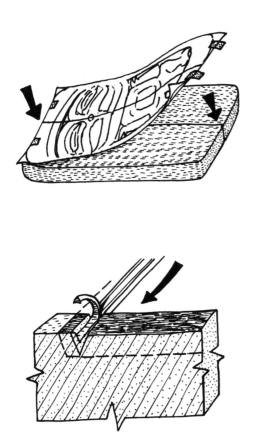

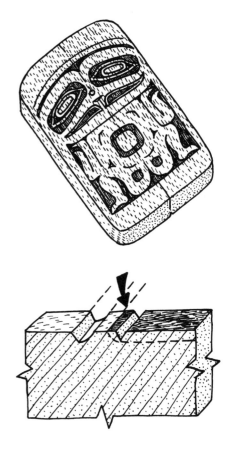

Illus. 5. Top left: Realign the tracing with the central line and secure it in place with tabs of masking tape. Top right: Shade in all the areas that need to be cut away. Bottom left: Cut a V-section trench around the design. The trench *should be about ⅛″ to the waste side of the line. Bottom right: Cut V-section trenches on either side of the narrow strip and use a small hollow-curve gouge to widen the trench on the waste side.*

160

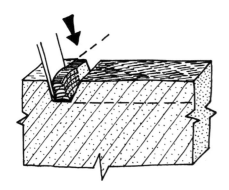

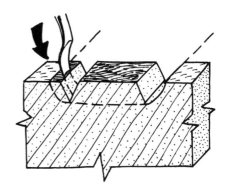

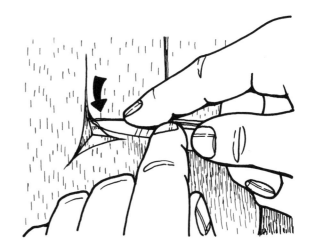

Illus. 6. Top left: Take the mallet and the straight shallow-curve gouge and set in a continuous stop-cut on the drawn line; then angle the tool over the design and remove the waste with short, sharp taps. Top right: Use a small spoon

gouge to scoop out the smooth curve of waste between the drawn line and the base of the lowered ground. Bottom: Use a knife to cut the triangular chip-carved pockets.

being careful to work about ⅛″ to the waste side of the drawn line, cut a V-section trench around the entire design (Illus. 5, bottom left).

As you are cutting around the various curves, you will, by necessity, be cutting both with and across the grain. Therefore, you will, for maximum control, need to hold the tool with both hands, one hand guiding and the other pushing and maneuvering. Work with long, slow, shallow scooping strokes, always being ready to brake and stop short if the tool starts to dig too deep, skid across the surface of the wood, or run away into end grain. Try to work to a uniform depth of about ¼″.

When you come to working the "eyes" and the "mouth," you will need to vary the technique somewhat. With the eyes, the problem is how to lower the various areas of waste without breaking off the fragile bands of short grain that delineate the shape of the eye. The best advice is to cut a V-section trench on either side of the narrow strip or ridge, and then to

use a small shallow-curve gouge to gradually widen the trench until you reach the drawn line (Illus. 5, bottom right). Of course, as you get closer and closer to the narrow strip of relief wood, you will have to work with increasing care, being all the while watchful that you don't cut into the high-relief wood. The mouth area is worked in much the same way, the only difference being that the trench on the relief side of the narrow band of high-relief wood is left as a permanent feature.

When you lower the sharp-cornered areas, take a mallet and a straight shallow-curve gouge, hold the gouge so that it is on the drawn line but is angled away from the waste, and then with short, sharp taps, work around the motif, setting in a continuous stop-cut (Illus. 6, top left).

When you work the curve-cornered or dished areas, such as the eye sockets, you first establish the depth of the waste with a small V-section trench, and then, instead of setting in a stop-cut, you use a small spoon gouge to scoop out the smooth curve between the drawn line and the base of the lowered ground (Illus. 6, top right).

Finally, use a knife to swiftly cut in the small incised arcs on the body and under the nose, and the little triangular chip-carved pockets on the body (Illus. 6, bottom).

LOWERING THE GROUND AND CLEARING THE WASTE

When you have established the depth and breadth of the lowered ground with a V-trench, and cleaned out the various corners, curves, steps, and angles, then take the shallow-curve spoon gouge and scoop out the waste to a uniform depth of about ¼". When you come to the edge of the lowered area, slide the tool into the initial stop-cut so as to leave the angle looking sharp and clean (Illus. 7, top right). Now use a combination of spoon chisels and gouges to take the ground to a good finish. Try to leave the lowered area looking smooth and crisply cut, but not so overworked that you can't see the tool marks.

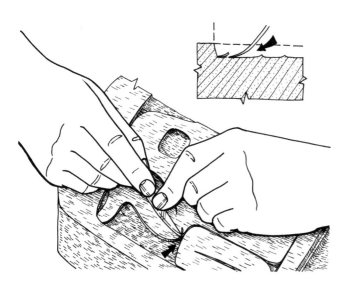

Illus. 7. Top right: Use the shallow-curve spoon gouge to lower the waste ground. Slide the tool into the initial stop-cut and leave the angle looking sharp and clean. Bottom: Use a small knife to clear the angles and curves between the high-relief areas and the lowered ground.

Take a small delicate tool, say, a small knife, and spend time making sure that all the angles and curves between the relief area and the ground are clean and free from bits and pieces of debris (Illus. 7, bottom).

Finally, take a sheet of fine-grade sandpaper, and supporting it in your open palm, rub selected areas, such as the curve of the eye sockets and the edges of the panel, down to a smooth finish.

PAINTING AND FINISHING

When you consider the panel well carved, take the acrylic paints—the red, light blue, and black—and mix them with water so as to make a wash of each color. Having studied the design and noted that several of the lowered areas around the body and the two curved lines above the eyes have been left unpainted, take a soft brush and block in the various colors that make up the design. Paint the body red, the lowered areas of the eyes and mouth light blue, and the relief areas of the claws (or hands), eyes, face, and eyebrows black.

When the paint is completely dry, give the workpiece a last rubdown with the fine sandpaper. Rub through the paint on high spots and edges so as to achieve a handled-and-worn look.

Finally, wipe away the dust, apply a generous coat of wax polish, and use a soft brush to burnish it to a sheen finish.

TROUBLESHOOTING AND POSSIBLE MODIFICATIONS

- Look for a well-seasoned slab of wood. If it feels and looks damp and unseasoned, then you run the risk of the slab warping and splitting.
- If by chance the slab does warp slightly and bow across its width, then use the convex side as the working face.
- In painting, aim for a well-worn look. To this end, apply the paint in thin washes. Let the paint soak into the wood, and then alternately rub it down and wax it. Ideally, you should be able to see the grain through the paint.

19
Totem Pole Miniature (*Haida*)

A clan pole—a prototype made prior to carving the full-size pole

Saw, chisel, gouge, and knife
Roughed out, deeply carved, relief-carved, and incised
Waxed and burnished

The biggest wood carvings of all time were the totem poles that were made by the Indians who lived along the Northwest coast of North America. Made traditionally from the red cedar tree, and deeply carved and painted with all manner of real and legendary creatures—including wolves, ravens, thunderbirds, bears, and fish—totem poles were three-dimensional proclamations of clan ancestry, entitlements, and status.

Totem poles can be compared with European coats of arms, in that they both show family lineage and triumphs. Totem poles were basically erected to commemorate special events and to make statements about power, prestige, and affluence. The more powerful the chief, then the taller and more elaborately carved the pole.

The poles also served a number of secondary purposes. For instance, a platform high up on the pole might be the last resting place for a chief's coffin, a cavity in the pole might hold a dead chief's ashes, and the base of the pole might form part of the entrance to a house.

The carvings in the totem poles would often portray, in order of importance, from the top to the bottom, the rights and privileges of the chief, his wife's family, related families, and the greater family. A totem pole would be erected in front of the owner's house to testify to his clan and his status. Because the pole symbolized all the entitlements of the clan, it was considered to be of inestimable worth.

The totem pole miniature, as featured in this project, would have been a prototype made prior to carving the full-size pole. The original pole, which was found by Europeans on Queen Charlotte Island in 1900, is almost 21 feet high.

DESIGN, STRUCTURE, AND TECHNIQUE CONSIDERATIONS

Take a look at the project pictures (Illus. 1) and the working drawings (Illus. 2), and see how, at a scale of slightly over one grid square to 1″, the pole is about 31″ high, 4″ wide, and 3¾″ from the front to the back. Note that the top of the pole is carved with a stylized chief, and that the various other carvings illustrate all the clan crests that have to do with the tribe's lineage. See also how, with this particular pole, the back is more or less flat, and the width is greater than the depth. However, if you look at the side view, you will notice that the distance from the back of the pole to the tip of the beak indicates how the design needs to relate to the initial bulk of wood.

In side view, you will see that the front face of the pole angles back into the wood until, at a point just below the jutting beak, it has cut halfway through the initial thickness of the side view. Although, at first glance, the pole might appear to be a bit top heavy and weakened by the beak and the neck under the beak, you can also see that the jutting beak and the rather delicate taper of the chief nicely counters what would otherwise be an off-balanced form. The sum-total carving is extremely stable, in that the center of gravity occurs about one quarter of the way up from the pole's base.

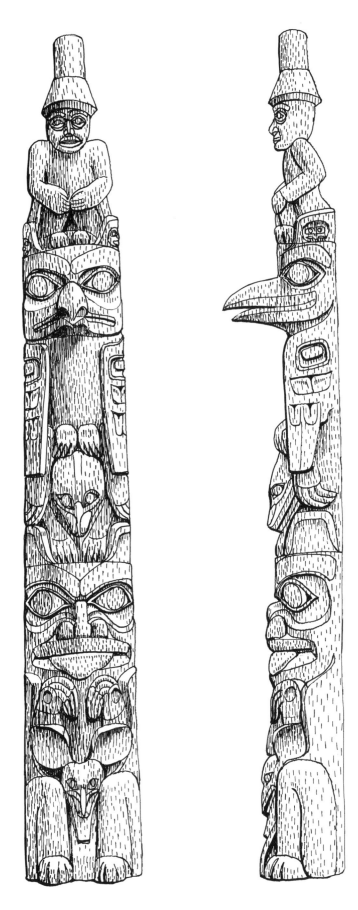

Illus. 1. Project pictures—Haida totem pole prototype, front and side views.

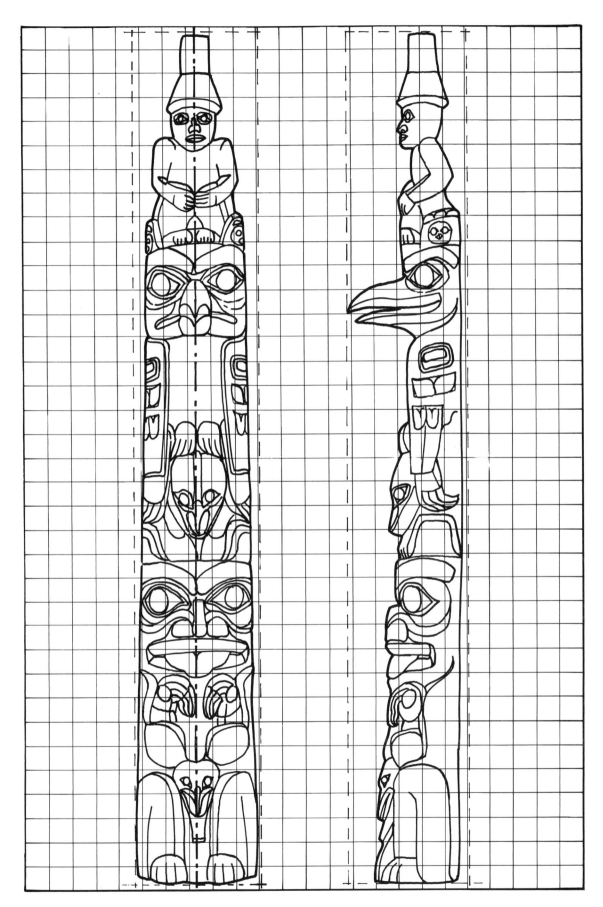

*Illus. 2. Working drawings—front and side views. The grid
scale is slightly over one square to 1″.*

TOOLS AND MATERIALS

For this project you need:

- a prepared 4 × 4″ section of wood that is 36″ long—it's best to use a smooth-grained, knot-free type such as lime, holly, or sycamore

- a workbench with a vise and hold-down

- a pencil and ruler

- a large straight saw—it needs to be sharp

- a good selection of chisels and gouges

- a selection of knives, including a heavy-duty craft knife, a crooked knife, and a scalpel

- a mallet

- a pack of graded sandpapers

SETTING OUT THE DESIGN AND CLEARING THE WASTE

When you have studied the project pictures (Illus. 1), the working drawings (Illus. 2), and the various details, and have a clear understanding of just how the project needs to be worked, check the wood over to make sure that it is free from faults. If by chance the wood does show signs of having slight end splits, knots that appear to be a bit of a problem, or whatever, then spend some time working out how best to avoid them. If, for example, there is a small split at one end, make sure that the split occurs at the top rather than the bottom so that the potential problem is cut away with the waste.

Establish end central points by drawing crossed diagonals, and then run central lines down all four faces of the wood. Pencil in the various faces "top," "front," "back," "side left," and "side right." Make a tracing of the profiles. Then take a "side" tracing, make sure that it is aligned with the central line, tape it in position, and pencil-press-transfer the traced lines through to the wood. When the side profiles are clearly mapped out on the wood, one on each side, draw simple straight-line saw guides, have a last check to make sure that everything is correct, and then shade in the areas that need to be cut away as waste. Now secure the wood in the vise and then, making sure that the line of the cut is well to the waste side of the drawn line, use the straight saw to clear away the bulk of the waste (Illus. 3, left). Take the front tracing,

cut it at the "beak" area, align the two halves with the side profile, press-transfer the traced lines through to the wood, and draw straight-line guides (Illus. 3, right). Finally, cut away the waste on either side of the chief on top of the totem.

CARVING THE PRIMARY FORMS

Once you have cleared away the waste, set the workpiece down on the bench and use a pencil and ruler to run the main design lines around the wood. Link up such details as the brim of the chief's hat, the chief's shoulders, the point of the jutting beak, the points just above and below the beak, and so on, all the way down the wood.

Now, with the wood secure front-up on the bench, take a medium shallow-curve straight gouge and work down the workpiece, cutting away the areas of corner waste (Illus. 4, bottom right). Keeping one eye on the shape of the "side" profile, and being watchful not to cut too deeply, work from the "front" face down to the "side," until the areas above and below the beak look generally rounded.

When you come to clearing away the waste from each side of the beak, again be very cautious not to chop too deeply into the wood. Having noted how the eye sockets and the cheeks run in a smooth curve to the point of the beak, and how the grain runs up and down through the beak, slice away the waste accordingly (Illus. 4, top left).

At this stage the task is not so much to carve deeply but more to rough out the overall surfaces and to establish the broad primary shapes that make up the design. So, from the top to the bottom of the pole, you need to chop in for the top of the chief's hat, clear the waste from around the chief's face, shoulders, and waist, establish the shape of the areas above and below the beak, clear away the waste from between the large wings, and so on, all the way down the pole. As you cut, carve, and work over the various forms that make up the design, you will need to keep pencilling in and reestablishing the guidelines. Of course, as you get closer and closer to your envisaged form, you will, in light of your progress, have to keep modifying the forms and details. This is in no way to say that you should radically change the design, but only that by the very nature of wood carving, some of the shapes and planes will almost invariably waver from the working drawings. And so you continue, until you have achieved the main raised surfaces that make up the design.

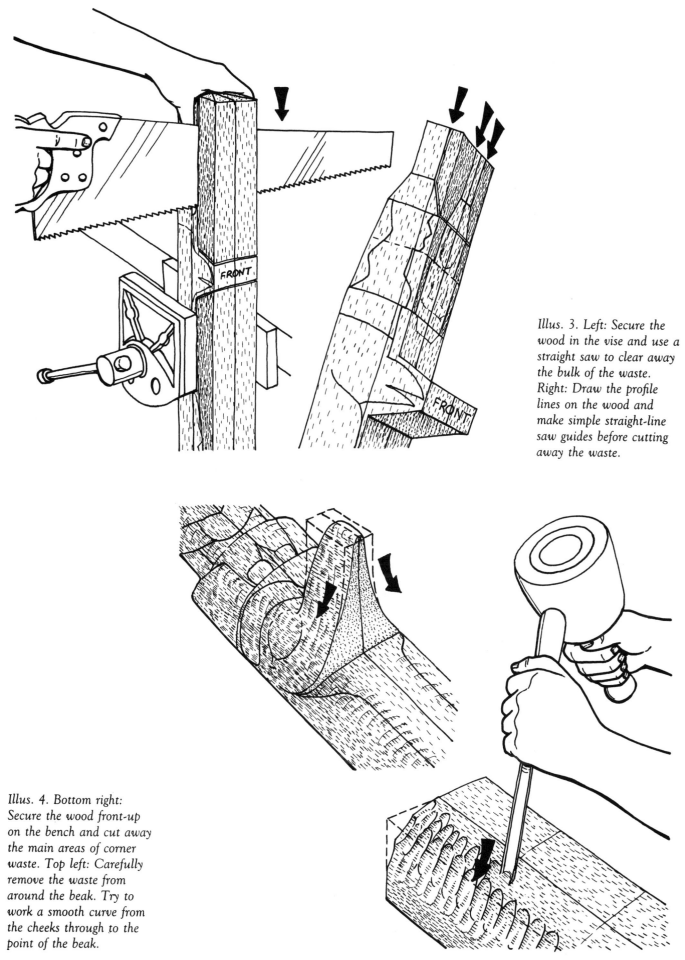

Illus. 3. Left: Secure the wood in the vise and use a straight saw to clear away the bulk of the waste. Right: Draw the profile lines on the wood and make simple straight-line saw guides before cutting away the waste.

Illus. 4. Bottom right: Secure the wood front-up on the bench and cut away the main areas of corner waste. Top left: Carefully remove the waste from around the beak. Try to work a smooth curve from the cheeks through to the point of the beak.

CUTTING IN THE DETAILS

Now comes the rather tricky task of cutting in all the details that go into making up the incised areas of the design. Starting with, say, the beaked image towards the top of the pole, clearly pencil in the line dividing the beak, and the shape of the outer eye socket, the inner eye, the pupil, and the eyebrows. When this is done, take a knife and set in the main stop-cut lines. Again, don't cut the lines too deep; in this first instance, just cut in to, say, a depth of about 1/8″.

Once you have set in the stop-cuts, then, starting with the outer eye socket (meaning, the moated area between the top rim of the socket and the inner eye), take a small shallow-curve spoon gouge and scoop out the waste. Aim to keep the sharp line of the top rim, but to run the lower socket area in a smooth line into the cheek and beak (Illus. 5, top right).

Use a knife to cut in and detail the line that divides the beak.

When you come to detailing the large pair of stylized wings that occur just below the beak, again, start by setting in the shape of the leading edge of the wings with a stop-cut. Have the stop-cut running in a smooth line, from the back of the pole, forward under the beak (or cheek), straight down either side of the breast, and then out and around and on towards the back of the pole. Set in the line of the claws with a stop-cut and then start to clear away the waste area between the wings. With the workpiece secured with the front face-up on the bench, take a small spoon gouge and lower the wood between the wings by about 1/4″ (Illus. 5, bottom). Try to keep sharp-angled steps on the leading edges of the wings and to have the breast running in a smooth curve up the throat and through to the underside of the beak.

Now continue establishing the shape of what looks like a bear cub's head just below the large bird's claws, carving the shape of the large beaver head that occurs below the bear cub, and so on, down to the mouselike head and the large pair of knees at the base of the pole.

CUTTING IN THE INCISED MOTIFS AND FINISHING

When you have detailed the various images and generally cut away the waste ground in and around the forms, and when you are basically satisfied with the

carving, take the graded sandpapers and rub all the surfaces down to a smooth finish. Be careful not to blur the crispness of the carving.

Having looked closely at the relatively few motifs that decorate the wings (Illus. 6, left), carefully establish the position of the details and then draw them in with a pencil. When you are happy with the shape and position of the details, cut them in with the point

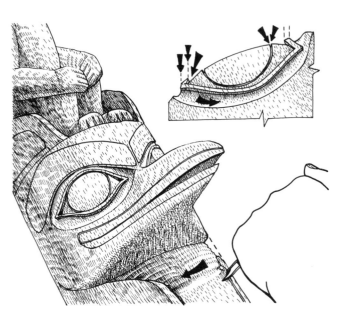

Illus. 5. Top right: Use a small shallow-curve spoon gouge to scoop out the moated area around the eye. Note how the wood is sliced down from the edge of the eyeball and into the corner of the eyelid. Bottom: Define the edge of the wings with a continuous smooth-running stop-cut; then remove the waste between the wings and the throat.

of a sharp knife or scalpel (Illus. 6, top right). The carving is straightforward—it's really nothing more than slight V-section stop-cuts, U-section trenches to establish the depth of the carving, and then the waste is cut away to create the dished hollows (Illus. 6, right—top to bottom). Again, the chief's head is basically a series of slight V-sections and dished hollows. First aim for the form's overall roundness, and then cut back the various V-sections and hollows that make up the details. Be watchful that you approach the grain to the best effect (Illus. 7).

Finally, rub down with a fine-grade sandpaper, brush the debris from all the cracks and crannies, make sure that the pole stands firm and true, apply a couple of coats of wax, burnish to a good finish, and the job is done.

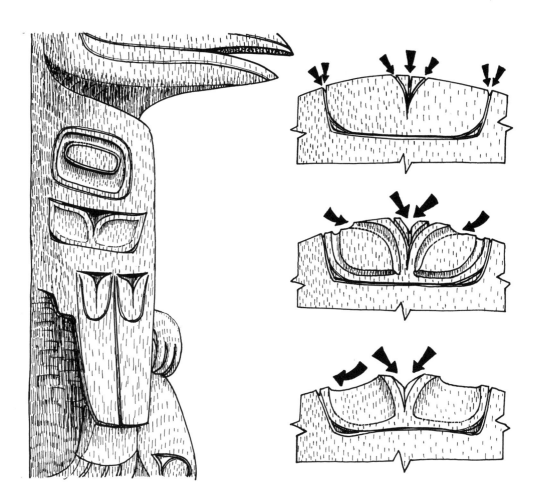

Illus. 6. Left: Wing details. Top right: Use a knife to cut in the lines of the wings. Middle right: Use a small spoon gouge to remove the waste from the dished areas, and work the V-section cut with a knife or chisel. Bottom right: Complete the V-cuts and finish the delicate dished area. Leave the shapes looking crisp with smooth edges.

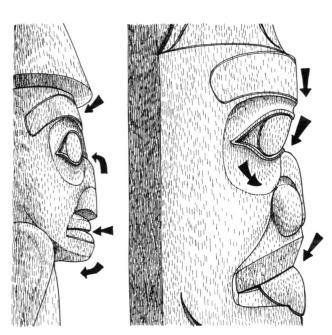

Illus. 7. Left: Detail of the chief's head, showing the various planes and the directions of cut—note the vigorous lines of the nose and the strong jutting jaw. Right: The beaver's (or bear's) head—the eyes are angled downwards, the eye sockets are deeply moated, and the tongue protrudes over the bottom lip.

TROUBLESHOOTING AND POSSIBLE MODIFICATIONS

- If you like the general idea of this project, but you want to make a larger pole, all you do is blow up the scale of the drawings and use different tools. For example, if you decide to carve a pole twice this size, then instead of using a knife and gouge, you would use a mallet, chisel, gouge, and adze.

- Many of the images, details, and techniques featured in this project are covered in greater depth in other projects—see projects 2, 8, 12, and 14.

- If you want to try your hand at carving a good-size pole, say, one at about 12″ or more in diameter, it's best to start by carving a short, chunky practice piece. You could select a detail, say, the image at the bottom of the pole, and use a short length of large-diameter wood.

- If you are ambitious and want to carve a full-size pole, have the pole lying down but set up off the ground and supported on a row of sawing trestles. Spend time considering just how the finished pole is going to be moved.

20
Blanket Chest (Tlingit)

A kerf-cut and steam-bent chest used for storage

Saw, gouge, and knife
Sawn, kerf-cut, relief-carved, incised, and steam-bent
Painted, waxed, and burnished

Of all the wooden items made by the *Tlingit* Indians, their large storage chests are perhaps the most curious. They are special, not so much for the way they are decorated—which is amazing in itself—but more for the way they are made and put together. The chests are actually made from just two planks: a single slab for the bottom, and a single wraparound kerf-cut and steam-bent plank for the four sides.

On close inspection, it can be seen that the box sides bulge slightly in the middle, run around three

Illus. 1. Project picture—a Tlingit *kerf-cut, steam-bent blanket chest.*

of the four corners in a smooth steam-bent curve, and then come together at the fourth corner to be recessed, pegged, and shaped.

The joints in these chests are so stable and close fitting that the Indians used them not only for dry storage but also for holding liquid commodities such as oil and hot water.

Old first-hand accounts describe how a plank was first split off the living tree and then surfaced and prepared with an adze so that it was thinner at the corners, grooved and kerf-cut at the corners of the inside face, soaked in a mixture of water and urine, steamed in a pit of hot seaweed, folded and clamped with ropes, pegged end to end, and finally fitted with a recessed and pegged bottom. The combination of the thin wood at the corners, the kerf-cut groove on the inside face, and the steam treatment not only allowed the fibres of the wood to stretch at the bends without breaking but also allowed the small amount of undercompression wood at the inside corners to be taken up by the kerf-cut groove.

DESIGN, STRUCTURE, AND TECHNIQUE CONSIDERATIONS

Take a look at the working drawings (Illus. 2 and 3) and see how the chest measures 24″ long, slightly over 12″ wide, and 12″ high. Study the details and see how the corner kerfs, or grooves, relate to the three straight-sided $\frac{1}{2} \times \frac{1}{2}$″ channels on the inside face of the box being undercut along one side to a depth of $\frac{1}{2}$″. Note the way the undercut allows for compression take-up on the inside corners when the wood is being folded (Illus. 2 and 3). Prior to steaming and folding, the 2″ thickness of the plank is reduced at the corners to 1″ and then further reduced at the kerfs to $\frac{1}{2}$″.

Study the working drawings and details and note how the box is best carved after it has been put together. Our research suggests that from tribe to tribe, at least a dozen types of kerf corners were made—everything from a simple 90° V-section channel to a very complicated, deeply worked, and undercut "swallow-tail."

Finally, if you have any doubts at all as to how the technique works, it would be best to go through a dry run with a piece of scrap wood.

TOOLS AND MATERIALS

For this project you need:

● an 80″ length of 2″-thick plank wood at 12″ in width, to allow for wastage—it's best to use prepared cedar

● a slab of 2″-thick wood at about 28 × 16″ for the bottom, to allow for wastage

● a pencil, square, and measure

● a sheet each of work-out paper and tracing paper for each side of the chest that you want to carve

● a straight saw

● a good selection of gouges and chisels

● a workbench with a hold-down or large clamps

● a sandbag or a couple of pieces of old carpet felt

● acrylic paint in red and black

● a couple of paint brushes—one broad and the other fine-point

● a plastic-bag-and-electric-kettle steamer—see Illus. 6

● a pair of thick leather work gloves

● a small hand drill with a $\frac{1}{4}$″ bit

● a handful of 4″-long, $\frac{1}{4}$″-diameter dowel pegs

● all the usual workshop items, such as cord, ropes, battens, and glue

MARKING OUT AND PREPARING THE WOOD

Set the 80″-long plank down on the work surface and check it over for problems. Ideally, it should be completely free from stains, dead knots, and splits. If you do have to settle for wood that contains knots, make sure that they occur well away from what will eventually be the corners of the box.

Now, having squared off the ends of the plank, and starting with a 1″ strip for the link-up corner recess, set the plank out left to right along its length with the following carefully measured step-offs: 1″ for the link-up corner recess, 12″ for the first side, 1″ for the first corner kerf, 24″ for the second side, 1″ for the second corner kerf, 12″ for the third side, 1″ for the third corner kerf, and finally 24″ for the fourth side

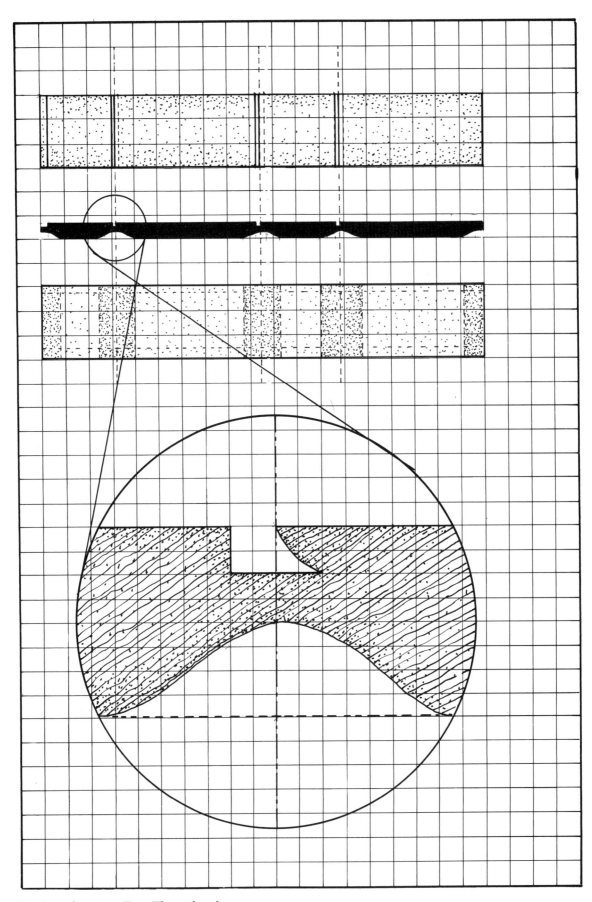

Illus. 2. Working drawings. Top: The grid scale is one square to 4″. Bottom detail: The grid scale is four grid squares to 1″—note the shape of the kerf-cut.

172

*Illus. 3. Working drawings. Top and middle: The grid scale
is one square to 1″. Note the detail showing a section
through a kerf-cut, steam-bent corner.*

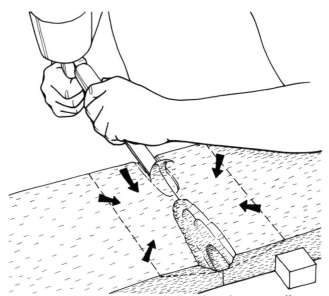

Illus. 4. Secure the wood to the bench and use a mallet and a shallow-curve straight gouge to hollow out the "valleys." Grasp the gouge in the middle and use your elbow to steady and pivot it—clear the waste from the side to the middle.

(Illus. 2). Divide each 1″-wide corner kerf into two ½″-wide strips and run a central line down the middle and right around the plank. Now, with the recessed end of the plank to the left, shade in the left-hand side of each of the three kerf channels. Label this face of the plank "inside."

Flip the board over and label the other face "outside." Set this side of the plank out with measured step-offs so that there is a 2½″-wide strip to the left and the right of each of the three central lines, and a 2½″-wide strip on each end of the plank (Illus. 2). If all is well, the "outside" face of the plank should be set out, left to right along its length: 2½″, 7½″, 5″, 20″, 5″, 8″, 5″, and finally 19½″. Now, thinking of each of the 2½″ and 5″ strips as valleys or dips, secure the workpiece with a clamp and use the shallow-curve straight gouge of your choice to waste the wood at each of these areas. Hollow out the valleys to a depth of 1″ in the middle of the kerf corners, and then shape up the total surface so that from end

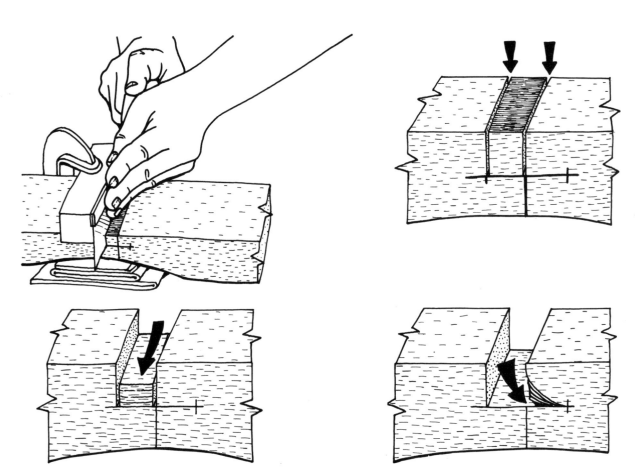

Illus. 5. Top left: Use a strip of wood for a saw guide. The strip should be of such a height that the brass rib on the back of the saw hits the top of the guide when the cut is the correct depth. Top right: Make sure that the cuts are to the waste side of the drawn lines. Bottom left: Use the ½″-wide straight chisel to clear away the waste. Bottom right: Slice down and under to clear away the waste from the kerf-channel overhang.

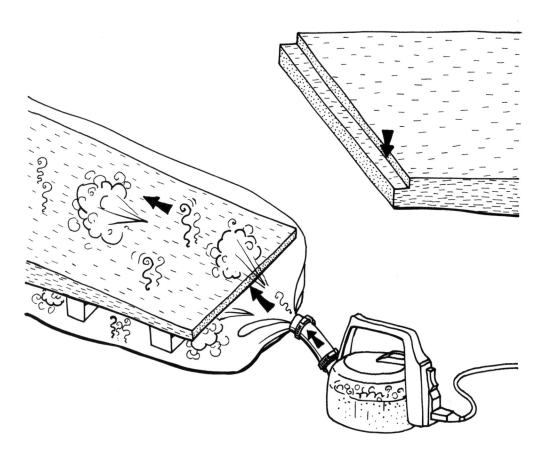

Illus. 6. Top right: Cut a ½"-deep, 1"-wide recess on the inside face of the panel's 12" end. Bottom: Rest the plank on blocks inside the plastic steamer bag. Link the mouth of the bag to the kettle spout with a length of plastic tube and clips. You could speed things up by having two kettles, one on each end of the bag.

to end the plank undulates in a series of smooth hill-and-valley dips and peaks. Each of the four peaks should indicate the position of the middle of the four box sides (Illus. 4).

CUTTING THE KERFS

Turn the plank over so that the "inside" face is uppermost, support it on the piece of old carpet felt, and secure it with the clamps. Now take the straight saw and, being careful not to go deeper than ½" (Illus. 5, top left and right), make six saw cuts, one on each side of the three shaded-in corner-kerf channels. Make sure that the cuts are to the waste side of the drawn lines. Use the ½"-wide straight chisel to clear the waste from the kerf channels (Illus. 5, bottom left), which need to be ½" wide and ½" deep. Take a look at the working drawings and details and see how the central-line side of the kerf channel needs to be undercut to a side depth of ½" so as to make a half-fishtail, or half-fantail, profile. With a bent chisel and a knife, work on the central-line side of the channel, and undercut the vertical face so that it runs in a smooth curve under the central line. Carefully whittle down and under, until the base of the channel is an inch wide (Illus. 5, bottom right). Left

to right, label the three kerf channels 1, 2, and 3. Finally, cut the ½"-deep, 1"-wide recess on one end of the plank (Illus. 6, top right) and reduce the thickness of the other end to a little over an inch.

STEAMING AND BENDING

Having studied Illus. 6 and having a good, clear picture in your mind's eye of just how the steaming apparatus needs to be set up, place the shaped, kerf-cut, and recessed plank in the steamer bag. Make sure that the kettle is at least three-quarters full of water and then switch it on. Being ready to switch off the power and to fill the kettle up if it appears to be running dry, reckon on steaming the plank for at least an hour. Note: The kettle needs to have a spout and should not switch off automatically.

While you are waiting, set out the cord, ropes, work gloves, and battens so that they are all close at hand.

When the kerfs are flexible, remove the plank and set it on the floor so that it is kerf side, or inside face, up. Now, one corner at a time, set the foot batten across the wood, loop the rope around the plank, stand on the foot batten, and gently heave up on the rope (Illus. 7, top left). Work the corners in the order 1, 3, and 2. When you have achieved the complete

175

wraparound box form, set the box right-side up, set sticks on either side of the corners, wind the tourniquet-cord clamp around the box, and adjust with wedges and the twist stick until the two ends of the plank come together with the 1″ end plane notching and coming to rest in the recess (Illus. 7, top right). Working with controlled haste, drill half a dozen holes on each side-face of the recess, dribble glue in the holes, and bang the dowel pegs home (Illus. 7, bottom left). Finally, when the wood has cooled down and the glue has set, use the rasp and the sandpaper to rub the link-up corner of the box down to a smooth, rounded, and matching finish.

FITTING THE BASE, CARVING, PAINTING, AND FINISHING

Set the box down on the slab base, run a pencil line around the inside and outside of the box bottom, and with a pencil label both of the box sides and the base slab with match-up points. Draw another line about ½″ to the waste side of the line outside the box. Now, with the saw, mallet, gouge, and chisel, cut the base slab to a ½″-overlap fit, and lower the box side recess to a depth of an inch (Illus. 7, bottom right). Aim for a tight friction fit. Finally, flip the box up-side down, smear glue on all mating surfaces, bang the base slab into place, and secure it with dowel pegs (Illus. 7, bottom right).

Note: A recessed-slab lid is optional.

Take a good look at the project picture and see how, in the main, only the white part of the design is cut away and lowered. Decide how many sides of the box you want to carve (in the original, the front and back were carved while the ends were painted); then trace off the design (Illus. 3) and pencil-press-transfer the traced lines through to the wood. Shade in the areas that need to be lowered (Illus. 8, top left), set the profiles in with stop-cuts and V-section trenches (Illus. 8, top right), and then use one of the spoon gouges to clear away the waste (Illus. 8, bottom

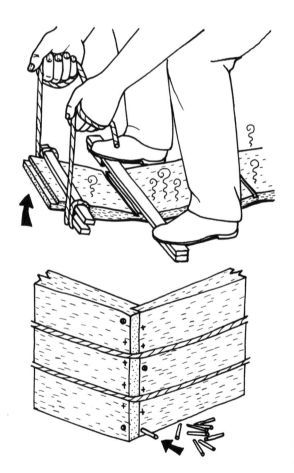

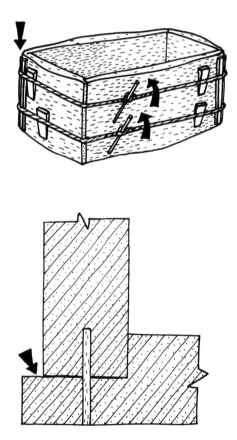

Illus. 7. Top left: Stand on the batten and pull the plank upwards. Top right: Have protective batten strips on either side of the corners. Use the twist stick to wind up the tourniquet cord; then adjust with wedges until the ends of the plank come together in a good fit. Bottom left: First drill and peg three holes, at the top, middle, and bottom. Bottom right: Cut the base slab to a ½″-lap-over-edge fit.

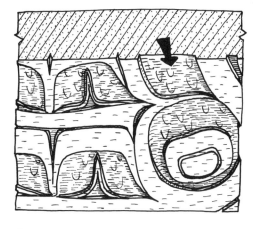

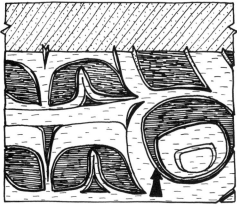

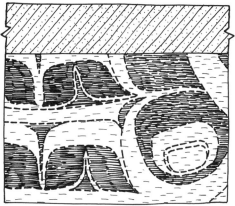

Illus. 8. Top left: Shade in the areas that need to be lowered. Top right: Set the design in with stop-cuts and V-section trenches. Bottom left: Use a spoon gouge to clear away the waste. Bottom right: Bring the work to a good

finish by cleaning up the dished areas and the various incised cuts. Try to leave the carving looking smoothly curved and crisp.

right). Use a knife to work difficult tight-angled areas. (Work the carving details as with other projects—see projects 8, 14, and 18.)

Once you have lowered selected areas, cut in incised lines and details, and generally brought the carving to a good completion, wipe away all the dust and debris, and move the workpiece to the area that you have set aside for painting. Mix the acrylic paints to a thick wash and then carefully pick out the areas that make up the design. Use black for the primary forms such as the eyebrows and the pupils, and red for the secondary details such as the lips and nostrils.

When the paint is completely dry, rub the workpiece down with the graded sandpapers—just enough to break through the paint at "wear" points. Finally, apply a coat of wax and bring the wood to a dull-sheen finish.

TROUBLESHOOTING AND POSSIBLE MODIFICATIONS

- If you are concerned about cutting the kerfs and steam-bending the corners, then it would be best to go through a trial run before starting the project.
- If you like the idea of the project but want to make a smaller box, then change the thickness of the wood accordingly.
- It's most important that the plank be free from flaws such as splits and knots. A knot on or near one of the corners could result in the wood splitting when you are steaming and bending.
- If you want to ensure tight, secure corner joints, you could dribble glue into the kerfs just prior to bending.

Additional Patterns and Motifs

Illus. 1. Tsimshian *carved-and-painted chest panel (front)*.

Illus. 2. Templates for ovoid eyes, eyes and wings, and fins and wings.

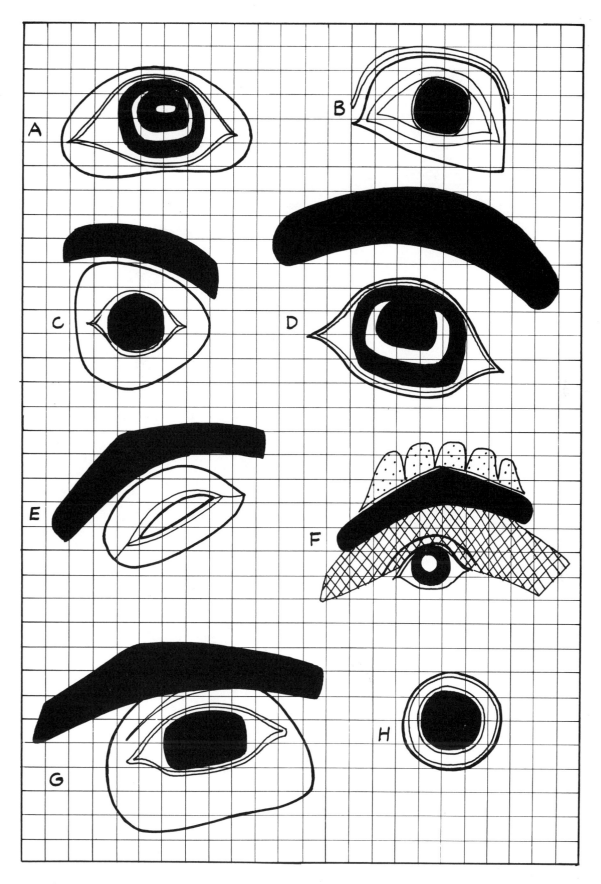

Illus. 3. Motifs: *(A) frog's eye, for salmon clan,* Tlingit; *(B) sparrow-hawk's eye,* Haida; *(C) bear's eye,* Tlingit/Haida; *(D) bear's eye,* Haida; *(E) raven's eye,* Tlingit-Chilkat; *(F) female spirit's eye,* Tlingit; *(G) wolf eye,* Tlingit; *(H) seal/fish eye,* Tlingit.

181

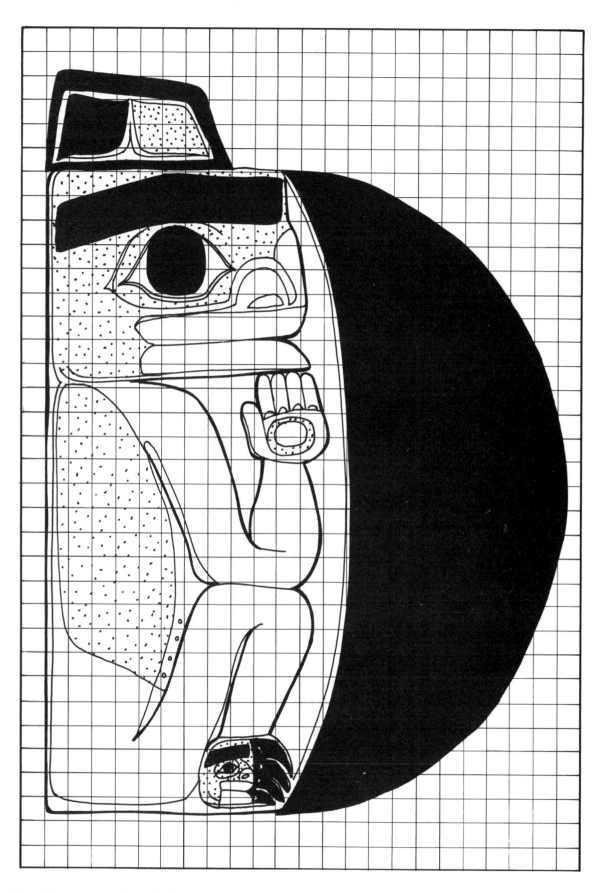

*Illus. 4. Carved house post—95½″ high—collected from the
Moon House, Port Mulgrave Yakutat, 1916–17. It's one of
four house posts, representing the moon and a wolf.*

182

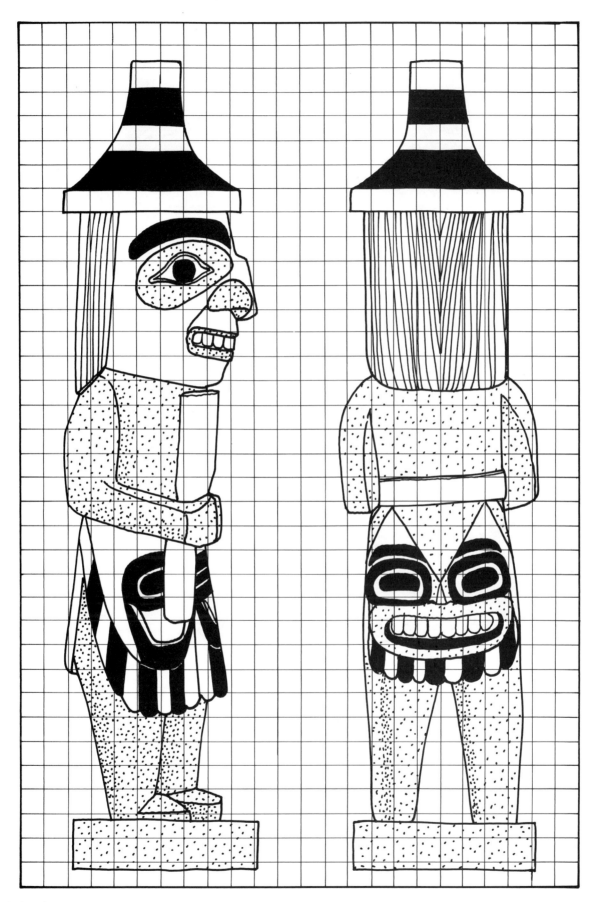

Illus. 5. Haida *spirit of death in the form of a man—27½″ high and 6¼″ wide—painted blue, black, and red.*

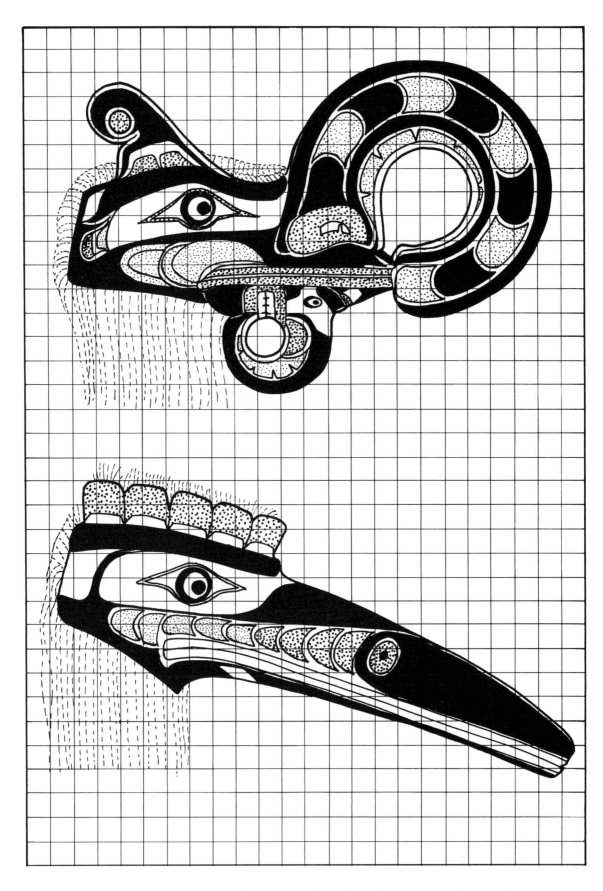

Illus. 6. Top: Crooked-Beak Hamatsa mask, made by Willie Seaweed in 1940. It's 40″ long and painted black, white, red, and brown. Bottom: Raven mask (the broken lines show fibre decoration), painted black, white, red, and orange.

184

Illus. 7. Top: Kwakiutl *mask, painted black, red, and white. Bottom:* Kwakiutl *thunderbird mask, made by Jim*

Howard in 1918. It's 19″ long and painted blue, white, red, and black.

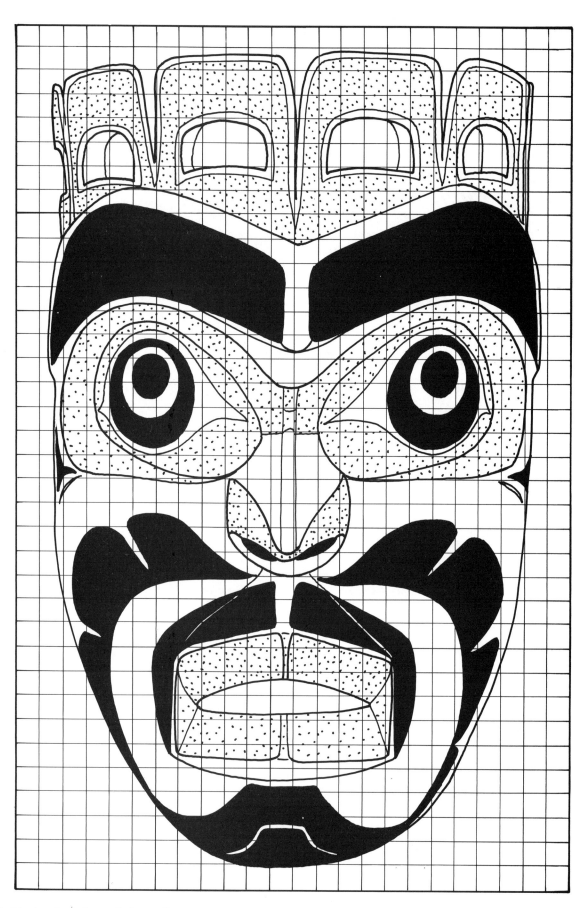

Illus. 8. Kwakiutl mask, made by Willie Seaweed in 1938.
It's 16″ high and painted white, black, green, and red.

*Illus. 9. Kwakiutl sun mask, with closed rays, carved by
Arthur Shaughnessy in 1918.*

Metric Equivalents

INCHES TO MILLIMETRES AND CENTIMETRES

MM—millimetres   CM—centimetres

Inches	MM	CM	Inches	CM	Inches	CM
⅛	3	0.3	9	22.9	30	76.2
¼	6	0.6	10	25.4	31	78.7
⅜	10	1.0	11	27.9	32	81.3
½	13	1.3	12	30.5	33	83.8
⅝	16	1.6	13	33.0	34	86.4
¾	19	1.9	14	35.6	35	88.9
⅞	22	2.2	15	38.1	36	91.4
1	25	2.5	16	40.6	37	94.0
1¼	32	3.2	17	43.2	38	96.5
1½	38	3.8	18	45.7	39	99.1
1¾	44	4.4	19	48.3	40	101.6
2	51	5.1	20	50.8	41	104.1
2½	64	6.4	21	53.3	42	106.7
2	76	7.6	22	55.9	43	109.2
3½	89	8.9	23	58.4	44	111.8
4	102	10.2	24	61.0	45	114.3
4½	114	11.4	25	63.5	46	116.8
5	127	12.7	26	66.0	47	119.4
6	152	15.2	27	68.6	48	121.9
7	178	17.8	28	71.1	49	124.5
8	203	20.3	29	73.7	50	127.0

Museums

The earliest Pacific Northwest Indian wood carvings were collected by Captain Cook in 1778 and ever since they have continued to be avidly appreciated and collected the world over. Examples of Pacific Northwest Indian totems, masks, and boxes can now be found in just about every major city and university museum. However, we know for certain that the following museums have very good collections:

American Museum of Natural History, New York.
British Library, London.
Centennial Museum, Vancouver.
Denver Art Museum, Denver.
Field Museum of Natural History, Chicago.
McCord Museum, Montreal.
Museum of Anthropology, University of British Columbia, Vancouver.
National Museum of Man, Ottawa.
Provincial Museum of British Columbia, Victoria.
Royal Ontario Museum, Toronto.
University of Pennsylvania Museum, Philadelphia.
University of Washington Museum, Seattle.

Bibliography

Barbeau, M. *Totem Poles of the Gitksan Upper Skeena River.* Ottawa: National Museum of Canada, 1973.

Boas, Franz. *Primitive Art.* Mineola, New York: Dover Publications, 1955.

Drucker, P. *Indians of the Northwest Coast.* Garden City, New York: The Natural History Press, 1963.

Feder, N. *American Indian Art.* New York: Abrams, 1973.

Garfield, V. *The Tsimshian Indians and Their Arts.* Seattle: University of Washington Press, 1950.

Gunther, E. *Indian Life of the Northwest Coast of North America.* Chicago: University of Chicago Press, 1972.

Hawthorn, A. *Art of the Kwakiutl Indians.* Vancouver: University of British Columbia Press, Vancouver, 1967.

Holm, Bill. *Northwest Coast Indian Art.* Seattle: University of Washington Press, 1965.

Inverarity, R. *Art of the Northwest Coast Indians.* Berkeley, California: University of California Press, 1973.

King, J. C. *Portrait Masks from the Northwest Coast of America.* New York: Thames & Hudson, 1977.

Krause, A. *The Tlingit Indians.* Seattle: University of Washington Press, 1956.

Maurer, Evan. *The Native American Heritage.* Lincoln, Nebraska: University of Nebraska Press, 1977.

INDEX

About the Authors

A unique husband-and-wife team, Alan and Gill (for Gillian) Bridgewater are rapidly gaining an international reputation as producers of crafts books of the highest calibre. Gill does all the step-by-step illustrations, while Alan does the more technical illustrations, the research, and the writing. Other Sterling books by the Bridgewaters are *Making Noah's Ark Toys in Wood* and *Folk Art Woodcarving: 823 Detailed Patterns.*

The Bridgewaters met at an art school, where both of them taught, and have two children. They live in a quayside captain's cottage in Cornwall, England.